The Book of Guy Hawkes Day And its BONFIRE NIGHT

Volume I: The Grand Blast

Theoretical Orientations, Primary Documents

The Book of Guy Fawkes Day and Its Bonfire Night Volume I: The Grand Blast, Theoretical Orientations, Primary Documents

PART 1

Conrad Jay Bladey, Hutman Productions, © 2020

ISBN: 9781732083080

Dedicated to the spirit of bonfire and to eternal mysteries that it discloses and especially to Mary C. Bladey my editor wife and bonfire girl!

Cover Illustration:

From: To God in Memory of his Double Deliverance from the Invincible Navy, (1588) and the Unmatchable Powder Treason (1605), "by a Transmariner" (1689) In: Ward, Samuel, "Improved and embellished by a Transmariner in 1689), Source: Gerard, John, What Was the Gunpowder Plot, 189, p. 229.

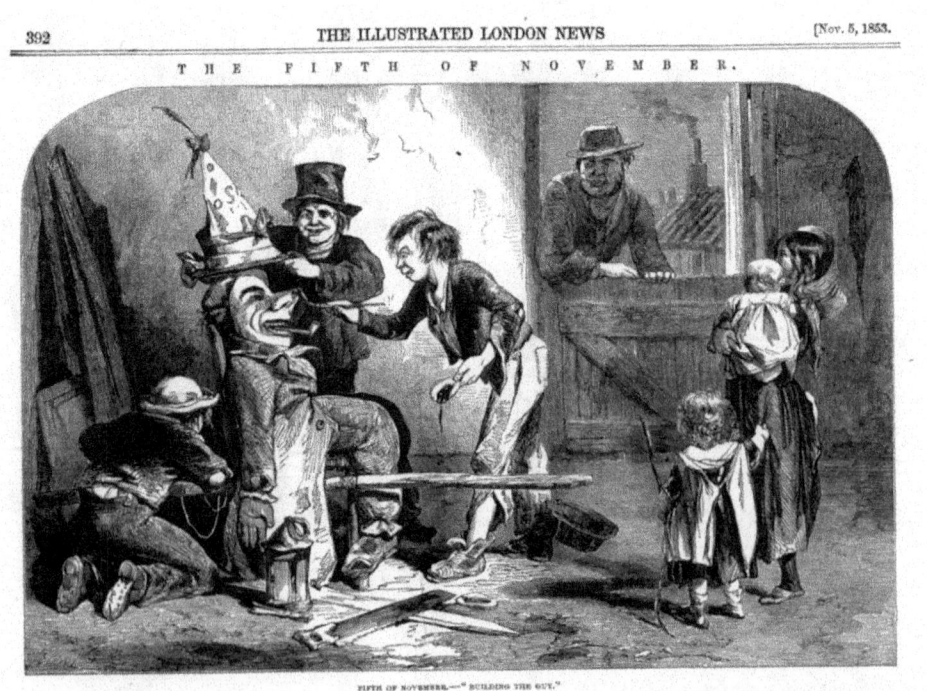

Foreward

As I begin this work I would like to direct you to the primary unifying purpose of all celebration: the disclosure of mystery. We celebrate to acknowledge the unknown and unexplainable. We disclose it to get out of its way and to adapt to its existence in order to support the common good.

Richard Feynman wrote: "What is the pattern or the meaning or the why? It does not do harm to the mystery to know a little more about it."— Richard P. Feynman, The Feynman Lectures on Physics (1964), Volume I, 3-10, *"The Relation of Physics to other Sciences."*

Despite all of the asking, mystery still remains.

Humans are obsessed with turning mystery and wonder into stories and histories. These are taken as explanation. History explains nothing. It is simply an account of the state of knowledge, and often such accounts are only intelligible to learned experts. With the writing of every history, mystery does not shrink, it grows. There is always the next question. We should continue creating histories and scientific explanations, but we should also engage in the acceptance of mystery and wonder. Mystery and wonder continue to exist beyond the realms of faith and scientific knowledge. Once this has been achieved we can manage our relationships with mystery and wonder more efficiently. We can then maximize the beneficial effects of the treasures which are our celebrations.

This work collects artifacts that have been created to assist in the disclosure of mystery and wonder. Put them to use, create your own and enjoy the freedom from the unknown that celebration provides.

1930's Batgers Cracker Tin

They made that House which is the hyve of this kingdome, from whence all her Hony comes, That House, where justice herselfe is conceyvd, in their preparing of good laws, and inanimated and quickned and borne by the Royall assent then given, they made that whole house, one Murdring peece: and having put in their powder, they charged that peece with Peers, with people with Princes, with the King, and ment to discharge it upward at the face of heaven, to shoote god at the face of god, Him, of whome god had sayd, *Dij estis*, you are gods, at the face of that god who had said so: as though they would have reproched the god of heaven, and not have been beholden to him for such a king, but shoote him up to him and bid him take his king againe, for *Nolumus hunc regnare*, we will not have this king to reigne over us.

--Shami, Jeanne, <u>John Donne's 1622 Gunpowder Plot Sermon</u>., Duquesne University Press, Pittsburgh, Pennsylvania, 1996, pp.95-97.

Contents

Foreword 3

Contents 6

Preface 9

Purpose 11

    Theoretical Orientation 12

        Defining- What do I Mean? 13

        The Folkloric "Big Bang"---- A Dream of Processes at the Beginning of Time and the Activist Approach to Folklore 16

        The Birth of Relationship and Process 18

        Management and Preservation 18

        Bonfire as Complex Disclosing Artifact of Celebration 19

        Is it "Pagan" or "Origins Unknown"? 20

        The Impending End of Bonfire Forces the Beginning of Study 20

        The Mission 21

    Dreams, An adventure in abstraction and a Warning! 22

        The Cultural Vision. Disclosing the "Invisible Entities:" The Mystery of Providence and the Wonder of Seasonal Transition 23

        The Vision of the Celebration Marching Through Time 24

        The Vision of Dynamic Artifacts 25

        Celebration as Pinball 26

        26

        Applying Theory to Celebration 28

Nationalism - What Was this England? 34

    The Great Chain of Being 34

    The Chain is Challenged 37

        Via Media 38

        Stories Vs. Explanation 38

Background Arguments 41
    The Book of Esther. Bible, King James Version 42
    The Sacrifice of Thanksgiving- Sacrifice Defined in the Old Testament 50
    God Looking Down and Laughing- Inspiration for Iconography and Verse 51
    Psalm 37 52
    Regnans In Excelsis, Pope Saint Pius V, April 27, 1570 53
    Papal Bull 53
    The tradition of tolerance toward English Catholics under Elizabeth was destroyed by the forceful pursuit of the Counter Reformation by Pope Pius V 55
    A Treatise of Equivocation, Henry Garnet, c. 1595 56
    Comes James: James IV of Scotland Crowned King of England 62
    The Shepheards Spring Song, in gratulation of the royall, happy, and flourishing Entrance, to the Majestie of England, by the most potent and prudent Souveragne, James king of England, France and Ireland, Henry Chettle,. 1603. 62
    Accession Speech to Parliament, James I, March 19, 1603 65
    Simaancas, Archivo General, Sección de Estado 840/126, Guy Fawkes, 1603 67
    Measure for Measure, Act 2 Scene 2 Shakespeare, 1604 71
    Treaty of London, James I, 1604 74
    Instructions from the Nuncio at Brussels to Dr. William Giffordi Dean of Lisle, OCTAVIUS, Bishop of Trica, August 1, 1603. 76
    To Henry Garnet, Claudio Aquaviva, the General of the Jesuits, June 25, 1605. 78
    Henry Garnet to Claudio Aquaviva, Henry Garnet, July 24, 1605 79
    To Claudio Aquaviva, Henry Garnet ,July 24. 1605 80
    Letter from Henry Garnet to Robert Persons. October 4, 1605 81

The Explosion 83
    The Mounteagle Letter 86
    House of Commons, Journal, Vol. 27, fol. 4, Parliament, November 5, 1605 92
    Warrants By the King, King James I, 1605 93
    By the King, King James I, 1605 94
    Descriptions of Robert Winter and Stephen Littleton by Robert Baker, 1605 95

By the King, King James I, 1605 95

Diary, Sir Roger Wilbraham, The 5 of Nov. 1605 96

To Sir Thomas Edwards, Ambassador at Brussells, Sir Edward Hoby, Gentleman of the Bedchamber, 1605 97

Letter, John Chamberlain, November 5, 1605 98

The King's Speech 100

The King's Book, James I, 1605. 110

Image: "Guy Fawkes Before and after Torture", Nye, Comic History.

Preface

One clear, crisp Fifth of November in London, an American of thirteen years of age looked out on what seemed to be another ordinary day, if one can have ordinary days in the City of London. I had not been prepared for what was to unfold as darkness approached. Suddenly on either side of our house, bonfires the size of the houses themselves were lit. Then the skies were lit up by rockets and the silence was broken by hundreds of explosions taking place all around us. My first reaction was to take cover because as far as I was concerned the big war had started. It did not occur to me that the fireworks did not represent a war, but rather the thanksgiving for our continued deliverance from the threats which confront us daily. The next year I had my own fireworks and my lifetime fascination with the holiday known as Guy Fawkes Day and its Bonfire Night had begun.

"Powder Plot 1 W.E. exc. 1605, From: Gerard, John, What Was the Gunpowder Plot, 1897, frontispiece.

Later as a student at Durham University in the 1970s I attended my first bonfire, cooked roasted potatoes in the coals, ate my first Yorkshire parkin watching the crackling fire surrounded by clouds of sparks. I felt linked to that night in 1605 when Providence looked down with the eye of God and saved a country and preserved the evolutionary path which has produced our culture, institutions and way of life.

Decades later I find myself living in a society which has seen unparalleled progress in science and technology. Miracles of medicine and technology happen daily. Our understanding of the universe has grown significantly. One thing however has not been accomplished. We still do not know how, without human intervention and often despite it, we continue to be delivered, somehow, from the dangers that seem to appear daily. We still stand like the people of the 17th century in the presence of the awesome mystery of Providence. This is why the study of the human relationship to this mystery is so important.

Calendar customs are much more than artifacts designed for amusement and entertainment. They have been used for centuries to give form to abstract mystery and to create a dialog with it. They help us to do what we can to cross over and connect with the mystery, to understand it as best we can, and to do our best to relate to it in the most positive way. This work is here so we can make progress on this old frontier with our ever present neighbor the watchful eye of God.

What can you do to more fully develop the treasure that is the celebration of Guy Fawkes Day and its Bonfire Night?

Image: Cartoon, Doyle, 1832

Purpose

This work examines and describes a complex calendar custom that has taken place each year, celebrated all over the world for over four hundred years. The celebrations are cultural and individual reactions to the perceptions of mysteries and wonders in the environment. My purpose is to document and understand the annual re-appearance of this celebration. It is only after the customs have been documented that we can begin to understand the complex processes and relationships involved in the construction of artifacts of disclosure of mysteries and wonders from artifacts of celebration, and their maintenance through the manipulation of principles, processes, relationships and variables. When we understand how calendar customs work we can begin to optimize their ability to function to improve the human condition and strengthen our political, social and cultural institutions.

A powerful network of artifacts of all kinds emanated from the national horror of the intended treason known as the Gunpowder Plot. Following the horror came the wonder of the mysterious great deliverance. The network of artifacts sharing constituent parts took root in society, extending outward, serving potentially as many interpretations, meanings and functions as there could be participants or ideas. The network began with a traditional cultural response to the horror and deliverance- bonfires and bells. Then it was given energy by government mandates and religious liturgy. Yet throughout, the most important motivating force was the horror and awe felt by the people in general. This motivated them to, despite their local and regional cultures, unite to "Remember and Remember." The roots of the network extended to all levels of society and permeated all aspects of culture both in the United Kingdom and worldwide. Music and chant are but one dimension of that extensive network. The collection of artifacts presented here is just a start.

The celebration continues in a world in which the danger of terrorism looms large. I hope you will find some of these artifacts of assistance for your own expressions and celebrations. Don't stop there. Compose some of your own.

This work is designed to gather together artifacts created from those of the Gunpowder plot. It brings them from many obscure and hard to access places. This makes of many, one; *E pluribus unum* so to speak.

It is the first step toward meaningful analysis and explanation. I hope it facilitates future work.

Image: Victorian Scrap

Theoretical Orientation

Although explanation is beyond the scope of this work, it is possible here to put forth a few general observations based upon the materials which have been assembled. These observations do not take the form of absolute pronouncements but rather as dreams and thoughts which have occurred to me and have proved helpful to me in the course of the assembly of the material contained in this work. I encourage you to come to your own conclusions.

We must take care with the way we describe any cultural institution or production, and calendar customs are no exception. Once historians and anthropologists and folklorists make their pronouncements and draw their conclusions. those pronouncements and conclusions become part of the tradition itself. They are fed directly into contemporary practice. It is amazing how much academic folklore, often-unsubstantiated conclusions and long-debunked theories remain alive today in folk memory, to in turn shape contemporary practice.

When we tell people what a custom is we are also telling others what the custom is not. In so doing we lose often as many celebrants as we gain. For example, by over emphasizing "pagan" aspects of traditions folklorists have turned away Christians even though the customs and traditions, described had been Christianized centuries ago. Whatever we conclude or wish to publish it should not unnecessarily limit participation or acceptance of the traditions.

Celebrations do not represent and never have represented any one thing to any one group or individual. They are complex artifacts in constant flux in many dimensions.

I have chosen to avoid labels and categorization. Bonfire must remain an artifact of disclosure of mystery and wonder accessible to all. Celebrations are beyond temporal definition. They are too dynamic. It is my opinion that we need to leave specific meaning to the people involved. Why settle on only one meaning or significance when in reality the number of meanings and significances can be as many as the number of celebrants? Instead, our role should be to discover how processes and relationships work to form, maintain and adapt traditions. Essentially, we must come to learn and explain how a celebration is constructed, adapted and manipulated rather than merely describe its form at a specific time. This is why it is important to embed our observations and specific histories within the larger context of the nature of celebration as the disclosing artifact of timeless mysteries.

Once we understand the processes and relationships involved we can better serve our host communities and come closer to the goals of the study: The active preservation of our treasured artifacts of celebration and the maintenance, continuation and growth of the tradition that discloses wonder and mystery, the celebration itself.

Before going further, it is important to isolate a few definitions.

Defining- What do I Mean?

Definitions are generally only appropriate for specific questions asked. It is best that you create your own to suit your own inquiries. It may be helpful to know what I mean in this work.

Ritual- A ritual may not be linked to any particular belief system. A ritual is something that is repeatedly re-enacted in roughly the same form, whenever celebrants see fit. Repetition is the key.

Disclosing Artifact of Celebration- Celebrations are constructed to disclose mysteries and wonders such as seasons, regional diversity and unexplainable deliverances. Through the construction of disclosing artifacts around invisible mysteries and wonders these wonders, can be given form and then can be adapted to or manipulated for the common good. For example, by disclosing a season through celebration, groups can prepare for planting. They can come to grips with mysteries such as unexplained extremes of weather or natural disasters which can destroy one community and leave another intact. The disclosing artifact is constantly changing to reflect expansion of knowledge. It is a complex artifact made up of smaller artifacts called artifacts of celebration.

Disclosing artifacts take us beyond scientific factual knowledge and explanation to acknowledge and adapt to that which is not yet known. They help us get beyond differences of particular faiths to reconcile humanity to that which that remains unknown beyond the frontiers of narrow theological discussion.

Artifact of Celebration- This is the basic element of the disclosing artifact or custom. Essentially, disclosing celebrations and customs are made up of artifacts, both material and non-material, such as songs, recitations, foods, bowls, recipes, costumes, torches, or tunes, held together or taken apart and adapted through relationships, processes and variables by celebrants, observers, and cultures.

Relationship- Relationships exist between people and artifacts of celebration and rituals. There is something within the people, community, culture, which links them to some aspect of the artifact of celebration or ritual. These are best described as parallel sets of variables. Relationships can be strong or weak. They can disappear, be created, and be renewed. Once there is a relationship between people and a variable it becomes meaningful to them and they can manipulate it. Relationships enable the structural change of artifacts of celebration and of disclosing artifact.

Folk Practice- That which people do. It is historical, temporal and finite. It describes one particular state of a changing artifact. This should have no special restriction to particular groups which should not have to adhere to historically recorded or contemporary practice as if frozen in time. Practice can be new, old or combinations of both. It is important to record and be aware of all practice because all practice should occur and be accommodated with reference to the same environment of relationships, processes and variables through time.

Process- There is no one "folk process." There are many processes working on many levels. Processes are the ways people and groups act upon artifacts of celebration and disclosing artifacts as guided by the relationships that exist between them.

"Performer" and "Audience"- It is often difficult to divide the two. The performer (children asking for "penny for the guy" for example) is often outside the site of celebration, for example the house, whereas the audience is generally inside, although this is not always the case. I would prefer the terms "co-performers" or "participants." This acknowledges that both parties bring something essential to the celebration, ritual or custom. Both sides must possess essential knowledge and prepare in advance. At times the audience co-performer brings more, at times less. In the case of Bonfire rituals those inside the house have to recognize and understand that the "penny for the Guy" house visitors as non-threatening, know what they are seeking, and be ready for them. In the Lewes and Sussex Bonfire traditions the crowd plays an important complementary role to that of the specialists, the Bonfire Boys and

Girls of the Bonfire Societies. The crowd needs to, for example, distinguish the bonfire boys and girls from "criminal street thugs." As insiders, those traditionally known as performers usually know the tunes, lyrics and basis for traditions well. But at other times they may not know any more than the audience. One should be prepared to see many variables and values on those variables on both sides of the threshold and on both sides of the parade or bonfire barricades.

<u>Mystery</u>- Throughout human history the universe has been divided into three sections. First there is the scientifically known and understood portion. The second portion is that which is constructed based upon faith in what can be extrapolated from the known to the unknown. The mystery, the innermost portion, goes beyond faith and science. While in the past science and faith have traditionally been thought to be sufficient, these suppositions have led not to unity of belief and understanding but a distinct lack of unity and conflict of scientific paradigms and religious faiths. Unity may perhaps lie in the acceptance of the validity of the unknown and its role once disclosed by celebration in human cultural history.

Capture of Fawkes 1825

The Folkloric "Big Bang" ---- A Dream of Processes at the Beginning of Time and the Activist Approach to Folklore

The <u>Bible</u>, one of our earliest references, describes the creation of life and of the seasons. It is one starting point in the quest for understanding. I cite it as it was used as an important source for the construction of artifacts of celebration and disclosure of the mysteries and wonders associated with the Gunpowder Plot and its season.

"In the beginning was the Word and the Word was with God, and the Word was God. The same was in the beginning with God. All things were made by him and without him was not any thing made that was made. In him was life and the life was the light of men. And the light shineth in darkness, and the darkness comprehended it not" – Bible, John 1: 1--14.

It is, perhaps, difficult for us to comprehend the darkness at the beginning of time. As John noted, man had no word. Even the light of the life of men could not be comprehended by the darkness that surrounded men. Today for us to comprehend it is a difficult task.

"And God said, Let there be lights in the firmament of the heaven to divide the day from the night; and let them be for signs, and for seasons, and for days, and years" –Bible, Genesis 1:14.

The <u>Bible</u> is not much help to those wishing to understand how we are to comprehend the seasons and manage our relationship to them---- they just happened and had some relationship to stars.

It took God until Leviticus 23 to come to Moses and provide him with the initial set of calendar customs:

"Speak unto the children of Israel, and say unto them, Concerning the feasts of the LORD, which ye shall proclaim to be holy convocations, even these are my feasts." – Bible, Leviticus 23:2.

One thing is certain: at the very beginning of time there was no folklore, no rituals, no artifacts of celebration, no customs, no folk practices. There was only the physical environment. There was no environment of ideas, perhaps even no gods.

What happened next should be a major concern of folklorists---- the "folkloric big bang." We do not need to go back in time. We do not need to see it. We need, however, to know how it worked and how it continues to work through time and space to aid in the creation, decay, rediscovery and revival of the artifacts of celebration, of disclosure and folk practice. Folklorists were late--comers and have had to start by picking up the pieces, but perhaps it is more than pieces of historical accounts but forces and relationships that we must also discover and understand.

In the beginning of the study of folklore there were unsupported inferences drawn from folk practice. Scholars viewing folk practices as transcripts or histories would think creatively about them, meditate on them and attach their musings, their fictions, their dreams to the folk practices. Scholars then became the myth builders. They examined, for example, the mummers play which involved a sword fight, the death of one of the participants and his restoration to life, and found in their musings and dreams unsupported fictions related to human sacrifice, death and rebirth and the change of seasons. They looked at other practices and found fertility relationships; the list can go on and on. Scholarly mythologies were extrapolated. Analysis was made out of whole cloth. Scholars became principals in the extension of folklore by exercising their own folk processes. There was no direct evidence linking the ceremonial practices to fertility or to human sacrifice, yet they were interpreted as such. When a diverse range of possible meanings may have existed, they narrowed their explanation. This does not mean that the activities of fiction engaged in by scholars were unimportant or should be rendered obsolete but that in their work scholars had become caught up in the folk processes. They had created their own artifacts to add to the tradition, not only as academic exercises but as real myths. These myths became artifacts of celebration and we see their important role in the construction of folk revivals. A survey of participants in bonfire activities throughout the British Isles will reveal that a fair number of participants cite the myths of scholars as the purposes of their contemporary celebrations. Therefore scholarly musings, dreams, fictions, add an equally important set of contributions to the mix which inform and cause human behaviors and ritual practices. We cannot dismiss them. These processes have occurred through time.

The Birth of Relationship and Process

After the "folkloric big-bang" we find not only the birth of artifacts of celebration. We also must acknowledge the birth of relationships and processes. These link people to the artifacts. They do not tell us what was done but why and how. As we move from past observations, musings and descriptions of celebrations, we should consider focusing upon these dimensions of the question. An important goal should be the development of understandings and explanations which will enable us to work dynamically with the processes and relationships we find around us today. If, as many maintain, the artifacts of celebration are important treasures, we must be able to build relationships to them. While earlier scholars have merely described artifacts, we must find ways through mastery of the processes to build the relationships that will keep rituals and celebrations running efficiently. There are many important reasons for the development of these skills.

Management and Preservation

The first and perhaps most important purpose before us is the preservation of known or imagined folk practice and artifacts of celebration. While we can achieve some level of preservation and curation in museums and publications, it can be argued that the active use of the artifacts and practices is another important dimension leading to preservation. It leads not only to preservation but to further development and evolution of folk practice and the inventory of artifacts of celebration.

Another important purpose is the management of the process of creation, evolution, decay and revival of folk practice. This process is inefficient. Destruction, re--discovery and rebuilding could be seen as wasteful and a burden when left unmanaged. Perhaps an important function of folklorists is to make themselves obsolete by finding a way to adjust and repair the celebrations so that they will continue more efficiently. Essentially, we need to discover ways to keep people from destroying and burying their artifacts.

A third purpose relates to the value of our subject matter. If scholars believe it is important to collect, describe, organize and meditate upon folk practices and artifacts of celebration, we must develop means of bringing the values we discover to bear in contemporary practice. When we have discovered processes and functions we must be able to activate them so that perceived value can be realized by contemporary groups.

Once we have done all this we can return to our meditations, description and collecting, our dreams and our fictions. We must still exercise the pursuit of the task to disclose and manage mystery and wonder to creatively develop even more artifacts and practices that will inform future behavior and serve cultures and peoples yet to come.

Bonfire as Complex Disclosing Artifact of Celebration

Bonfire is too much of a dynamic cluster of relationships, processes and artifacts to be explained by a single definition. Everything is in flux. Artifacts change and come and go. The constants are not the disclosing artifacts but the mysteries and wonders they help us to relate to. Historical accounts are merely snapshots in time and definitions good only for the moment. Explanation and understanding are to be found at a higher level.

Guy Fawkes Day and its Bonfire Night are composed of many parts. Such a part can be a house visiting custom, procession, fire celebration or occasion for ritual foods and chants. It can be filled with religious significance for some but strictly political and nationalistic for others. For large numbers the attraction is the warmth of the bonfire, and the "Ohs and Ahs" of the fireworks. Purposes can be shared or entirely personal. Then all this changes in both content and emphasis through time.

As soon as one attempts to comprehend bonfire it becomes cloudlike, a constellation, a kaleidoscope within a spinning vortex. Songs, recipes, bits and pieces, memories, artifacts, all and nothing at once. But that is exactly as it should be. Narrow historical, descriptive explanations are finite, limited, limiting, and divisive. They often serve limited purposes and are often imposed from outside. Wonders and mysteries, on the other hand, dwarf in size and complexity the explanations applied only to specific configurations of the disclosing artifacts on their surfaces. They exist independently of them and despite them continue through time. Our focus is not what an artifact or practice is but how it works, moves and changes. How does it disclose the mystery or wonder? How well does it help us to relate to it?

Is it "Pagan" or "Origins Unknown"?

I suppose we could take the safe route and simply state that Bonfire was all just "pagan." It is "out there" in another mysterious culture. Bonfire does have its sensually timeless qualities but is that simply a physical reaction and not a reflection of cultural continuity? The burning of bonfires is an artifact of celebration that was employed generally to mark important occasions. Guy Fawkes Day was set on November fifth because that just happened be the date Parliament met. It turned out that due to the weather it was a good time for a bonfire. The event coincided with seasonal change.

The strategy of pagan attribution has little potential for explanation. The very use of word "pagan" indicates a failure to realize the complexity of millennia of pre--Christian history of countless distinct cultures, traditions and transitions. Using the word pagan is only to say "unknown" or "ancient" and that we know already. Perhaps we need to abandon beginning for the end? While it is important to record what is known of origins, it is the presence and inner workings of artifacts of celebration that is central.

Clearly we should consider other ways to process bonfire that go beyond history and origins. I suggest that analysis of how artifacts of celebration are created, adapted, and lost will be most helpful. So too is understanding how these artifacts articulate with the mystery that they help to define and disclose.

The Impending End of Bonfire Forces the Beginning of Study

Many scholars have been motivated by the fear of the end. Bonfire, however, knows no end. It dies, and with the change of cultural circumstances is reborn-- re--generated. This feeling of imminent demise comes from the founding of study not in process but in history. It is acceptable to worry that history may be lost and accounts forgotten. If one is dealing in re-creation these may be done inaccurately. If one views bonfire as a disclosing artifact and as relationships, variables, structures and processes then it is clear that it is as immortal as the mysteries and wonders it is designed to disclose. Bonfire is created from the artifacts of celebration around new relationships of culture with mystery and wonder it is never re-created. Attempts at re-creation will be short lived and ineffective.

None the less there has historically been a profound worry amongst scholars that Bonfire and Guy Fawkes Day celebrations will disappear. Yet they never do, and they continue here and there like sparks that rekindle wildfires long after the fire is thought extinguished. The celebration will not end as long as the mysteries and wonders, the seasons and the human condition, persist. The change we see is in the artifacts of celebration that clothe and reveal the abstraction and not the wonder and our timeless relationship to it. Perhaps we need not worry so much about the demise of the phenomenon but rather concentrate upon the interfaces between the artifact of disclosure and celebration and wonder and mystery and between the artifacts and the cultures that produce them. The concern about apparent demise should be replaced with a concern that the celebrations and their artifacts more efficiently survive the inevitable cycles of death and rebirth with which they are confronted.

The Mission

So, what can I do here that others have not already done? Well, to start out I can assemble the historic artifacts of celebration. Here I have tried to pull together more artifacts, more observation and more histories and more interpretations than have been found elsewhere. I have as it were cast a broad light illuminating the contents of museums and library shelves. I have brought as much of it as is possible together.

It is hoped that gathering up the artifacts will help to slow further deterioration for a while. The collection will potentially help others to avoid having to start anew. Recycling will link them to those who have come before. I have included not just the ancient artifacts but have added in the artifacts of Bonfire I have found in our ethno-present. I have attempted to be as complete as possible, often including multiple descriptions of the same observations for the benefit of those who wish to survey all versions in one place.

While it is helpful to know how, when and why new parts are added, we are not here to censor them or hold one more important than another.

The most important place for bonfire's artifacts of celebration is in the active lives of celebrants. It is a place where the celebrations can live and develop. It is in this active life where they can help to comfort, energize, and benefit real people. I encourage all who read these pages to take up these artifacts and put them to use, teach them to others and practice what is written here. Books and museums do their work but they have never been sufficient.

As I conclude, I too feel pulled like scholars before me to dream of a way to explain and interpret the artifacts of celebration which I have collected. So I shall begin my collection by inserting a dream sequence. Please feel free to consult this section later or ignore it completely. Perhaps it can form a sort of background fantasy for the artifacts presented here. I hope my musings will expose even deeper mystery, even more complexity and that this new--found sense of mystery will make these treasures of celebration much more inviting to future celebrants. Keep in mind that the number of questions and dreams that can be constructed around these artifacts is infinite. Create your own!

Dreams, An adventure in abstraction and a Warning!

I begin with a strong warning. Although we can identify environmental forces and historical trends, everything is local! Any perception of cultural unity is an illusion. After all there can be as many purposes for celebration and ritual as there are celebrants. There can be as many reactions to the environment, as many traditions, as there are families, villages, counties and regions. One should expect to find an amazing amount of variation caused by many particular reactions of particular groups and individuals to the environment and the processes which work through history. Additionally, with time, and respecting the inability of human beings to avoid errors, change must be thought of as being more likely than consistency. That said, it is even more amazing to find correlations and common threads running through the many traditions of bonfire. How does the movement through time of a wonder such as bonfire occur? What does it look like? How is continuity maintained?

Just as cultural unity is an illusion so too is the concept that we have some how evolved beyond our ability to learn and practice past cultures. Anthropologists have taught us that culture is learned. If these volumes contain treasures, then we must be willing to put them to work in our lives. While it is important to acknowledge cultural roots it is also very important not to limit the use of these treasures to a single region or group.

Perhaps the most important warning-- While museums and libraries are wonderful institutions, the institution that has served folklore best has been the human family. We must encourage the living tradition to grow and prosper!

The Cultural Vision. Disclosing the "Invisible Entities:" The Mystery of Providence and the Wonder of Seasonal Transition

Things happen. Hours of daylight change in number, temperatures change, the natural world responds around us. When we are alone we reach out to others. When we feel our dependence upon others we should help them to survive. We should adapt to cold. We should plan ahead for the season to come. We have to have ways to expect and relate to the unexplainable- the disaster which destroys one and not another. All of these changes are, however, quite invisible and abstract. How do we take something so invisible and give it form? What is this feeling of longing for others and of mutual dependency? How do we remember the recurrence of something we cannot see nor understand?

Perhaps the answer is that we treat it as "Kemp," the "invisible man" of the book and movie. (Original Novel: H.G. Wells, The Invisible Man: A Grotesque Romance, 1897. Movie: Invisible Man, Universal, 1933.)

As with the Invisible Man we must provide the mystery with bandages and wrappings to give it shape. We give it a calendar setting. We prepare for it. The bandages are the rituals, customs, and artifacts of celebration. Some are ancient and perhaps of some unknown theological origin, some are Christian, some are the outpourings of the individual human spirit in song and verse. They are all attached to the invisible man, "the dark matter" of seasonal change to give it form. When we clothe the invisible entity we can see it coming, escape its grasp and even fight back. The mystery is in part also our ability to give form to the abstract and unknown.

Sometimes artifacts fall off. Sometimes they are replaced, sometimes lost. From time to time new artifacts are created and added. Despite all of the improvements of "human progress," our clocks and our calendars and weather reports, without them, the invisible entity still would slip our grasp. Even today we would soon lose our way and become crushed by the march of the seasons. We would lose the hope of deliverance and the benefits of providence. In terms of Bonfire we would lose philosophies such as that of the Great Chain of Being that unite people one with another and guide us to common purposes and goals. If Bonfire did not help us to disclose seasonal change we would be less prepared for the season that followed. Celebration of deliverance makes the future hope of deliverances possible. Our celebrations give shape to and preserve our relationships to the mysteries and wonders.

The goal of the celebrant is to make sure that the invisible entity is adequately clothed and that positive relationships with the mysteries are maintained.

How can we understand how the clothes and wrappings are created? How can we keep them from wearing out? How do we keep them in place? Equally as invisibile as the mystery of providence and seasonal transition are the relationships between people, communities and cultures which accomplish these tasks--the dark invisble matter of folklore. The artifacts are just the starting point in this mystery. On the other hand perhaps it is just another dream.

The Vision of the Celebration Marching Through Time

Picture a band of bonfire boys and girls on the road. They walk through the mire, through the cold, and bring their torches and effigies, chants, songs and foods. The bonfire tradition with all of its artifacts of celebration travels like an over-loaded tinker's cart. It rolls through time. At one place on the road it is rewarded and the bonfirers are encouraged by hospitality, food and drink. Other places are not so welcoming. The bonfire celebrants are stoned, chased out of town or perhaps ignored. (At times this has worked the other way, a good example being the enemy of bonfire the Rev. John Newton, author of Amazing Grace, who lost his position by persecuting bonfire,) In some instances the celebrants are picked up like a toy train no longer needed and stored in a box where they await discovery. Sometimes the toy is cared for or curated. Perhaps the toy is not found and is neglected, to decay and be forgotten. Often this is how we find these artifacts of celebration, forgotten and fragmentary. Sometimes the effigy is left to deteriorate in the barn. Sometimes the Guy Fawkes Mask is found and put back into service within the tradition. Perhaps it is rescued by a museum. Often they are left to rot away entirely. My task here is to gather up what we still have and put it back on the shelf for later discovery by other people to use to create their own celebrations. We must be confident that the values we attach to the things we treasure can be shared with others.

The Vision of Dynamic Artifacts

The artifacts of celebration which clothe the mystery are dynamic. When, for example, a bonfire is lit, or torches enter a public square, behaviors change. Mental processes are invoked, visions are given material form. Artifacts are versatile. Any artifact that fits can be given a role. Once involved in celebration, artifacts acquire new dimensions. They are not static, they inspire behaviors.

Illustration: Guy Fawkes Asleep, <u>Green's Characters & Scenes in Harlequin and Guy Fawkes or the Fifth of November</u>

Celebration as Pinball

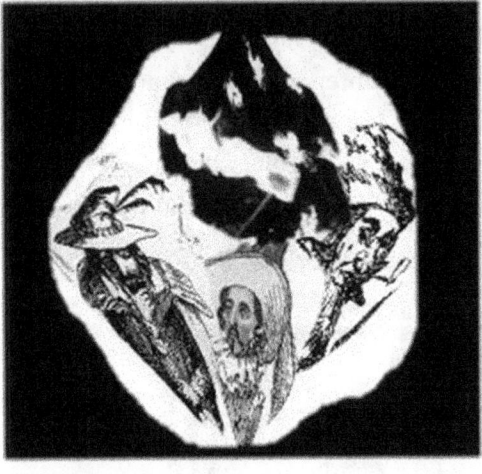

Celebration-as a ball of component artifacts

While no analogy is perfect, this one may be useful for some.

We are at the very beginning of a complex path toward explanation, understanding and effective intervention. The celebration of the Great Deliverance of 1605, Guy Fawkes Day and its Bonfire Night, can be thought of as a pinball game ball that has been kept in play for over 400 years.

People gather the component artifacts of celebration into a malleable ball. Parts can be added, adapted, removed, preserved, lost or re-discovered. The ball is launched as celebration into a complex world filled with all manner of special interests, cultural identities and social complexity. Often this environment conflicts with the values and interests of the groups who create the celebration.

From the ball's initial launch people act together like pinball game flippers to save the ball of celebration, flipping it upward, giving it more energy and staying power.

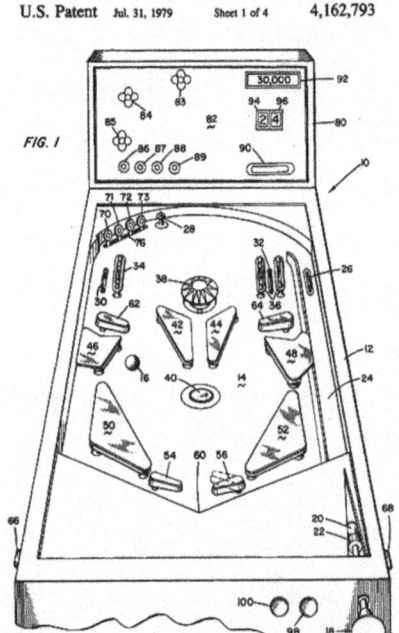

Flippers represent strategic re-direction as the new position of the ball is determined by the thoughtful skill of the flipper operator. Sometimes a flipper can be skillfully manipulated to hit a target to score and or

Cummings, Gary, J., Game Scoring System, Patent number: 4162793, Filing date: Mar 27, 1978, Issue date: Jul 31, 1979, U.S. Patent Office.

obtain more energy, just as celebration can be targeted to, for example, raise funds or accomplish national unity. The celebration can be re-energized based upon a re-designed cultural paradigm, or perhaps a marketing strategy, theological goal or political scheme.

Other people or groups serve as bumpers. When the ball hits the bumper it is propelled outward without the ability of the player to alter its direction strategically. In this way pure fun motivates the boost of energy of celebration. Coincidental events may also provide unplanned boosts of energy. For example the coincidence of the Great Deliverance with the change of seasons as well as the landing of William and Mary at Torbay, fulfilled this role, adding to the energy of the celebration.

In certain places on the playfield the ball of celebration can sink into holes. While out of play momentarily, the celebration can be adapted and modified. Parts are added, the celebration may be made more politically correct or more relevant to the times, before the hole shoots out the ball with increased energy and staying power.

An important aspect of the model is the complexity of the circuitry which is used to operate the device. We must be prepared for an equally complex and detailed mechanism governing the movement of celebration through culture, society and time.

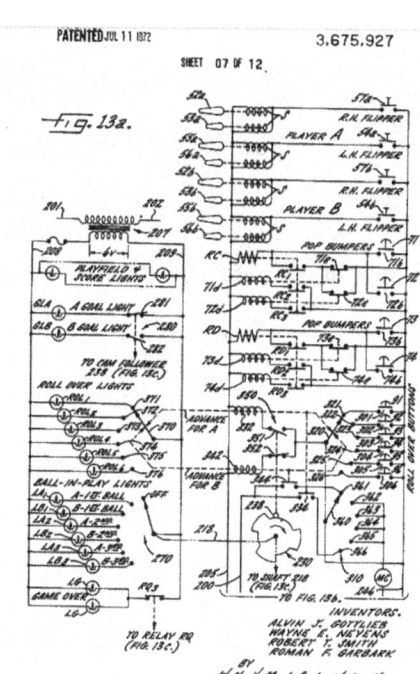

We begin here by tracing the celebration, the ball if you will, over an unseen playfield, and its path year after year. As we study its movements we should

1Gottlieb; Wayne E. Neyens et al, TWO-PLAYER PINBALL MACHINE, Patent number: 3675927, Filing date: Jun 10, 1970, Issue date: Jul 1, 1972, U.S. Patent Office.

eventually develop an understanding of the playfield and then of the mechanism that operates it. This work gathers essential evidence: snapshots of the ball and its constituent parts taken through time. It is the first step.

Applying Theory to Celebration

What do we do with this theory? Some recommendations.

1. Because revival based upon history alone is essentially static and taken alone there is no relationship to wonder or mystery, revival should be tempered with "enactment." Revival must be founded upon a conscious belief in the underlying mystery and wonder. While it can be entertaining, celebration must be rooted in belief. It should be essential and not optional.
2. Enactment is active. Celebration should be allowed to adapt to reflect the relationship between culture and the mysteries and wonders. It is not a re-enactment of an historical account. It is to be allowed to adapt.
3. Artifacts of celebration as opposed to the artifact of disclosure are the nuts and bolts, the hardware from which the celebration as disclosing artifact is constructed. At this level re-use and re-enactment are legitimate and valuable. One should not have to re-invent the basics. It is impossible to use them all every year. Yet, they must be respected as the investments they are. In this context history, recording of observation and curation are of greatest importance. Historic artifacts of celebration should be carefully curated and rotated in and out of celebration proportionally with newly created artifacts.
4. Avoid at all cost a narrowing of purpose. The numbers of reasons for celebration must be held as infinite. Selecting a single purpose, for example fund raising or tourism puts. all celebration at a selective disadvantage.

If we focus upon the wonders and mysteries rather than historical accounts our dedication to the task of disclosing them and working with them via artifacts of disclosure will be just as timeless.

A Fusion of Mysteries

What does this have to do with the celebration of Guy Fawkes Day and its Bonfire night? Not hard to tell!

The Gunpowder Plot Celebrations have been important and strong for over 400 years, permeating all aspects of culture from music to literature to foodways to politics, because they harnessed the power of relationships to two important shared mysteries: The Mystery of Providence and of Seasonal transition.

In purely historical terms the Great Deliverance saved not only the Parliament but also the King, so as the two institutions exchanged power through time the celebration could continue in the good favor of one or the other.

Culturally and politically the celebrations of the deliverance called for by the King, the Parliament and Clergy addressed the relationship of a political and cultural entity to the mystery of Divine providence. All was regarded within the framework of the Great Chain of Being. Why was the Parliament and nation preserved? The deliverance was not man-made. The deliverance re-enforced contemporary paradigms which were used to disclose the mystery of Providence. It was necessary to renew efforts to satisfy the requirements of those paradigms.

Essentially the Great Chain of Being which linked all aspects of creation including human beings to God was to be be carefully maintained. But first, the artifacts of celebration had to be prescribed and constructed. How do you stay in God's favor? Consultation with the Bible indicated that it was necessary from time to time to make sacrifices of thanksgiving. Therefore, annual celebrations were in order. They would plant trees in the orchards of future deliverances and be guided by the practices of the Old Testament of the Bible.

Just as this mystery was being addressed another approached. Guy Fawkes and the conspirators were discovered during an important time of seasonal change.

Had the plot gone forward as originally planned it would have occurred at the time of the opening of Parliament, February 7, 1605. The king delayed its opening for several reasons including the presence of the plague in London. So it is coincidence rather than "pagan" cultural continuity that linked the two events. The mystery of seasonal change, in this case from Fall to Winter, was already being marked by hiring fairs and other customs. It was a time of preparation for the challenges of the dark and cold months ahead. The transition had long been a period significant for ancient Celtic cultures, which knew it as the beginning of the season of darkness or Samhain. While the transition was significant in many dimensions, Bonfires were generic artifacts of celebration taken as it were "off the shelf" for important occasions of all kinds, such as births, coronations, and religious holidays. Fire was also looked upon as an iconic element in the Old Testament of the Bible. Other artifacts of celebration utilized to construct the disclosing artifact for the mystery of seasonal change such as the souling house visitation custom and Yorkshire parkin a.k.a. "soul cake," as well as the effigies and artifacts of chariviari and rough music, were also on the shelf ready for re-use in the new disclosing artifact of celebration of the Great Deliverance from the Gunpowder Treason. The nuts-and-bolts hardware of celebration was well known, documented and ready for action. Some of them may have been quite ancient although much of their presumed history has been lost.

Celebrations were designed to disclose the two mysteries complemented each other harmoniously. There was a good fit. On one hand the nation and culture prepared for future blessings and a good relationship with Providence, and on the other they worked to ensure survival through preparation to do battle with the harsh seasons ahead. Combined with these shared cultural motivations went all of the personal ones such as simply going out for a good time, meeting friends, and having fun. This combination of motives helped to make the celebrations durable.

The study of Guy Fawkes Day Celebration is the study of the adaptation and re-consideration of the paradigms used to disclose the two abstract mysteries. It is important to understand that it is inappropriate to use the term "evolution" in this context. Evolution implies a positive teleological development moving toward a better fit, an improved product or a higher state. This is absolutely not the case with these celebrations. Adaption of the paradigms came periodically and took the form of assembly, disassembly and re-assessment of purpose. Along the way elements are discarded, and opinions concerning the mysteries change radically. Today we find ourselves with paradigms that are vastly different from the ones employed in the 17th century.

Museums and libraries are filled with cast-off artifacts and traditions. As we study the processes and relationships involved, we have to be sure to remember that ours is just one answer and is not necessarily the best. Once we are open to the adjustment of the celebrations we can work with the processes and relationships we will discover to utilize the available artifacts, customs and treasures to achieve the best possible fit between our celebrations and their ability to disclose and respond to the mysteries that we confront.

Artifacts of celebration are complex. They can be seen as being individual universes serving many roles and providing for many functions in addition to the ones they are selected to accomplish. Bonfire, for example, is much more than a simple fire. It provides free fuel for those for whom fuel was costly. The celebrants could cook and see at night as they gathered around the bonfire. Using the leisure time that celebration provided, they could check in with their neighbors, share news, exchange assistance and coordinate their lives. Bonfires were funded along with drink by wealthy citizens who through their position had evaded the grasp of the law. The pay-back of food and drink and warmth and light kept the imperfect system of government functioning by providing balance. Each custom brought to bear to disclose the mysteries intensified the meaning of the day for the culture as a whole. The greater the number of complex artifacts of celebration utilized, the greater the number of relationships with potential celebrants that could be created. The artifacts bring relationships that form a multi-stranded interwoven root system linking one to the other and to people. Connecting at many levels and at great social depth insured the continuation of the celebration. As celebrations became more complex the question arises: How well did they continue to function in their intended roles as disclosers of the mysteries? That is one potential way of evaluating successor paradigms.

As this work unfolds we shall see how a strong case for relevance can be made for celebrations which effectively help human beings acknowldedge, disclose and generally relate to ever-present and unchanging mysteries which continue to shape our world today.

The bottom line is this: Does your celebration effectively disclose certain mysteries in our environment in such a way that our continued relationship to them will be as positive, efficient and beneficial as possible? Don't stick to just one mystery-the more the better.

As it was in the beginning

As I studied Guy Fawkes Celebration and its Bonfire night I began by trying to determine how I should celebrate. I gathered up traditions and enacted them. My quest lead me to the Bonfire Boys of Sussex. They taught me their traditions. I learned how to make torches, build effigies, cook traditional foods. I found them inspiring even though they were lamenting the transition of the customs that they experienced growing up as I had in London. They hoped for a return to what they called "the old traditions." But it turned out, as I pursued further research, that their experience was only that of a few generations out of over four hundred years of the march of the celebration through time. For Celebrants of earlier centuries, fancy dress was tattered women's dresses and blackface. Celebrations were more like threatening mobs than organized, regulated and safe processions. "People power" rather than municipal power prevailed and Riot Acts were read. I determined that it might be helpful to return to the start and discover how it all unfolded and maybe discover some treasures lost or discarded on the way, dropped by the "Guys" in their trudge through time.

This volume is designed to help future celebrants to return to the very beginning. Here in this volume you will observe the birth of celebration.

Some parts will be found to be archaic or dated but I hope that you will also discover timeless aspects. Once they were loud and bright, relating to the two mysteries, but are often now faint and tarnished. Yet they can help give life to celebrations to come.

Remember, Remember.....here's how!

Nineteenth Century Print

Nationalism – What Was this England?

The Great Chain of Being and other Essential Life Support Systems

Above: Illustration 1579 drawing of the great chain of being from Didacus Valades, Rhetorica Christiana

The Great Chain of Being

England in 1605 was a unique land, tethered to God via the *scala naturae* or Great Chain of Being. This order of the universe would condition the English reaction to all events in 1605 and can later be used to evaluate the transformation of the people and state over time. This concept of the structure of the world remained important in one form or another until the revolution caused by Darwin in the 19th century. Although the concept persisted the Chain looked quite different in the 19th century than it had in the 17th. Indeed although its parts are still with us today it may be very difficult to see the chain at all.

Everyone and everything was categorized, according the beliefs of the time and place in their own link of the chain. At the top of the chain in heaven was God the creator. Beneath him were the angels, worldly and spiritual. The humans, fallible and mutable, clung to the link beneath them. Beneath man came the beasts, the fish and then the plants, then the elements and rocks. The chain therefore literally extended from heaven to the earth itself. Everything fit somewhere.

The role of Kings, Churchmen, Politicians and the people was to maintain the Great Chain or at least do nothing to upset it. Just as all things were part of the chain, all actions, events, and philosophies were interpreted in such a way as to harmonize with the chain as it was interpreted in any given time. If the chain held sway and was strong everything would be well and of course celebrations could go onward. In addition to being a people linked to God via their King and the chain, England in 1605 was a country and people in pursuit of nationalism but frustrated by diversity of religions, theories, schemes, and special political interests. Beginning with the Reformation and Renaissance multiple models of chains had evolved and competed with each other to control politics and underwrite celebrations.

In his fundamental work on the Great Chain of Being Arthur Lovejoy concluded:

"...as many historic examples show- the utility of a belief and its validity are independent variables; and erroneous hypotheses are often avenues to truth.....I may,...close by a reminder that the idea of the Chain of Being, with its presuppositions and implications, has had many curiously happy consequences in the history of western thought..."

-Lovejoy, Arthur O., <u>The Great Chain of Being,</u> 1936, p.233.

I propose that the paradigm of the Great Chain of Being can be employed as an effective tool to understand the evolution of celebration and its changing relationship to the cultures which have created and adapted it. In particular the evolution of the paradigm is helpful in explaining instability in the celebration which has led to continual cycles of decline and re-invention. In addition, analysis and reconstruction of the paradigm has a great potential to produce a strong, lasting foundation for continued celebration based upon eternal mysteries rather than fluctuating cultural reassessments.

Lovejoy describes the Great Chain of Being (Latin: *scala naturae*, literally "ladder or stair-way of nature"), as originating in the <u>Republic</u> and <u>Timareus</u> of Plato. The paradigm evolved and was systematized by the Neo-Platonists. Essentially the Great Chain is a categorization of all creation from the earth up to God in a chain based upon the state of knowledge and belief at the time. Categorization was done by specialists and perhaps even intelligible only to them, however, the foundations of the chain in the deity at the top and material creation at the bottom provided a comprehension of the mysteries which could comfort all people in their daily struggles between them.

Most analysis of the chain has focused upon the nature of the deity and the justification for the method of classification employed. Significant debate has surrounded the timing and evolution of the process of creation. Other moral issues have arisen relating to the ranking of social classes and races in relationship to the perfection of the deity. There has been significant debate as to whether creation is finite or ongoing. For my purposes I would suggest that the categorization and ranking found within the Great Chain of Being is a temporal artifact dependent upon the state of knowledge and belief at the time of its creation. If we recognize that change is ongoing through processes such as evolution and that our knowledge is constantly expanding we can be justified in allowing our specialists to rehabilitate the categorization within the chain to reflect current knowledge. Given constant rewiring of relationships within the chain based upon the evolution of our knowledge of the truth we need not destroy the chain or continually construct entirely new ones. In order to accomplish this rewiring, we must make a fundamental conceptual change. We must remove the deity from the process of categorization. We should allow our specialists to create categories based upon knowable complexity and or evolutionary sequence defined by the state of knowledge. In this way the linkage of the mysteries by the chain is preserved.

I would suggest that, agreeing to disagree as to the nature of the deity and the nature of our knowledge of all creation, we would be well served by redefining them as mysteries which continue to defy our knowledge. If we accept that the mystery of the deity is timeless and as yet not understood and if we accept that creation is not as yet fully defined by our limited scientific knowledge and that the concept of "infinity" is at best a stop-gap concept waiting for knowledge to expand, then we can envision a Great Chain of Being which is eternally founded yet adaptable, its content updateable. I see in the two mysteries, that of deity and of creation reflections of the two concepts of "God" or mystery described by Lovejoy. At the end of the chain known as deity was the kind of being:

..."Absolute of otherworldliness- self-sufficient, out of time, alien to the categories of ordinary human thought and experience, needing no world of lesser beings to supplement or enhance his own eternal self-contained perfection." At the bottom end, that of creation, is the "God Mystery" "who emphatically was not self-sufficient nor, in any philosophical sense , ""absolute""": one whose essential nature required the existence of other beings, and not of one kind of these only, but of all kinds which could find a place in the descending scale of the possibilities of reality- a God whose prime attribute was generativeness, whose manifestation was to be found in the diversity of creatures and therefore in the temporal order and the manifold spectacle of nature's processes." (Lovejoy,1936, p.315.)

Although a paradigm tailored for my purposes, this paradigm holds the chain constant and universal. If this is the case, all of creation including celebration will be set within the mysteries of deity and creation. The paradigm allows us to place our explanations and analysis upon a foundation independent of time. This will allow us to adapt our celebrations so that they will become more stable through time, founded upon relationships to our environment of mysteries rather than upon constant cultural reassessment.

The Chain is Challenged

Historically, the Great Chain of Being once served as a disclosing artifact for two important mysteries: the Creation, and God. In the late 15th century Renaissance science began to attack our relationships to earth. The earth could be understood through science without reference to mystery of creation. The bottom end of the great chain was disconnected. It was replaced by constant scientific debate which continues to this day.

In 1517 Martin Luther began a religious reformation that attacked the top end of the Chain of Being- the relationship to the mystery of God which flowed through the clergy and absolute monarchy to the people. Rather than to replace the Pope with a unified reformed church, Luther's reformation produced many alternative Protestant denominations. There was no one top anchor of the chain. Each denomination established its own different disclosing artifact for relating to the mystery of God. Nations such as England, for example, created a national church, their own individual disclosing artifact for the relationship. Once the chain linking people to God was severed, mercantile nation-states maintained for a time a link, through the absolute monarch, to the mystery of the deity. With the execution in England of Charles I by Parliament even this replacement for the top end of the chain had been severed.

Beginning with Henry VIII and continuing under Elizabeth I the monarchy represented the union of Church and State. England was a nation for which the sovereign played the role of moderator rather than that of dictator. The great blessing of Nationalism required that harmony be maintained between all groups: cultural, political, and spiritual. The goal was that of holding the pendulum motionless in the center so that the horrors of drastic change such as were seen in the Reformation of Henry VIII and Bloody Mary would no longer threaten prosperity and national unity. Religion was purposefully left ambiguous in the Book of Common Prayer. Allowing personal interpretation would benefit unity and nationalism.

There were, however, limits. These were political: one could not flaunt the law or promote sedition. It was important that religion not be allowed to cross the political line in support of other nations against one's own state. Religion therefore had a dual role. It was permitted to be spiritual but it could not become political. Ambiguity of religion, however, would not only lead to the prospering of underground radicals but would also force the state to deal with constantly competing religious and moral philosophies, each of which would strive for political support. It can be said that the history of the 17th century

England is that of the battle for control of the pendulum and the preservation of the Great Chain of Being from political manipulation. The solution, it was thought, was for the church to seek the middle way or *Via Media*.

Via Media

The Anglican church under Elizabeth I saw itself in the middle. It was neither extremely Protestant, that is, Calvinist or Genevan, nor was it Catholic or Roman. This compromise provided for a degree of national stability. It was based upon the role of the absolutist monarch which had replaced the disputed nature of the link to the deity which had anchored the Great Chain of Being at its top. By sticking to the *Via Media,* radical thinkers could be marginalized and confrontation with their political surrogates could be defined and focused. Nationalism could define itself in relation to its political enemies on either side. The church, with the absolute monarch at its head, was free to make concessions to Catholics in the areas of liturgy and ritual, and was kept politically independent by Acts of Supremacy and Uniformity. The primary interest of the government was the preservation of the Chain of Being and the maintenance of strong nationalism. It was not the placating of Protestant extremists or Catholics as neither group was satisfied. The important point for them was that they were allowed to survive to manipulate politics another day. Thus the arrangement paved the way for great stability while at the same time leaving the Great Chain of Being vulnerable to political winds.

We proceed to view the events of 1605 and the changing celebrations of the great deliverance that followed, our way illuminated by the ever-present Great Chain of Being, English Nationalism and the Via Media. We shall see how celebration of the Fifth of November evolves within this unique political, cultural, and spiritual environment.

Stories Vs. Explanation

Analyses of disclosing artifacts, such as celebrations, when created independently from their relationships to mysteries and wonders, lose dynamic explanatory vitality. They become simple stories, artifacts of celebration, which can only be told and re-told, that is, reenacted. They lose their ability to disclose because mysteries and wonders are not static but constantly changing. Appearing to be tools of explanation, these static scripts and stories denying mystery and wonder they do not actually explain but rather lead only to the next set of questions. Until we reach some sort of end point where the "deity" and creation are completely known, wonder and mystery will grow as fast as explanation expands. While the stories allow us to know the wonder, they do not assist us in the manipulation of the relationships to wonder and mystery. They are temporally specific. This is perhaps the underlying cause for the shock felt that scientific progress, while expanding knowledge of the wonder also leads to unforeseen negative consequences such as the capability for mass destruction and pollution.

For the purposes of revival the model which I am proposing anthropologists and folklorists should encourage the development of strong networks of complex relationships between the people and the disclosing artifacts and the wonders and mysteries they disclose. These relationships should be shared by the largest segment of the population as is possible. The more relationships the stronger the celebration will become. The relationships need to be specific, function at many levels and be well developed.

The many individually-defined, personal, motivating purposes such as having fun, seeking the heat of the bonfire, socializing, as well as those related to the stories of the plot, the wonder and mystery of national deliverance and the mystery of seasonal change and natural disasters as well as unexplained deliverances, must all be intertwined, and networked together just as the roots of a large tree. The more complex the web of relationships developed between these purposes the stronger the disclosing artifact of celebration will become.

This suggestion contradicts the trend currently prevailing of viewing celebrations as primarily defined individually, or personally rather than by large groups and limited to the lower level goals such of having fun. At this level enactment fades and re-enactment prevails. Often the unification of of relationships to the mystery is confused with unregulated nationalism. This danger is the result of the degradation of the Chain of Being which produced absolute monarchy following the destruction of the "deity" end of the chain and its replacement with nation-specific absolutist rulers. Just as we have agreed to disagree as to the nature of the "deity" we also must recognize that the mysteries are not nation-specific. Once we embed individual groups, cultures and nations within the larger mystery, the danger of uncontained nationalism can be eliminated from the model.

The role of historians and folklorists may be not to simply safeguard the story, the script of celebration but to manage the active use of the artifacts of celebration (of which stories and scripts are only some examples) within the artifacts of disclosure of which they are constituent parts. Their task is the insertion and attachment the greatest number of the artifacts within the web of relationships which support, change and maintain the artifact of disclosure.

In this way we might make up for the loss of the monolithic, state/culture specific great chain of being by building individual networks between groups of celebrants and the original mysteries and wonders avoiding constant localized cultural reassessment.

A Nearly Exploded Idea.

Punch, 1885

Background Arguments

Of course it was a blessed land! Had not the Armada been beaten back by the very hand of God so that his favored people might be saved? Was not the country blessed by a Divine monarch whose path was guided by God? Did not England have a Parliament which provided for the rule of law and justice? Were not the Christian people of the realm the true descendants of the Israelites of the Old Testament– and likewise God's chosen ones? Believe it or not, more importantly it was real in the hearts and minds and souls of the people and their rulers in England in the 17th century..

An important part of that reality was the firm belief that England shared as one people the historical legacy of the Israelites of the Old Testament. In fact it was much more than an historical legacy, it was believed to be real continuity. The English were therefore required to continue the ancient traditions, walking the walks, talking the talks and celebrating the celebrations, the Old Testament being their guide. Why not? Why would they ever risk the loss of God's favor and become "the other?"

One part of this shared history, a part that we must know and understand well was the Book of Esther- because as all were to come to know and understand well– this portion of history would repeat itself in 1605.

So I have provided portion of that history for you to know and understand below:

The Biblical Foundation of Politics and Reaction

The Book of Esther. Bible, King James Version

The story thus far. Suffice it to say that Esther, a Jew, after winning a beauty contest was selected by the King Ahasuerus (who was not a Jew) to become his queen. She did not tell him that she was a Jew. Esther's next of kin, Mordecai, also a Jew, had instructed her not to tell the king that she was a Jew.

Now we can return to the story:

Esther 2

21 In those days, while Mordecai sat in the king's gate, two of the king's chamberlains, Bigthan and Teresh, of those which kept the door, were wroth, and sought to lay hands on the king Ahasuerus.

22 And the thing was known to Mordecai, who told it unto Esther the queen; and Esther certified the king thereof in Mordecai's name.

23 And when inquisition was made of the matter, it was found out; therefore they were both hanged on a tree: and it was written in the book of the chronicles before the king.

Esther 3

1 After these things did king Ahasuerus promote Haman the son of Hammedatha the Agagite, and advanced him, and set his seat above all the princes that were with him.

2 And all the king's servants, that were in the king's gate, bowed, and reverenced Haman: for the king had so commanded concerning him. But Mordecai bowed not, nor did him reverence.

3 Then the king's servants, which were in the king's gate, said unto Mordecai, Why transgressest thou the king's commandment?

4 Now it came to pass, when they spake daily unto him, and he hearkened not unto them, that they told Haman, to see whether Mordecai's matters would stand: for he had told them that he was a Jew.

5 And when Haman saw that Mordecai bowed not, nor did him reverence, then was Haman full of wrath.

6 And he thought scorn to lay hands on Mordecai alone; for they had shewed him the people of Mordecai: wherefore Haman sought to destroy all the Jews that were throughout the whole kingdom of Ahasuerus, even the people of

Mordecai.

7 In the first month, that is, the month Nisan, in the twelfth year of king Ahasuerus, they cast Pur, that is, the lot, before Haman from day to day, and from month to month, to the twelfth month, that is, the month Adar.

8 And Haman said unto king Ahasuerus, There is a certain people scattered abroad and dispersed among the people in all the provinces of thy kingdom; and their laws are diverse from all people; neither keep they the king's laws: therefore it is not for the king's profit to suffer them.

9 If it please the king, let it be written that they may be destroyed: and I will pay ten thousand talents of silver to the hands of those that have the charge of the business, to bring it into the king's treasuries.

10 And the king took his ring from his hand, and gave it unto Haman the son of Hammedatha the Agagite, the Jews' enemy.

11 And the king said unto Haman, The silver is given to thee, the people also, to do with them as it seemeth good to thee.

12 Then were the king's scribes called on the thirteenth day of the first month, and there was written according to all that Haman had commanded unto the king's lieutenants, and to the governors that were over every province, and to the rulers of every people of every province according to the writing thereof, and to every people after their language; in the name of king Ahasuerus was it written, and sealed with the king's ring.

13 And the letters were sent by posts into all the king's provinces, to destroy, to kill, and to cause to perish, all Jews, both young and old, little children and women, in one day, even upon the thirteenth day of the twelfth month, which is the month Adar, and to take the spoil of them for a prey.

14 The copy of the writing for a commandment to be given in every province was published unto all people, that they should be ready against that day.

15 The posts went out, being hastened by the king's commandment, and the decree was given in Shushan the palace. And the king and Haman sat down to drink; but the city Shushan was perplexed.

Esther 4

1 When Mordecai perceived all that was done, Mordecai rent his clothes, and put on sackcloth with ashes, and went out into the midst of the city, and cried with a loud and a bitter cry;

2 And came even before the king's gate: for none might enter into the king's gate clothed with sackcloth.

3 And in every province, whithersoever the king's commandment and his decree came, there was great mourning among the Jews, and fasting, and weeping, and wailing; and many lay in sackcloth and ashes.

4 So Esther's maids and her chamberlains came and told it her. Then was the

queen exceedingly grieved; and she sent raiment to clothe Mordecai, and to take away his sackcloth from him: but he received it not.

5 Then called Esther for Hatach, one of the king's chamberlains, whom he had appointed to attend upon her, and gave him a commandment to Mordecai, to know what it was, and why it was.

6 So Hatach went forth to Mordecai unto the street of the city, which was before the king's gate.

7 And Mordecai told him of all that had happened unto him, and of the sum of the money that Haman had promised to pay to the king's treasuries for the Jews, to destroy them.

8 Also he gave him the copy of the writing of the decree that was given at Shushan to destroy them, to shew it unto Esther, and to declare it unto her, and to charge her that she should go in unto the king, to make supplication unto him, and to make request before him for her people.

9 And Hatach came and told Esther the words of Mordecai.

10 Again Esther spake unto Hatach, and gave him commandment unto Mordecai;

11 All the king's servants, and the people of the king's provinces, do know, that whosoever, whether man or women, shall come unto the king into the inner court, who is not called, there is one law of his to put him to death, except such to whom the king shall hold out the golden sceptre, that he may live: but I have not been called to come in unto the king these thirty days.

12 And they told to Mordecai Esther's words.

13 Then Mordecai commanded to answer Esther, Think not with thyself that thou shalt escape in the king's house, more than all the Jews.

14 For if thou altogether holdest thy peace at this time, then shall there enlargement and deliverance arise to the Jews from another place; but thou and thy father's house shall be destroyed: and who knoweth whether thou art come to the kingdom for such a time as this?

15 Then Esther bade them return Mordecai this answer,

16 Go, gather together all the Jews that are present in Shushan, and fast ye for me, and neither eat nor drink three days, night or day: I also and my maidens will fast likewise; and so will I go in unto the king, which is not according to the law: and if I perish, I perish.

17 So Mordecai went his way, and did according to all that Esther had commanded him.

Esther 5

1 Now it came to pass on the third day, that Esther put on her royal apparel, and stood in the inner court of the king's house, over against the king's house: and the king sat upon his royal throne in the royal house, over against the gate of the

house.

2 And it was so, when the king saw Esther the queen standing in the court, that she obtained favour in his sight: and the king held out to Esther the golden sceptre that was in his hand. So Esther drew near, and touched the top of the sceptre.

3 Then said the king unto her, What wilt thou, queen Esther? and what is thy request? it shall be even given thee to the half of the kingdom.

4 And Esther answered, If it seem good unto the king, let the king and Haman come this day unto the banquet that I have prepared for him.

5 Then the king said, Cause Haman to make haste, that he may do as Esther hath said. So the king and Haman came to the banquet that Esther had prepared.

6 And the king said unto Esther at the banquet of wine, What is thy petition? and it shall be granted thee: and what is thy request? even to the half of the kingdom it shall be performed.

7 Then answered Esther, and said, My petition and my request is;

8 If I have found favour in the sight of the king, and if it please the king to grant my petition, and to perform my request, let the king and Haman come to the banquet that I shall prepare for them, and I will do to morrow as the king hath said.

9 Then went Haman forth that day joyful and with a glad heart: but when Haman saw Mordecai in the king's gate, that he stood not up, nor moved for him, he was full of indignation against Mordecai.

10 Nevertheless Haman refrained himself: and when he came home, he sent and called for his friends, and Zeresh his wife.

11 And Haman told them of the glory of his riches, and the multitude of his children, and all the things wherein the king had promoted him, and how he had advanced him above the princes and servants of the king.

12 Haman said moreover, Yea, Esther the queen did let no man come in with the king unto the banquet that she had prepared but myself; and to morrow am I invited unto her also with the king.

13 Yet all this availeth me nothing, so long as I see Mordecai the Jew sitting at the king's gate.

14 Then said Zeresh his wife and all his friends unto him, Let a gallows be made of fifty cubits high, and to morrow speak thou unto the king that Mordecai may be hanged thereon: then go thou in merrily with the king unto the banquet. And the thing pleased Haman; and he caused the gallows to be made.

Esther 6

1 On that night could not the king sleep, and he commanded to bring the book of records of the chronicles; and they were read before the king.

2 And it was found written, that Mordecai had told of Bigthana and Teresh, two of the king's chamberlains, the keepers of the door, who sought to lay hand on the king Ahasuerus.

3 And the king said, What honour and dignity hath been done to Mordecai for this? Then said the king's servants that ministered unto him, There is nothing done for him.

4 And the king said, Who is in the court? Now Haman was come into the outward court of the king's house, to speak unto the king to hang Mordecai on the gallows that he had prepared for him.

5 And the king's servants said unto him, Behold, Haman standeth in the court. And the king said, Let him come in.

6 So Haman came in. And the king said unto him, What shall be done unto the man whom the king delighteth to honour? Now Haman thought in his heart, To whom would the king delight to do honour more than to myself?

7 And Haman answered the king, For the man whom the king delighteth to honour,

8 Let the royal apparel be brought which the king useth to wear, and the horse that the king rideth upon, and the crown royal which is set upon his head:

9 And let this apparel and horse be delivered to the hand of one of the king's most noble princes, that they may array the man withal whom the king delighteth to honour, and bring him on horseback through the street of the city, and proclaim before him, Thus shall it be done to the man whom the king delighteth to honour.

10 Then the king said to Haman, Make haste, and take the apparel and the horse, as thou hast said, and do even so to Mordecai the Jew, that sitteth at the king's gate: let nothing fail of all that thou hast spoken.

11 Then took Haman the apparel and the horse, and arrayed Mordecai, and brought him on horseback through the street of the city, and proclaimed before him, Thus shall it be done unto the man whom the king delighteth to honour.

12 And Mordecai came again to the king's gate. But Haman hasted to his house mourning, and having his head covered.

13 And Haman told Zeresh his wife and all his friends every thing that had befallen him. Then said his wise men and Zeresh his wife unto him, If Mordecai be of the seed of the Jews, before whom thou hast begun to fall, thou shalt not prevail against him, but shalt surely fall before him.

14 And while they were yet talking with him, came the king's chamberlains, and hasted to bring Haman unto the banquet that Esther had prepared.

Esther 7

1 So the king and Haman came to banquet with Esther the queen.

2 And the king said again unto Esther on the second day at the banquet of wine,

What is thy petition, queen Esther? and it shall be granted thee: and what is thy request? and it shall be performed, even to the half of the kingdom.

3 Then Esther the queen answered and said, If I have found favour in thy sight, O king, and if it please the king, let my life be given me at my petition, and my people at my request:

4 For we are sold, I and my people, to be destroyed, to be slain, and to perish. But if we had been sold for bondmen and bondwomen, I had held my tongue, although the enemy could not countervail the king's damage.

5 Then the king Ahasuerus answered and said unto Esther the queen, Who is he, and where is he, that durst presume in his heart to do so?

6 And Esther said, The adversary and enemy is this wicked Haman. Then Haman was afraid before the king and the queen.

7 And the king arising from the banquet of wine in his wrath went into the palace garden: and Haman stood up to make request for his life to Esther the queen; for he saw that there was evil determined against him by the king.

8 Then the king returned out of the palace garden into the place of the banquet of wine; and Haman was fallen upon the bed whereon Esther was. Then said the king, Will he force the queen also before me in the house? As the word went out of king's mouth, they covered Haman's face.

9 And Harbonah, one of the chamberlains, said before the king, Behold also, the gallows fifty cubits high, which Haman had made for Mordecai, who spoken good for the king, standeth in the house of Haman. Then the king said, Hang him thereon.

10 So they hanged Haman on the gallows that he had prepared for Mordecai. Then was the king's wrath pacified.

Esther 8

1 On that day did the king Ahasuerus give the house of Haman the Jews' enemy unto Esther the queen. And Mordecai came before the king; for Esther had told what he was unto her.

2 And the king took off his ring, which he had taken from Haman, and gave it unto Mordecai. And Esther set Mordecai over the house of Haman.

3 And Esther spake yet again before the king, and fell down at his feet, and besought him with tears to put away the mischief of Haman the Agagite, and his device that he had devised against the Jews.

4 Then the king held out the golden sceptre toward Esther. So Esther arose, and stood before the king,

5 And said, If it please the king, and if I have favour in his sight, and the thing seem right before the king, and I be pleasing in his eyes, let it be written to reverse the letters devised by Haman the son of Hammedatha the Agagite, which he wrote to destroy the Jews which are in all the king's provinces:

6 For how can I endure to see the evil that shall come unto my people? or how can I endure to see the destruction of my kindred?

7 Then the king Ahasuerus said unto Esther the queen and to Mordecai the Jew, Behold, I have given Esther the house of Haman, and him they have hanged upon the gallows, because he laid his hand upon the Jews.

8 Write ye also for the Jews, as it liketh you, in the king's name, and seal it with the king's ring: for the writing which is written in the king's name, and sealed with the king's ring, may no man reverse.

9 Then were the king's scribes called at that time in the third month, that is, the month Sivan, on the three and twentieth day thereof; and it was written according to all that Mordecai commanded unto the Jews, and to the lieutenants, and the deputies and rulers of the provinces which are from India unto Ethiopia, an hundred twenty and seven provinces, unto every province according to the writing thereof, and unto every people after their language, and to the Jews according to their writing, and according to their language.

10 And he wrote in the king Ahasuerus' name, and sealed it with the king's ring, and sent letters by posts on horseback, and riders on mules, camels, and young dromedaries:

11 Wherein the king granted the Jews which were in every city to gather themselves together, and to stand for their life, to destroy, to slay and to cause to perish, all the power of the people and province that would assault them, both little ones and women, and to take the spoil of them for a prey,

At this point the Jews with the permission of the king took revenge against their tormentors and killed them.....most importantly they celebrated.....

15 And Mordecai went out from the presence of the king in royal apparel of blue and white, and with a great crown of gold, and with a garment of fine linen and purple: and the city of Shushan rejoiced and was glad.

16 The Jews had light, and gladness, and joy, and honour.

17 And in every province, and in every city, whithersoever the king's commandment and his decree came, the Jews had joy and gladness, a feast and a good day. And many of the people of the land became Jews; for the fear of the Jews fell upon them.

Esther 9

17 On the thirteenth day of the month Adar; and on the fourteenth day of the same rested they, and made it a day of feasting and gladness.

18 But the Jews that were at Shushan assembled together on the thirteenth day thereof, and on the fourteenth thereof; and on the fifteenth day of the same they rested, and made it a day of feasting and gladness.

19 Therefore the Jews of the villages, that dwelt in the unwalled towns, made the fourteenth day of the month Adar a day of gladness and feasting, and a good day, and of sending portions one to another.

20 And Mordecai wrote these things, and sent letters unto all the Jews that were in all the provinces of the king Ahasuerus, both nigh and far,

21 To stablish this among them, that they should keep the fourteenth day of the month Adar, and the fifteenth day of the same, yearly,

22 As the days wherein the Jews rested from their enemies, and the month which was turned unto them from sorrow to joy, and from mourning into a good day: that they should make them days of feasting and joy, and of sending portions one to another, and gifts to the poor.

23 And the Jews undertook to do as they had begun, and as Mordecai had written unto them;

24 Because Haman the son of Hammedatha, the Agagite, the enemy of all the Jews, had devised against the Jews to destroy them, and had cast Pur, that is, the lot, to consume them, and to destroy them;

25 But when Esther came before the king, he commanded by letters that his wicked device, which he devised against the Jews, should return upon his own head, and that he and his sons should be hanged on the gallows.

26 Wherefore they called these days Purim after the name of Pur. Therefore for all the words of this letter, and of that which they had seen concerning this matter, and which had come unto them,

27 The Jews ordained, and took upon them, and upon their seed, and upon all such as joined themselves unto them, so as it should not fail, that they would keep these two days according to their writing, and according to their appointed time every year;

28 And that these days should be remembered and kept throughout every generation, every family, every province, and every city; and that these days of Purim should not fail from among the Jews, nor the memorial of them perish from their seed.

29 Then Esther the queen, the daughter of Abihail, and Mordecai the Jew, wrote with all authority, to confirm this second letter of Purim.

30 And he sent the letters unto all the Jews, to the hundred twenty and seven provinces of the kingdom of Ahasuerus, with words of peace and truth,

31 To confirm these days of Purim in their times appointed, according as Mordecai the Jew and Esther the queen had enjoined them, and as they had decreed for themselves and for their seed, the matters of the fastings and their cry.

32 And the decree of Esther confirmed these matters of Purim; and it was written in the book.

The Sacrifice of Thanksgiving- Sacrifice Defined in the Old Testament...

As for celebrations according to the Bible: Let us consider the "Sacrifice of Thanksgiving"

Leviticus 7:12
If he offer it for a thanksgiving, then he shall offer with the sacrifice of thanksgiving unleavened cakes mingled with oil, and unleavened wafers anointed with oil, and cakes mingled with oil, of fine flour, fried.

Leviticus 7:13
Besides the cakes, he shall offer for his offering leavened bread with the sacrifice of thanksgiving of his peace offerings.

Leviticus 7:15
And the flesh of the sacrifice of his peace offerings for thanksgiving shall be eaten the same day that it is offered; he shall not leave any of it until the morning.

Leviticus 22:29
And when ye will offer a sacrifice of thanksgiving unto the LORD, offer it at your own will.

Leviticus 7:12
If he offer it for a thanksgiving, then he shall offer with the sacrifice of thanksgiving unleavened cakes mingled with oil, and unleavened wafers anointed with oil, and cakes mingled with oil, of fine flour, fried.

Leviticus 7:13
Besides the cakes, he shall offer for his offering leavened bread with the sacrifice of thanksgiving of his peace offerings.

Leviticus 7:15
And the flesh of the sacrifice of his peace offerings for thanksgiving shall be eaten the same day that it is offered; he shall not leave any of it until the morning.

Leviticus 22:29
And when ye will offer a sacrifice of thanksgiving unto the LORD, offer it at your own will.

Chronicles 16:8 Give thanks unto the LORD, call upon his name, make known his deeds among the people.

Psalm 95:2
Let us come before his presence with thanksgiving, and make a joyful noise unto him with psalms.

Psalm 69:30 30. I will praise the name of God with a song, and will magnify him with thanksgiving.

Nehemiah 12:46
For in the days of David and Asaph of old there were chief of the singers, and songs of praise and thanksgiving unto God.

Jeremiah 30:19
And out of them shall proceed thanksgiving and the voice of them that make merry: and I will multiply them, and they shall not be few; I will also glorify them, and they shall not be small.

God Looking Down and Laughing- Inspiration for Iconography and Verse

Deuteronomy 26:7

7 And when we cried unto the Lord God of our fathers, the Lord heard our voice, and looked on our affliction, and our labour, and our oppression:

8 And the Lord brought us forth out of Egypt with a mighty hand, and with an outstretched arm, and with great terribleness, and with signs, and with wonders:

Psalm 102:19-20

19 For he hath looked down from the height of his sanctuary; from heaven did the Lord behold the earth;

20 To hear the groaning of the prisoner; to loose those that are appointed to death;

Deuteronomy 11

11 But the land, whither ye go to possess it, is a land of hills and valleys, and drinketh water of the rain of heaven:

12 A land which the Lord thy God careth for: the eyes of the Lord thy God are always upon it, from the beginning of the year even unto the end of the year.

17 Which said unto God, Depart from us: and what can the Almighty do for

them?

18 Yet he filled their houses with good things: but the counsel of the wicked is far from me.

19 The righteous see it, and are glad: and the innocent laugh them to scorn.

20 Whereas our substance is not cut down, but the remnant of them the fire consumeth.

21 Acquaint now thyself with him, and be at peace: thereby good shall come unto thee.

-<u>Bible</u>, King James Version, "Job 22," 17-21.

<u>Psalm</u> 37

¹¹But the meek shall inherit the earth; and shall delight themselves in the abundance of peace.

¹²The wicked plotteth against the just, and gnasheth upon him with his teeth.

¹³The LORD shall laugh at him: for he seeth that his day is coming.

¹⁴The wicked have drawn out the sword, and have bent their bow, to cast down the poor and needy, and to slay such as be of upright conversation.

¹⁵Their sword shall enter into their own heart, and their bows shall be broken.

¹⁶A little that a righteous man hath is better than the riches of many wicked.

¹⁷For the arms of the wicked shall be broken: but the LORD upholdeth the righteous.

--<u>Bible,</u> King James Version, "Psalm 37," 12-17.

In Conclusion

As you think of the people of England, remember that they may appear to be English but they are called to walk, talk, celebrate and behave like God's chosen people the Israelites of the Old Testament, or at least they try to. Or, they wish to make you think that they do.

Tolerance Destroyed~ Papal Intervention

Regnans In Excelsis, Pope Saint Pius V, April 27, 1570

Papal Bull

Pius, servant of the servants of God, for the perpetual remembrance of the fact.

He Who reigneth on high, to Whom all power had been given, alike upon earth and in heaven, has intrusted one alone, that is to say, to Peter, prince of the Apostles, the care of governing, the Catholic Church, One, Holy, out of which there is no salvation.

He has constituted it alone over all the nations, and over all the kingdoms, that it should root out, destroy, overturn, plant, and edify, in order that it should continue in the unity of the Holy Ghost, and that it should deliver to the Saviour, safe and free from all danger, the faithful people, bound together in the bond of mutual charity.

We, being, by the great goodness of God, called to hold the helm of the Church, devote ourselves unceasingly to our charge, and omit no labor to preserve intact the unity, and the Catholic religion, which its Author has left exposed to tempest, in order to try the faith of His people and correct us for our faults. But the numbers of the impious has usurped so much power, that there is no place in the world which they have not endeavored to corrupt with their perverse doctrines. Among others, Elizabeth, the servant of crime, and pretended Queen of England, has offered them an asylum in which they find shelter.

This same Elizabeth, after seizing the throne, has usurped throughout England the authority of supreme head of the Church. She has monstrously exercised that power and that jurisdiction, and she has again cast into the way of a despicable perdition that kingdom, once devoted to the Catholic faith and the recipient of its blessings.

Elizabeth has destroyed the worship of the true religion, which was overturned by Henry VIII, and which the legitimate Queen Mary, so commendable to the respect of posterity, had succeeded in establishing by the efforts of her own powerful hand, and with the assistance of the Holy See. Elizabeth, embracing and following the errors of the heretics, has dismissed the royal council of England, composed of the English nobility, and has replaced them with obscure heretics. She has oppressed those who cultivated the Catholic Faith, and has replaced them by evil speakers and ministers of impiety. She has abolished the sacrifice of the Mass, prayers, fasting, distinctions of meat, celibacy and

Catholic rites. She has ordered the circulation of books containing a system of manifest heresy, and of impious mysteries. She has commanded her subjects to receive, observe, and preserve precepts which she has adopted from Calvin. She has dared to decree that the bishops, rectors of churches, and the other Catholic priests, be driven from their churches and deprived of their benefices. She has disposed of them and of other ecclesiastical things in favor of the heretics; and she has also decided upon causes the decision of which rightly only belongs to the Church. She has forbidden the prelates, clergy, and people to recognize the Roman Church, and to obey its laws and its canonical sanctions. She has constrained most of her subjects to recognize her culpable laws, and to abjure the obedience due to the sovereign pontiff. She has prescribed, that, by oath, they shall recognize her as sole mistress, alike in things spiritual and temporal. She has inflicted penalties and punishments upon those whom she could not persuade, and those who persevered in the unity of the faith and in obedience. She has also thrown into prison bishops and rectors of churches, and many of them have perished there in misery.

These things are well known to all nations; they are proved by the gravest testimony, and no room is left for tergivesation, excuse or defence. We, seeing these impieties multiplied, and seeing that still other crimes are added to the first; seeing that the persecutions against the faithful are increasing, in consequence of the compulsion and self-will of the said Elizabeth, we are persuaded that her heart is more than ever hardened. Not only does she despise the pious prayers of good Catholics, that she should be converted and brought back to her right mind, but, further, she has even refused to receive in England the nuncios whom we have sent. We, then, forced by necessity to resort to the arms of justice against her, cannot soften our grief that we have not severely dealt with a princess whose ancestors had so well deserved the praise of the Christian republic.

We, therefore, supported by the authority of Him Whose will has called us to the throne, although we are unworthy of such a charge, in the name of the apostolic authority, we declare the said Elizabeth a heretic, and aider and foster of heretics, and that her adherents, in the above cited acts have incurred the sentence of anathema, and are separated from the unity of the body of our Lord Jesus Christ.

We declare her deprived of the pretended right to that kingdom, and of all domain, dignity and privilege. We declare the subjects, the nobility and people of that kingdom, free from their oaths, and from all debt of subjection, of fidelity, and of respect; and by the authority of these presents, we deprive the said Elizabeth of the right to her pretended kingdom. By this prescription we further forbid all nobles, people, subjects, and others, to venture to obey the orders, advice, or laws of the said Elizabeth. As to those who shall act otherwise than as we have here authorize and order, we include them in the same sentence of anathema.

As it is difficult to carry these presents wherever necessary, we will command that a written notarial copy, under the seal of a bishop and of this court, have the same authority in any tribunal and without, and have like force and value as if these actual presents were exhibited.

Given at Rome, near Saint Peters, the 28th of February, in the year 1576, and of our pontificate the 6th.

PIUS PP. V

-De Montor, <u>Lives of he Popes in the Early Middle Ages</u>, 1902, pp. 791-4.

The tradition of tolerance toward English Catholics under Elizabeth was destroyed by the forceful pursuit of the Counter Reformation by Pope Pius V.

This papal bull is credited for inspiring the following plots against the monarchy in England.

The Northern Rebellion -1569
The Ridolfi Plot – 1571
The Throckmorton Plot - 1583
The Babington Plot – 1586
The Lopez Plot - 1594
The Stafford Plot - 1586
The Somerville Plot- 1583
Poisoned Pommel Plot - 1598
The Essex Rebellion - 1601
The Bye and Main Plots - 1603

Pope Pius V, Missal,1600

A Dangerous and Foreign Logic
A Treatise of Equivocation, Henry Garnet, c. 1595.

Chap. 5

Of Some other ways of Equivocation Practiced by the Sayntes of God, Besides that which Principally we Defended in the Chapter Before.

Besides these kyndes of propositions which we have hitherto defended not to be lyes, although by them always some trewth is concealed, there be some other wayes, whereby without a lye a trewth may be covered, which I will briefly sett down.

1. First, we may use some equivocall words which hath many significations, and we understand it in one sense, which is trewe, although the hearer conceave the other, which is false. So did Abraham and Isaac say, that their wives were their sisters, which was not trewe as the hearers understood it, or in the proper meaning, whereby a sister signifyeth one borne of the same father or mother, or both, but in a general signification, whereby a brother or a sister signifyeth one neere of kynred, as Abraham called Lott his brother, who was but his brother's sonne; and our Lord is sayed to have had brothers and sisters whereas properly he had neyther. The like unto this were if one should be asked whether such a straunger lodgeth in my house, and I should aunswere, "he lyeth not in my howse," meaning that he doth not tell a lye there, althoughe he lodge there.

2. Secondly, when unto one question may be given many aunsweres, we may yeelde one and conceale the other. So Samuel, being comaunded by God to go to Bethlehem to anoynte David kinge, sayed unto God, "How shall I goe? For Saul will heare of it and kyll me." And our Lord sayed, "Thou shalt take a calfe out of the hearde and shalt say, I come to do sacrifice to our Lord." And Samuel did as our Lord sayed unto hym, and came into Bethlehem. But the auncients of the cittye, wondering thereat, met hym and sayed, "Is thy coming peaceable?" who aunswered, " It is peaceable; I am come to do sacrifice unto our Lord." Here Samuel uttered the secondary cause of his coming, and warely dissembled the principall, which not withstanding they principally intended to knowe, and by this answere were put out of suspition thereof. So may it happen that one coming to a place to heare masse may answere them who aske the cause of his

cominge, that he came to dynner or to visit some person which is there, or with some other trewe alleaged cause satisfye the demaunders.

3. Thirdly, the whole sentence which we pronounce, or some word thereof, or the maner of pointing or devidinge the sentence, may be ambiguous, and we may speake it in one sense trewe for our own advantage. So it is recorded of St. Frauncis, that being asked of one who was sought for death, whether he came not that way, he answered (putting his hand into his sleeve, or as some say into his eare), "He came not this waye." St. Athanasius, first flying by water his persecutors, and beying so narrowly pursued that he coulde not escape, turned his course backwards, and meeting the enemyes ship, asked whome they sought for; who aunswering that they sought for Athanasius, he toulde them that he was a little before them, flying as it seemed some which pursued him. And the angell Raphael being demaunded of what stocke or linage he was, aunswered, " I am Azarias, the sonne of great Ananias," which the good old Toby so verily believed, that he sayed he was of a great stocke. But the angell meant it in a misticall sense, according to the signification of those names. Neither were it reprehensible in one which had just cause to say his fathers name were Peter or Paule, because the apostles are the spirituall fathers of the worlde. After which maner also Jacob sayed he was Esau his brother, because mystically he was so in deede; whereas God had ordeyned that the elder should serve the younger, signifying, by spirit of prophesye, that the people of the Gentylls, which was figured by Jacob, should be preferred before the Jewes. So if one should say to a theefe, "Juro tibi numeraturu me 200 aureos, " the word (tibi) maye be joined with (iuro) or with numeraturu. In like manner a man may cunningly alter the pronuciation, as if, according to the Italian manner of pronunciation, a man should say, "tibi vro," for "tibi juro," which two examples Bellarmin bringeth in his Dictates 2.2.q.89. ar. 7. Dub 2º (as also before, q. 69. Ar, 2. Dubio 2.). he allowed equivocations without oath bringing for proffer the speech of our Saviour, Non ascend, &c.

4. To these three wayes of concealing a trewth by words if we adde the other of which we spoke before, that is, whan we utter certaine words, which of themselves may engender a false conceite in the mynde of the hearers, and yet with somewhat which we understand and reserve in our myndes maketh a true position, than shall we have fower wayes how to concceale a trewth without making of a lye.

--Garnet, Henry, <u>A Treatise of Equivocation</u>, Ed.: David jardine, 1851,(c. 1595) pp. 48-53.

On the Succession

Breve of Pope Clement VIII. To the English Catholics, Concerning the succession to the English Crown, Pope Clement VIII, July 5, 1600.

To the English Catholics. Beloved children, health and benediction. In these most difficult times for the Christian comonwealth, in which he, who hath chosen the weak things of the world that he may confound the strong, hath appointed our lowliness to preside over his holy Catholic Church, many are the cares that oppress our mind, many the solicitudes that torture our heart; though, supported by his grace who comforteth us in all our tribulation, we lose not courage. But it is for your salvation, beloved children, and for the salvation of the once most flourishing kingdom of England, that we are specially anxious: it is to this that our thoughts and heart continually turn. For, though separated from us by a wide interval of land and sea, you still are near to us in Christ, still so intimately united to us in the spirit of charity, that you dwell, as it were, in the very midst of our affections; nor does anything impart more comfort and consolation to our mind than the assurance of your faith, and constancy, and agreement, and unity in the bond of peace: whence also we give more abundant thanks to God and the Father, and constantly beseech him to bestow on you strength and courage in the inward man, and abundance of divine grace, that you may not faint in your tribulations, but may make also with temptation issue, walking with one mind and with consent in the house of the Lord, which is the church, being rooted and founded in charity, one body and one spirit, as you are called in one hope of your calling. This, however, know, beloved children, that nothing is more dreaded by Satan, of whose multifarious craftiness we are not ignorant, than the concord and union of brethren, who, held together by the attractions of charity, which is the bond of perfection, serve God alone in the sincerity of their hearts, and seek, not the things that are their own, but the things that are Jesus Christ's. Many are the sufferings which you have undergone for the name of Christ and for the Catholic faith,—that precious deposit which your forefathers received from the Roman Church, the mother and mistress of all churches, and which you have so nobly laboured to preserve inviolate, so that, giving glory to God, we may say to you in the language of the apostle,—You have endured a great fight of afflictions, troubled, grieved, spoiled of your inheritance, driven from your country, and made a spectacle to God, and to angels, and to men. Wherefore, lose not your confidence, your courage, or your patience, which at all times, but now especially, is necessary for you, that, doing the will of God, you may receive the promise and the reward of your perseverance. Yet a little while, and he that is to come will come, and will not delay: for so we confide in him who is rich in mercy, that, for the glory of his name, and moved by your prayers, and the prayers of his other servants,. he will arise and judge his own cause, and, after long-continued storms, will command the winds and the sea, and the desired calm will come. Wherefore, be not wearied, fainting in your minds; but be ye strong and constant, and with all diligence preserve your concord in the love of Christ. But, above all things, take care that no earthly motive, no human passion or affection, induce you to follow the counsels, or to join the party, of those, who are either openly separated from the Catholic faith, or have incurred even the suspicion of heresy. Light, remember, hath no fellowship with darkness, nor can the Catholic have part with the heretic: surrounded by impiety, and entangled in error, they can have no portion with you. Look, therefore, alone to the honour of God, to the preservation of Catholic religion, to those true interestsof your country, which are indissolubly connected with the integrity of faith, and, finally, to that happiness in Christ, that ancient privilege of your ancestors, whose brightest glory was found in the preservation of true and uncorrupt religion. God will never desert you, if with that piety and zeal in which we trust, that resolution to which we address our paternal admonitions, you are careful before all things to promote his honour and worship: and, for our own part, embracing you, as we do, as most dear children, in the bowels of Christ, wherever and whenever we can be of service to you in the Lord, we will be at hand to aid you, to the utmost of our power, and with every exertion of our means. Stand fast, therefore, most dearly beloved, with one mind in the Lord, and the peace of God, which surpasseth all understanding, keep your hearts and minds in Christ Jesus. And this indeed we write to you, not that we doubt your religion, or piety, or constancy, or prudence, but rather that we may satisfy our duty, and in turn be consoled by you in every affliction. The God of all consolation comfort you ; while we who, however unworthily, represent him upon earth, impart to you our apostolical benediction, with every feeling of paternal love. Given at Rome, at St. Peter's, under the Ring of the Fisherman, on the 5th of July, in the year of Jubilee 1600, and of our Pontificate the ninth. *Endorsed,* "Breve of Clement VIII. to the Catholics of England, for procuring a Catholic successor in England."

---Lingard, John, <u>A True Account of the Gunpowder-Plot...</u>, 1851, p.123.

February 8, 1601
The Essex Rebellion

The Earl of Essex by Marcus Gheeraerts the Younger

The Essex rebellion was the most important plot relating to the Gunpowder Plot. In early 1601 the 2nd Earl of Essex, Robert Devereux, began to fortify his mansion, the Essex House, in London. On the morning of Feburary 8 he marched out of Essex House with nobles and gentlemen intent on a forced audience with the queen. Robert Cecil proclaimed him a traitor. The rebellion received no public support. Essex House was besieged and Essex surrendered. He was tried for treason on February 19, 1601 and, was executed on February 25, 1601.

The plot, linked to Catholic dissent, further set back the cause of tolerance. Most importantly it involved several who were to were to play major roles in the Gunpowder Plot after being spared execution for their roles in the Essex Rebellion.

Robert Catesby

Thomas Percy

Thomas Winter

John Wright

Christopher Wright

John Grant

Though not a plotter, William Parker Baron Monteagle was also involved.

The survival of these plotters to plot again attests to the philosophy that even though prominent Catholics had proven disloyal, their importance to the functioning of the state guaranteed the tolerance of even these dangerous individuals.

I will now direct your attention to the Eye of God, as it looked down upon London in 1603.

Actually a later illustration but the same eye! (Book of Common Prayer)

July 25, 1603

Comes James: James IV of Scotland Crowned King of England

The Shepheards Spring Song, in gratulation of the royall, happy, and flourishing Entrance, to the Majestie of England, by the most potent and prudent Souveragne, James king of England, France and Ireland, Henry Chettle,. 1603.

James IV of Scotland I of England, by: Paulus Van Somer, c. 1621

Collin Thenot and Chloria, red lipt Driope,
Shepheards, Nymphs Swaines, al that delight in field,
Living by harmlesse thrift your fat heards yeelde,
Why slacke yee now your loved company?
Up sluggards, learne, the larke doth mounted sing,
His cheerful Carrolls, to salute our King.
The Mavis, blacke-bird, and the little Wren,
The Nightengale on the hawthorne brire,
And all the winged Musicions in a Quire,
Do with their notes rebuke dull lazie men.
Up shepherds, up, your sloth breeds al your shames
You sleep like beasts while birds salute K. James.
The gray eyde morning with a blustring cheeke,
Like England's royall Rose mixt red and white,
Summons all eies to pleasure and delight,
Behold the evenings dews doe upward reeke,
Drawn by the Sun, which now doth gild the skie,
With his light-giving and world-cheering eie.
O that's well done; I see your cause of stay,

Was to adorne your temples with fresh flowers
And gather beautie to bedecke your bowers,
That they may seeme the Cabinets of Maie:
Honor this time, sweetest of all sweete Springs
That so much good, so many pleasures brings.
For now alone the livery of the earth
Gives not life, comfort to your bleating Lambes,
Nor fills the flowing udders of their dams,
It yeeldes another cause of gleesome mirth,
This ground weares all her best embrodery,
To entertaine her Soveraignes majestie.
And well she may, for never English ground
Bore such a Soveraigne as this royall Lord:
Looke upon all Antiquities Record;
In no Inrollment such a King is found.
Beginne with Brute, (if that of Brute be true,).
As I'le not doubt, but give old Bards their due.
He was a Prince unsettled, sought a Shore
To rest his long-tosst Troyan scattred Race:
And (as tis sed) found here a resting place
Grant this: but yeeld, he did false gods adore.
The Nations were not called to Christ that time,
Blacke Pagan clouds darkened this goodly Clime.
So, when dissention brought the Romans in,
No Ceasar till the godly Constantine,
(Descended truly from the British line)
Purged this Iles aire from Idoll-hated sinne;
Yet he in care of Rome left Deputies.
Our James maintaines (himselfe,) his dignities
The Saxon, & the Dane, scourged with sharp steele
(So did the Norman Duke) this beauteous Land;
Invading Lords raigne with an iron hand:
A gentler ruling in this Change we feele
Our Lion comes as meekely as a Dove.
Not conqring us by hurt, but harty love
Even as a calme to tempest toiled men,
As bread to the saint soule with Famine vext;
As a cool Spring to those with heat perplext,
As the Sunnes light into a fearfull denne,
So comes our King even in a time of neede,
To save, to shine to comforte and to feede.
O Shepherds, sing his welcome with sweete notes,
Nymphs, strew his way with Roses Red and White,
Provide all pastimes that may sense delight,
Offer the fleeces of your flockes white cotes:
He that now spares, doth in that saving spill
Where Worth is little, Vertue likes good will.
Now from the Orchades to the Cornish Iles,

From thence to Cambria, and the Hybernian shore,
The sound of Cruill warre is heard no more
Each Countenance is garnished with smiles,
All in one hymns with sweet contentment sing,
The praise and power of James their onely King.
Our onely King, one He, one Soverigne
O long-desired, and perfected good!
By him the heate of wrath, and boyling blood,
Is mildely quencht and Envie counted vaine,
That ties such mightie Nation to agree.
Shephearders, Ile not be tedious in my Songs
For that I see you bent to active sport;
To welcome him, whome we have wisht for long
Well done, dance on; looke how our little lambs,
Skippe as you spring about their fleecie damms.
Thus were yee wont to trip about the Greene,
And dance in ringlets, like our Faire Elves,
Striving in cunning to exceed your selves,
In honour of your late falne summer Queen:
But now exceed; this Maie excelles all Springs,
Which King & Queene and Prince & Princesse brings.
Showt joyfully, ye Nymphs, and rurall Swaines,
Your master Pan will now protect your foldes,
Your Cottages will be as safe as Holdes,
Feare neither Wolves nor subtill Foxes traines,
A Royal King will of your weale take keepe,
Hee'le be your Shepherd, you shall be his sheepe.
He comes in pompes; so should a King appear,
Gods Deputies shoiuld set the world at gaze;
Yet his milde lookes drive us from all amaze,
Clap hands for joy, our Soverigne draweth neere,
Sing, Io, Io, shepherds dance and sing,
Express all joy, in welcoming our King.
The aire, the season and the Earth accord
In Pleasure Order, both for sight and sense
All things looke fresh to greet his Excellence,

And Collin humbly thus salutes his Lord:
Dread and belouvde, live England's happy King,
While seasons last fresh as the lively spring.-Finis

-From: Chettle, Henry, <u>Englandes Mourning Garment</u>, London, 1603.

Accession Speech to Parliament, James I, March 19, 1603

Extracts on peace, the Union of the English and Scottish kingdoms and kingship.

On Peace

I resolve to call this Parliament ... That you who are here presently assembled to represent the body of this whole Kingdom, and of all sorts of people within the same, may with your own ears hear, and that I out of mine own mouth may deliver unto you the assurance of my due thankfulness for your joyful and general applause to the declaring and receiving of me in this seat (which God by my birthright and lineal descent had in the fullness of time provided for me,) and that, immediately after it pleased God to call your late Sovereign of famous memory, full of days, but fuller of immortal trophies of honour, out of this transitory life ... It is the blessings which God has in my person bestowed upon you all, wherein I protest I do more glory at the same for your weal, than for any particular respect of mine own reputation or advantage therein ... The first then of these blessings, which God has jointly with my person sent unto you, is outward peace, That is, peace abroad with all foreign neighbours: for I thank God I may justly say, that never since I was a King I either received wrong of any other Christian Prince or State, or did wrong to any. I have ever, I praise God, yet kept peace and amity with all ... for by peace abroad with their neighbours the towns flourish, the merchants become rich, the trade does increase, and the people of all sorts of the land enjoy free liberty to exercise themselves in their general vocations without peril or disturbance ... In the word of a King I promise unto you, That I shall never give the first occasion of the breach thereof, neither shall I ever be moved for any particular or private passion of mind to interrupt your public peace, except I be forced thereunto, either for reparation of the honour of the Kingdom, or else by necessity for the weal and preservation of the same, in which case, a secure and honourable war must be preferred to an unsecure and dishonourable Peace ...

On the Union of the kingdoms of England and Scotland

Although outward peace be a great blessing, yet is it far inferior to peace within, as civil wars are more cruel and unnatural than wars abroad. And therefore the second great blessing that God has with my person sent unto you, is peace within, and that in a double form. First, by my descent, lineally out of the loins of Henry VII, is reunited and confirmed in me the union of the two princely roses of the two houses of Lancaster and York, whereof that King of happy memory was the first uniter, as he was also the first ground-layer of the other peace ... But the union of these two princely houses is nothing comparable to the union of two ancient and famous kingdoms, which is the other inward peace annexed to my person ... Has not God first united these two kingdoms, both in language, religion, and similitude of manners? Yes, has he not made us all in one island, compassed with one sea, and of itself by nature so indivisible, as almost those that were borderers themselves on the late borders, cannot distinguish nor know or discern their own limits? These two Countries being separated neither by sea, nor great river, mountain, nor other strength of nature ... And now in the end and fullness of time untied, the right and title of both in my person, alike lineally descended of both the Crowns, whereby it is now become like a little world within itself, being entrenched and fortified round about with a natural, and yet admirable strong pond or ditch, whereby all the former fears of this nation are now quite cut off: The other part of the island being ever before now, not only the place of landing to all strangers that were to make invasion here, but likewise moved by the enemies of this State, by untimely incursions, to make enforced diversion from their conquests, for defending themselves at home, and keeping sure their back door, as then it was called, which was the greatest hindrance and let that ever my predecessors of the nation had in disturbing them from their many famous and glorious conquests abroad. What God has conjoined then, let no man separate ...

On Kingship

I do acknowledge, that the special and greatest point of difference that is between a rightful king and an usurping tyrant is in this: That whereas the proud and ambitious tyrant does think his kingdom and people are only ordained for satisfaction of his desires and unreasonable appetites; The righteous and just king does by the contrary acknowledge himself to be ordained for the procuring of the wealth and prosperity of his people, and that his greatest and principal worldly felicity must consist in their prosperity. If you be rich I cannot be poor: if you be happy I cannot but be fortunate: and I protest that your welfare shall ever be my greatest care and contentment: and that I am a servant it is most true, that as I am Head and Governor of all the people in my Dominion who are my natural vassals and subjects, considering them in numbers and distinct ranks; So if we will take the whole people as one body and mass, then as the head is ordained for the body, and not the body for the head; so must a righteous king know himself to be ordained for his people, and not his people for him.

And All Seemed to be Right With the World.

- The new king promised to bring a more tolerant and gentle nature to the country.
- National Prosperity had become more important than religion.
- The English Church remained independent.
- It was said that the king wanted to end the war with Spain.
- Catholic rebels, such as Thomas Percy, once part of the Essex rebellion, were once again serving the nation at court, forgiven.
- Jesuits had actually saved the king and country from the rebellious plot of a priest, William Watson
- As a result the king ruled that fines would no longer be collected from Roman Catholics until February 1605.
- Shakespeare might have been a source of wisdom for James who had promoted his players to more important roles at court

The Opinions of Catholics- Guy Fawkes Statement to the King of Spain c. July 1603

Simaancas, Archivo General, Sección de Estado 840/126, Guy Fawkes, 1603

(fo. I)

What the gentleman who came from England (Guy Fawkes, c. July 1603) confided to me to report by word of mouth to his Majesty is the following.

First he says that the king is a heretic and has demonstrated that he is one as it appears, for on his journey through England to London he granted pardon to many wrongdoers and others then in prison for debt when he ordered them to be freed from their prisons, but not to any Catholic although some Scotsmen who accompanied him begged this favor of him on behalf of some Catholics in the city of Durham and it was refused.

Farther along in his journey, when a Catholic priest named Hill found it convenient on the highway and presented to him a memorial in the name of everyone, he responded that he should attend him where he first had to make a halt which was in York where, when the priest came into his presence, they took him away under restraint before he could address the king. In the hope of offering help, a Catholic gentleman who thought that this had been done without the king's order went to inquire whether the king had commanded that the terms of the memorial's response be prepared. At the same moment he was arrested and taken under restraint to the city of London where he is being held until now without release.

After coming close to the city of London, the earl of Shrewsbury presented to him his relative from his own family, named Talbot, in the hope that he would grant the honor of knighting the gentleman. Since he was a Catholic he refused it. A gentleman named Carey upon hearing of the death of the queen caused a church to be closed for he did not want the preaching to continue until learning the king's will. For this he was fined 10,000 ducats and is being kept in prison. (fo.2) In word and in writing he is the head of the Church. He requires every one of his Council and everyone else who holds office in England to take an oath to that purpose.

He has ordered the collection of the fine of 200 florins a month which the queen ordered Catholics to pay.

A Scottish Catholic peer told a Jesuit in Brussels that he heard on that journey the king tell his Scottish friends that he hoped in a short time to have all of the papist sect driven out of England.

Many have heard him say at table that the pope is Anti-Christ which he wished to prove to anyone who believed the opposite.

He allows himself to be ruled by Sir George Home, his favorite who has always been one of the greatest heretics in all of Scotland.

How secure is the peace which he plans to negotiate with the king (of Spain) can be seen very well from the above and other similar things. It can be nothing else but a fiction and without sincerity on his part, for as a heretic he cannot avoid favoring the heretics and, on the contrary, scheme the ruin of those who are not.

At present he can well plan a peace, for after the summer months are gone he considers himself secure for this year. At present being very poor with nothing of his own, he awaits a large sum of money after the year has passed from the next parliament, and other revenues of his kingdom. Equally, he expects a large amount of money through the confiscations planned from Catholics.

(fo.3) Similarly, once secure from without, he will have a greater opportunity to tyrannize the poor Catholics of his domain, having convinced himself in his mind that by this way no enemy can harm him except by the act of Catholics from within, for without them he need not be afraid.

Similarly, once enriched with the property of Catholics and grown powerful from their names and lives, there will be a greater opportunity to join other heretics to wage war on the rest of the Christian princes who are not.

That he wants to gain time is clearly evident from the replies he has given to some Catholics who have dealt with him privately to receive a pardon to free themselves from prison. For them there is the one common response that they must observe what parliament has determined. As he requires of each one in parliament an oath concerning his supreme authority in the church it is well known that no Catholic may enter there, for they do not wish to take such an unjust oath. In this way he is secure in treating them as he wishes.

Furthermore the Dutch have done so much for (Robert) Cecil, George Home, (Edward) Bruce, Thomas Erskine and other heretics in his council that, either for their own advantage which they foresee through the promises of the Dutch, or out of a greater preference towards those of their own sect, they do not want to plan peace unless it is but pretense.

On the other hand the earls of Northumberland, Cumberland, Worcester, Shrewsbury do not want to plan peace unless it is under the condition of liberty of conscience. On this point they explain that they will obtain nothing in a peace (fo.4) while Catholics remain with their previous grievances, but rather it ought to be more dangerous when Catholics consider their hopes frustrated, and in that fashion trust in a search for any type of relief no matter how desperate it may be.

The grievances of the English Peers apart from the Catholics

He has granted many of the highest offices to Scots. To the earl of Mar he has handed the governance both of his son, the prince of Wales and of that province as we will. He made Lord Home, a Scot, the governor of the town of Berwick which is at the frontier of Scotland. Near his person everyone in his chamber are Scots, wherever there is an English official he has placed another Scotsman. He has made a Scot named Thomas Erskine the Captain of his Guard and this captain has dismissed 100 Englishmen who were outside of the muster, but he has not appointed others. The chancellor of the duchy of Lancaster is a Scot. He has given bishoprics to two Scotsmen. He has allowed the Scots, his favorites, to represent whomever they wish to their own profit. He has granted knighthood to them, receiving from some 300 ducats, from others 600 and in that fashion they become rich with the money of Englishmen.

The earl of Northumberland (who was the first to declare himself for him and who had said that he would have no other for king but the king of Scotland) had once planned to do something for the Catholics (as he told some persons later) but now finds himself discontented since the king has given him slight satisfaction.

The peers of England are seen to be unhappy with the Scots mainly for their crudity and particularly for the many quarrels at court. There, a royal page (fo.5) slew a page of the earl of Northumberland with a dagger. Another Scot struck an Englishman in the Presence chamber, yet they did not punish him but merely excused him as insane.

One day when it came to the king's notice that some quarrelling was going on between the English peers and the Scots in the Presence chamber, he promptly sent his lord chamberlain, an Englishman named Lord Thomas Howard, to command everyone to withdraw, in his name. At this lord Chandos replied that he did not believe that the king would speak such an order seeing that it was presumed to be for the peers, but for a lower sort (meaning some Scots) there might very well be a command to retire which did not include the peers. The chamberlain withdrew to the king with this reply, after which the Captain of the Guard, Thomas Erskine, a Scott came back with the announcement that they all should retire. To this came the response that a peer of their own realm had already said the same thing and was not believed, that he (the Captain) would give a command to any of them was much less to be believed. Erskine returned with this to inform the king who then came forth to say that he was unaware that such a company of peers was there. After this, the peers have retired from the court, little by little.

Some of the principal gentlemen have not wished to come to the court, although many of their friends have implored them to do so. It is certain if it were not for the Fathers of the Society, the schismatics in England would have long since taken up arms, (fo6) either because of these particular grievances or because of the slight satisfaction offered to the Catholic religion. A thing which they desire as much, or more, than the Catholics, as to end the war of conscience which kills them by degrees

There is a natural hostility between the English and the Scots. There has always been one, and at present it keeps increasing though these grievances, so that even were there but one religion in England, nevertheless it will not be possible to reconcile these two nations, as they are, for very long..

Measure for Measure, Act 2 Scene 2 Shakespeare, 1604

William Shakespere, Martin Droeshout, 1623

DUKE VINCENTIO

  Angelo,
    There is a kind of character in thy life,
  That to the observer doth thy history
  Fully unfold. Thyself and thy belongings
  Are not thine own so proper as to waste
  Thyself upon thy virtues, they on thee.
  Heaven doth with us as we with torches do,
  Not light them for themselves; for if our virtues
  Did not go forth of us, 'twere all alike
  As if we had them not. Spirits are not finely touch'd
  But to fine issues, nor Nature never lends
  The smallest scruple of her excellence
  But, like a thrifty goddess, she determines
  Herself the glory of a creditor,
  Both thanks and use. But I do bend my speech
 To one that can my part in him advertise;
  Hold therefore, Angelo:--
  In our remove be thou at full ourself;
  Mortality and mercy in Vienna
  Live in thy tongue and heart: old Escalus,
  Though first in question, is thy secondary.
  Take thy commission.-Act one scene one

CLAUDIO
Thus can the demigod Authority
Make us pay down for our offence by weight
The words of heaven; on whom it will, it will;
-Act 1 Scene 2

ISABELLA

Could great men thunder
As Jove himself does, Jove would ne'er be quiet,
For every pelting, petty officer
Would use his heaven for thunder;
Nothing but thunder! Merciful Heaven,
Thou rather with thy sharp and sulphurous bolt
Split'st the unwedgeable and gnarled oak
Than the soft myrtle: but man, proud man,
Drest in a little brief authority,
Most ignorant of what he's most assured,
His glassy essence, like an angry ape,
Plays such fantastic tricks before high heaven
As make the angels weep; who, with our spleens,
Would all themselves laugh mortal.

ISABELLA
Because authority, though it err like others,
Hath yet a kind of medicine in itself,
That skins the vice o' the top.

— Shakespeare, William, <u>Measure for Measure</u>, "Act 2, Scene 2," 1604.

Fawkes before King James, London Evening News, 1861

PEACE

The Somerset House Conference, Contemporary, artist unknown.

WE CANNOT ALL BE MASTERS, NOR ALL MASTERS CANNOT BE TRULY FOLLOW'D.

-Shakespeare, William, Othello. ACT I Scene 1. (c.1604-5)

On August 28, 1604 the nineteen-year Anglo-Spanish War ended with the Somerset House Conference which produced the Treaty of London of 1604

Treaty of London, James I, 1604

"KNOW all and every one, That after a long and most cruel Ravage of Wars, by which *Christendom* has for many Years been miserably afflicted, God (who has the Disposal of all Things) looking down from on high, and pitying the Calamities of his People (for whom he was pleas'd to shed his own Blood, that he might bring them Peace, and leave it with them) has powerfully extinguish'd the raging Flame by a firm Confederacy of the most potent Princes of the Christian World, and graciously made the Day of Peace and Tranquillity shine, which was hitherto rather wished for than hop'd. For by the Grace of the Omnipotent God, the Kingdoms of *England* and *Ireland* devolving, for extirpating the Seeds of Discord, upon the most serene Prince, *James* King of *Scotland,* and consequently those Causes of Dissension remov'd, which so long fomented and nourish'd War between the Predecessors of the most serene Princes *Philip* the .III. King of *Spain,* and *Albert* and *Isabella Clara Eugenia* Archduke and Archdutchess of *Austria-,* Duke and Dutchess of *Burgundy,* &c. and of the said King *James:* All the said Princes (God illuminating their Hearts) consider'd that there was no reason why they should have an Enmity at one another, who had never had any before, or why they should engage in War against one another, from which their Ancestors had always abstain'd, or why they should break off the most antient Confederacy which had been kept beyond the Memory of Man, and burst the Bands of the strictest Amity between the most serene Families of *Austria* and *Burgundy,* and the foresaid most serene King of *England,* and break the old Friendship which was daily cultivated with new and additional Offices or Love and Benevolence. Wherefore hearing of the Succession of the said most serene King of *Scotland* to the Kingdoms of *England* and *Ireland,* and *John Taxim* Count of *Villa Mediana* being sent on the part of the most serene King of *Spain,* and on the part of the said most serene Archduke and Archdutchess, *Charles* Count of *Aremberg,* to congratulate the said most serene King • of *England* upon his succeeding to the said Kingdoms, in the Name of the foresaid most serene Princes respectively • and that Embassy being most kindly taken, and the Ambassadors most amicably receiv'd:, the said most serene King of *Spain,* and the Archduke and Archdutchess were inform'd by their Ambassadors, That the most serene King of *England* was strongly inclin'd, not only to observe antient and former Treaties, but also to enter into more strict and firm ones. Wherefore they thought nothing was to be omitted by them, by which the common Tranquillity of *Christendom* might be promoted and the Interests of the People committed to them regarded.

-S.W., A General Collection of Treatys, Vol. 2, 1732. pp. 131-132,

And the plotters, due to the "interests of the People," had lost any chance of obtaining political support from abroad. They depended therefore upon the dedication of the Pope to the religious Counter Reformation for support for their forcible return to power.

London, 17th Century, c. 1615, Van Meer

There was great confidence that 1605 would be another grand year for the nation which was now blessed with peace just as it had earlier been delivered by God from the grasp of the Armada. The month of November would see the change of seasons bringing the festivities of the hiring fairs. The year would be punctuated by the ringing of bells and burning of bonfires, and a large number of creative rituals which marked the festive occasions of the chosen people. The King would hunt game, ponder a new translation of the bible and continue to rail against the evils of tobacco.

Little did he know that the history of the Old Testament was about to repeat itself and that the new Purim was to reveal the true nature of "the other" as never before. A new cause for bonfires, bells, and ritual would emerge.

Complex Politics

Instructions from the Nuncio at Brussels to Dr. William Giffordi Dean of Lisle, OCTAVIUS, Bishop of Trica, August 1, 1603.

Octavius, by the grace of God and favour of the Apostolic See, Bishop of Trica, Nuncio of our Lord Pope Clement VIII. and of the same Holy See in the provinces, cities, and other places of Belgium, with the powers of Legate *a latere,* and Vice-protector of the kingdoms of England, Scotland, and Ireland, to our beloved in Christ, William Gifford, priest, doctor of theology, and dean and canon of the collegiate church of Lisle, perpetual health in the Lord.

You have lately made known to us, that, as well from a zeal for the encrease of Catholic religion, as from a desire to manifest your respect for your serene princes, the King and Queen of England, you have determined to make a journey into that country, and to remain there for some time; and, on this account, you have humbly requested us to honour you with our letters: Wherefore, considering, what we have long known, how highly you have deserved of the Apostolic See, and confiding in that prudence and discretion, which, in matters of the greatest moment, and in circumstances connected not only with the duties of your office, but also with your reverence for the Holy See, we have so frequently witnessed; wishing, moreover, to give you the advantage of these our testimonial letters, We, by these presents, make known to our beloved in Christ, the Very Reverend George Blackwell, archpriest of England, and to all whom it may concern, that, by your reverence for the Apostolic See, by your faithful affection for your princes, the King and Queen of England, and by your ardent desire for promoting the cause of religion, you have ever rendered yourself most dear to us. Hence, we have thought it well to give it to you in special charge from ourselves, that, on your arrival in England, your first attention be directed to establish peace, and union, and concord amongst those Catholics who may still chance to be at variance, and that, in our name, or rather in the name of his Holiness himself, you exhort them to *mind not high things, but condescend to the humble,*—to walk with one mind in the house of God,—to promote the cause of religion in sincere and apostolic simplicity, —to exhibit all becoming attachment, and reverence, and obedience to their rulers, and thus to enable the very enemies of our faith to become judges of their holy and conscientious behaviour. We wish you, moreover, to entreat all who would deserve the name of Catholics, to commit no act which may disturb the public peace, which may offend their princes and magistrates, or bring their religion into hatred and suspicion; but to render to God the things that are God's, to Caesar the things that are Caesar's, and to abstain from mixing up the concerns of religion with the foreign affairs of state; that so they may never be exposed to the punishment of seditionaries and traitors (which in all were a disgrace, in churchmen a crime, and an atrocious wickedness), but may be able, should they suffer reproach for the name of Jesus, to consider it a joy and a gain. Further, we will and command you, if, without offence to the King, you can obtain admission to the presence of his royal consort, to assure her, from us, that our Holy Father has sought every occasion to manifest, by his actions, that paternal regard which he entertains for the King's Majesty: that no wish was ever nearer to his heart, than that he might see this same king, whom God, in his infinite goodness, and moved by the prayers of his royal mother, of happy memory, has already raised to a most powerful earthly kingdom, so united in this world to the mystical body of the church, as to secure the possession of a heavenly kingdom likewise: that he is ready to employ whatever authority he possesses over the Catholics, in promoting any measures which may conduce to the security either of the royal person or of the commonwealth, and will even withdraw from the country any of the missionaries of whose loyalty his highness may have conceived any rational suspicion : in a word, that he wishes to omit no office of friendship or affection, which his predecessors have ever performed towards the sovereigns of England, princes who have so highly deserved of the Holy See; and is anxious to let his majesty perceive with what sincere affection he embraces him, how perfectly he honours him, and how ardently he wishes him a long and happy life, a peaceful reign, a faithful people, and a state undisturbed by foreign or domestic broils. Finally, we wish you so to conduct yourself as becomes an ecclesiastic, who, having been educated from infancy in the holy city, has imbibed the piety of the Apostolic See, has become familiar with its rules of life, and knows, from long and constant experience, how fervently the Holy Father desires the prosperity and happiness of that kingdom, to which, by so many titles of gratitude and affection, his predecessors were pre-eminently attached. In conclusion, be careful to let your life and conversation be such, as to convince the world that, in supporting the foreign seminaries, the Holy Father has no other object but to gain souls to Christ, and, upon the principle of entire obedience to the sovereign, to secure the permanent happiness of that kingdom ;—which may Christ our Lord, in his mercy, vouchsafe to grant!—Given in our Palace at Brussels, August 1, 1603.

OCTAVIUS, Bishop of Trica, &c. &c.

[MS. in the English College at Koine, Scritture, iii. 17.]

-Lingard, John, <u>A True Account of the Gunpowder-Plot...</u>, 1851, p.73.

Concern in June of 1605

To Henry Garnet, Claudio Aquaviva, the General of the Jesuits, June 25, 1605.

[Copy in the State Paper Office.]

We have learned, though by a very private channel, what, 1 doubt not, your Reverence has there been informed of, that the Catholics are meditating some enterprise for their liberty: but, as such an attempt, especially at the present moment, is calculated not only to inflict the greatest injury on religion, but also to involve the Catholics themselves in the most serious danger, his Holiness has commanded me to write to your Reverence in his name, requiring you to employ whatever influence you possess with the principal persons in question, and particularly with the archpriest, in preventing even the discussion of such matters. These ideas should be abandoned, not only for the reasons which I have stated, but still more so, as an act of obedience to his Holiness, who, whilst he condemns the agitation of all such designs among Catholics, declares also that they will prove a serious obstacle to those greater and more important advantages which he is endeavouring to obtain for the body,—advantages which, as contributing to their peace and their security, it will ever be his unremitting study to ensure.

Wherefore, as your Reverence is well aware of the importance and necessity of the case, it will be your duty earnestly to dissuade them from all such designs; recollecting, besides the important reasons which I have already mentioned, that an abstinence from all intrigues of this kind will necessarily tend to the benefit of Catholics,—inasmuch as, should any violence occur (which God avert!) it would assuredly inflict the deepest injury on our Society, without whose consent the world will never believe that it could have taken place. June 25, 1605.

* [Eudaemon Joannes (249, 250), More (325), and others, profess to give this letter as it was written,—" rescripsit in haec verba;" but, besides other variations, they wholly omit the introductory part of the first sentence, which I have printed in italics, and then assure us that the letter was a reply to certain earnest representations made by Garnet, in the preceding month, as to the "desperate" designs of some Catholics. The words here supplied, however, distinctly show that Garnet had made no such representations, and that the intelligence, obtained at Rome, had been derived from a different source.—T.]

---Lingard, John, <u>A True Account of the Gunpowder-Plot...</u>, 1851, p.122.

Lingard provides two significantly different copies of the following letter.

Henry Garnet to Claudio Aquaviva, Henry Garnet, July 24, 1605.

In answer to the preceding

We have received your Paternity's letters with that reverence which is due to his Holiness and to your fatherhood. For my own part, I have already four times prevented a disturbance; nor is there a doubt that we shall be able to hinder any recourse to arms, since it is well known, with regard to a large number of Catholics, that, except in case of urgent necessity, they will attempt nothing of the sort without our consent. One thing, however, is a subject of no small anxiety to us,—it is, an apprehension lest others should fly to arms, and thus, by a kind of necessity, draw these also into the same courses. For there are many who will never be restrained by the bare commands of his Holiness. During the life of Pope Clement, they hesitated not to ask whether the pontiff could prohibit them from defending their lives: at the present moment, they declare that no priest shall ever be made acquainted with their secret purposes; and even among our friends there are some who make it, a subject of complaint against us that we oppose an obstacle to the completion of these men's deterent,. Therefore, to mollify these people in some degree, and also to gain time, so as, by a little delay, - to be able to apply a remedy to the evil, we have advised them to unite in deputing a representative to the Pope, &c. We must beseech God to apply the necessary remedy to these dreadful evils. We implore the blessing of his Holiness and of your Paternity. -London, 24 July, 1605.

[Copy in the State Paper Office.]

---Lingard, John, <u>A True Account of the Gunpowder-Plot...</u>, 1851, p.123.

To Claudio Aquaviva, Henry Garnet, July 24. 1605

"Excellent Sir,

"We have received your lordship's letters with that reverence which is due to his Holiness and to your paternity. For my own part, I have already four times prevented a disturbance; nor is there a doubt that we shall be able to hinder any recourse to arms, since it is well known, with regard to a large number of Catholics, that, except in case of urgent necessity, they will attempt nothing of the sort without our consent.

"There are, however, two subjects of no small anxiety to us. The first is an apprehension lest others should fly to arms, and thus, by a kind of necessity, draw these also into the same courses. For there are many who will never be restrained by the bare commands of his Holiness. During the life of Pope Clement, they hesitated not to ask whether the Pontiff could prohibit them from defending their lives: at the present moment, they declare that no priest shall ever be made acquainted with their secret purposes:—even among our friends there are some who make it a subject of complaint against us, that we oppose an obstacle to the completion of these men's designs.

"Well, to mollify these people in some degree, and also to gain time, so as, by a little delay, to be able to apply a fitting remedy to the evil, we have advised them to unite in deputing a representative to the Pope. This has been done; and I have directed the envoy to the Nuncio in Flanders, that by him he may be commended to his Holiness. I have also given him letters, setting forth the opinions of the parties in question, and the arguments by which those opinions are defended or opposed; and, as there will be no danger in the conveyance, I have written most fully and copiously on the subject.—So much for the first object of apprehension.

"The second is even more formidable; for the danger is, lest some treasonable violence be secretly offered to the king, and thus the whole body of Catholics be compelled to take up arms.

"Wherefore, in my opinion, two things are necessary: the first, that his Holiness should prescribe the course to be adopted in each of the above cases; the second, that, availing himself of the late unsuccessful rising in Wales, as a pretext for speaking, he should address a breve to the Catholics, and forbid them, under pain of censures, to resort to anything in the shape of violence. For the rest, seeing that things are daily growing worse and worse, we must beseech his Holiness to apply a speedy remedy to these dreadful evils, while we implore his blessing, and that of your reverend paternity.

81

"Your Excellent Lordship's servant,

"Henry Garnet.

"London, 24 July, 1605."

-Lingard, John, <u>A True Account of the Gunpowder-Plot...</u>, 1851, p.65.

Letter from Henry Garnet to Robert Persons. October 4, 1605

"My verie lovinge sir, we are to goe within fewe dayes neerer London, yet are we unprovided of a house, nor can find any convenient for any longe tyme. But we must be fayne to borrowe some private house, and live more privately untill this storme be overblowen; for most strict inquiries are practised, wherein yf my hostesse be not quite undone, she speedeth better than many of her neighbours. The courses taken are more severe than in Q. Elizabeth's tyme. Everie six weeks in a severall court, juries appointed to indite, present, find the goods of Catholicks, prize them, yea, in many places to drive away whatsoever they find (contra ordinem juris), and putt the owners, yf perhaps Protestants, to prove that they be theirs and not of recusants with whom they deale. The commissioners in all contreys are the most earnest and base Puritans, whom otherwise the kinge discountenanceth. The prisoners at Wisbich are almost famished: they are verie close, and can have no healpe from abrode, but the kinge allowinge a marke a weeke for eche one, the keeper maketh his gains, and giveth them meate but three dayes a weeke. If any recusant buy his goods againe, they inquire diligently yf the money be his own, otherwise they would have that toe. In fine, yf these courses hould, everie man must be fayne to redeeme once in six moneths the verie bedd he lyeth on: and hereof, that is of twice redeeminge, besides other presidents I find one in this lodginge where nowe I am. The judges nowe openly protest that the kinge nowe will have blood, and hath taken blood in Yorkshier: that the kinge hath hitherto stroaked the papists, but nowe will strike. This is without any least desert of Catholicks. The execution of two in the north is certayn, and, whereas it was done uppon could blood, that is, with so great staye after their condemnation, it argueth a deliberate resolution of what we may expect. So that there is noe hope that Pope Paulus V. can doe any thinge: and whatsoever men give owt there of easie proceedings with Catholicks, is mere fabulous. And yet I am assured notwithstandinge, that the best sort of Catholicks will beare all their losses with patience. But howe these tyrannicall proceedinges of such base officers may drive particular men to desperate attempts, that I can not answer for, the kinge's wisedome will foresee.

"I have a letter from Field in Ireland, whoe telleth me that of late there was a verie severe proclamation against all ecclesiastical persons, and a generall command for goinge to the churche; with a solemn protestation that the kinge never promised nor meant to give toleration."

October 4, 1605.

-Lingard, John, <u>A True Account of the Gunpowder-plot, extr. from Dr. Lingard's History of England, and Dodd's Church Jistory, with Notes by Vindicator</u>, 1851, p.63.

The Explosion

You are about to be witness to a Cataclysmic Explosion.

An explosion, of such magnitude that its shockwaves still loudly resound not only in the night air of the Fifth of November but throughout our very existence, our language, our literature and our world.

Yet, in reality, nothing actually exploded! The gunpowder was never actually lit.

The explosion was not of gunpowder but of a culture and nation confronted with the horror of the proximity of their very destruction.

For this reason this work is not merely a study the history of a treasonous sub-culture, nor of the procurement of gunpowder. We are not concerned with motives, of cover-ups, or of the mechanics of a failed plot and uprising.

This work considers something much more important: the reaction of the culture, the nation, the people and the world to the prospect of an ancient civilization, a form of government, independence, liberty and the very existence of the people, hanging by a thread over an abyss from which once entered there could be no return.

The explosion we will study was that of reaction. It is formed by the perceptions and documents of the time, not by historical analysis.

It began as a reaction to a very short, poorly written letter.

  Let us begin therefore, in its presence.

The day was a Saturday, October 26, 1605. William Parker 4th Baron, Lord Monteagle was the recipient. He had ordered supper to be prepared at his house at Hoxton. He was seated at the table when one of his pages brought him the letter which had been delivered by an unrecognizable man in the street who ordered him to give it directly to his master.

Image, left - William Parker by John de Critz, 1615.

Image: <u>Mischeefes Mysterie or Treasons Master-peece,</u>
<u>The Powder-Plot</u>, John Vickers, 1617.

The Mounteagle Letter

my lord out of the loue i beare to some of youere frendz i haue a caer of youer preseruacion therfor i would aduyse yowe as yowe tender youer lyf to devyse some excuse to shift of youer attendance at this parleament for god and man hathe concurred to punishe the wickednes of this tyme and thinke not slightlye of this advertisment but retere youre self into youre contri whyeare yowe maye expect the event in safti for thowyghe theare be no apparance of anni stirye i saye they shall receyue a terrible blowe this parleament and yet they shall not seie who hurts them this councel is not to be contemned becausse it maye do yowe good and can do yowe no harme for the dangere is passed as soone as yowe haue burnt the letter and i hope god will gine yowe the grace to mak good use of it to whose holy proteccion i comend yowe

To the ryght honorable
the lord mowteagle

-"Facsimile of the Letter to Lord Mounteagle and Superscripton of the same," In: <u>The Pictorial World,</u>. November 5, 1882, p.294.

To the ryht honorable the lord mounteagle

My lord out of the love I beare to some of youere frends I have a caer of youer preservacion therfor I would advyse yowe as yowe tender youer lyf to devys some excuse to shift of youer attendance at this parleament for god and man hath concurred to punishe the wickedness of this tyme and think not slightlye of this advertisment but retyre youre self into youre contri wheare yowe may expect the event in safti for thowghe theare be no apparence of anni stir yet I saye they shall receyve a terrible blowe this parleament and yet they shall not seie who hurts them this cowncel is not to be contemned because it maye do yowe good and can do yowe no harme for the dangere is passed as soon as yowe have burnt the letter and I hope god will give yowe the grace to mak good use of it to whose holy protection I comend yowe

Just in case you are not as gifted as King James I, here is the Modern English translation:

"My Lord, out of the love I bear to some of your friends, I have a care of your preservation. Therefore I would advise you, as you tender your life, to devise some excuse to shift of your attendance at this Parliament; for God and man hath concurred to punish the wickedness of this time. And think not slightly of this advertisement, but retire yourself into your country [county] where you may expect the event in safety. For though there be no appearance of any stir, yet I say they shall receive a terrible blow this Parliament; and yet they shall not see who hurts them. This counsel is not to be condemned because it may do you good and can do you no harm; for the danger is passed as soon as you have burnt the letter. And I hope God will give you the grace to make good use of it, to whose holy protection I commend you."

Monteagle saw nothing of Importance in the Letter

He did not understand it. King James I was at Royston hunting. Monteagle informed the king's ministers. The letter was given to the Earl of Salisbury, Robert Cecil. Cecil thought that it was the work of a lunatic but gave it to the king.

Portrait of Robert Cecil. Attributed to John de Critz, c. 1602.

It was then November 1, 1605

James Was Inspired.......

According to James the letter must refer to the blowing up of Parliament with gunpowder. The houses of Parliament must be searched.....but only at the last moment. That search was scheduled for November 4, 1605.

Image above left: James I, Nicholas Hillard, c. 1605

James I from a portrait of 1621. In: Sidney, Philip, History of the Gunpowder Plot, 1905, p.284

The Eye of God Had Gazed Down Upon the Plot and James was Blessed with its Vision.

THE POWDER PLOT. II.

King James I Paul Van Somer, 1620

-Eye of God From: Etching of 1605, W.E.,

In: Gerard, John, What Was the Gunpowder Plot, 1897, p.235.

Psalm 102:19-20

19 For he hath looked down from the height of his sanctuary; from heaven did the Lord behold the earth;

20 To hear the groaning of the prisoner; to loose those that are appointed to death;

Deuteronomy 11

11 But the land, whither ye go to possess it, is a land of hills and valleys, and drinketh water of the rain of heaven:

12 A land which the Lord thy God careth for: the eyes of the Lord thy God are always upon it, from the beginning of the year even unto the end of the year.

-Bible, King James Version.

The explosion has begun. From this time onward the details of the plot fade as the reaction of the culture, the government, the nation and the world takes center stage in our drama.

The Construction of the Official Artifacts of Celebration began...

Contemporary Dutch Print, Small portion, (British Museum, Political and Personal Satire, 63) In: Gerard, John, What Was the Gunpowder Plot, 1897, p. 227

BOOM

November 5, 1605

House of Commons, Journal, Vol. 27, fol. 4, Parliament, November 5, 1605

Martis, 5 Novembris, 1605 Gunpowder Plot.

This last Night the Upper House of Parliament was searched by Sir Tho. Knevett; and one Johnson, Servant to Mr. Thomas Percye, was there apprehended; who had placed Thirty-six Barrels of Gunpowder in the Vault under the House, with a Purpose to blow King, and the whole Company, when they should there assemble.

~House of Commons Journal Volume 1, 05 November -1605, Journal of the House of Commons : Volume 11802 Page 256 .

The Records of the Common Council of London record that the Citizens of London were to be permitted to light bonfires of celebration providing that: "this testemonye of joy be carefull done without any danger or disorder."

- "CLRO, Journal of Common Council, Vol. 27, fol. 4,", Cited by Nicholls, Mark, Investigating Gunpowder Plot, 1991, p. 13.

Warrants By the King, King James I, 1605

Whereas Thomas Percy Gentleman, and some other his Confederates, persons knowen to be so utterly corrupted with the superstition of the Romish Religion, as seduced with the blindnesse thereof, and being otherwise of lewde life, indolent disposition, and for the most part of desperate estate, have beene discovered to have contrived the most horrible treason that ever entred into the hearts of men, against our Person, our Children, the whole Nobilitie, Clergie, and Commons in Parliament assembled, which however cloaked with zeale of superstitious Religion, aimed indeed at the Subversion of the State, and to induce an horrible confusion of all things, In which they and all others of bankerupt and necessitous estate, might have those of better abilitie for a way to repaire their beggerly fortunes, and have proceeded so farre some of them in their devilish Attempts, as to assemble in Troupes in our Counties of Warwicke and Worcester, where they have broken up a Stable, and taken out horses of divers Noblemen and Gentlemen, within our towne of Warwicke, And no doubt but doe proceede further in their purposes, seeking to raise some Rebellion in our Realme, and will with many fained and false Allegations seeke to seduce divers of our Subjects, especially with shew of Religion: Although wee are by good experience so well perswaded of the Loyaltie of divers of our Subjects (though not professing true Religion) that they doe as much abhorre this detestable conspiracie as our Selfe, and will bee ready to doe their best endevours (though with expence of their blood) to suppresse all Attemptors against our safetie and the quiet of our State, and to discover whomsoever they shall suspect to be of Rebellious or Traiterous disposition: Yet have Wee thought good by this our open Declaration, to give Warning and advertisement to all our Subjects whatsoever, of that horrible purpose of Percies and his complices, and to distinguish betweene all others, calling themseves Catholickes, and these detestable Traitours: And therefore doe denounce and publish all the persons hereunder named, Adherents to Percy, to bee Traitours knowen, and that all others are in the same case, who shall in any wise either receive, abbette, cherish, entertaine, or adhere unto them, or not doe their best endevours to apprehend and take them.

Wherefore wee will and command all out Lieutenants, Deputy lieutenants, Sheriffes, Justices of Peace, Mayors, Bayliffes, Constables, and all other our Officers, Ministers and loving Subjects, to take knowledge thereof, and to doe their best duties herein, as they will answere the contrary at their uttermost peril: Not doubting, but that they all, without regard of their pretence of Religion, will with one heart and will, employ themselves for the suppressing, apprehending, detecting, and discovering of all sorts of persons any wayes likely to be privie to a Treason so hatefull to God and men, and implying in it the utter subversion of this Realme, and dignitie thereof.

By the King, King James I, 1605

Where amongst other Persons discovered to bee Confederates in the late horrible Treason, for the destruction of Our person and the whole estates of the Realme, one Robert Winter Esquire, is knowen to be a principall, who is fled so; the same, and being not found among the Companie taken and defeated by the Sheriffe of our Countie of Worcester, doeth lurke in some places of our Realme: Although we doubt not by that experience, which in this cause wee have had of the diligence of our Ministers in the apprehending of all persons, whome they shall have cause to suspect; yet because the said Winter is unknowen to many, we have thought it convenient to publish a description of him, to the ende hee may the sooner be found by those who shall lay waite for him, And to will and command all our Officers, Ministers and loving Subjects whatsoever, to make all diligent Search for the said Winter, and him to apprehend by all possible meanes, especially to doe their best to keepe him alive, to receive condigne punishment for his detestable crime. The like diligence wee doe also will and require them to use in the apprehending of Stephen Littleton Gentleman, whose description is also hereunder written.

Given at our Pallace of Westminster the xviij. day of November, in the third yeere of our Reigne of Great Britaine, France and Ireland.

God save the King.

Descriptions of Robert Winter and Stephen Littleton by Robert Baker, 1605

Robert Winter *is a man of meane stature, rather low than otherwise, square made, somewhat stouping, neere fourtie yeeres of age, his haire and beard browne, his beard not much, and his haire short.*

Stephen Littleton *is a very tall man, swarthy of complexion, of browne coloured haire, no beard or little, about thirtie yeares of age.*

-Imprinted at London by Robert Barker,
Printer to the Kings most Excellent Maiestie.
1605.

By the King, King James I, 1605

Forasmuch as it appeareth now in part, who were the Complices of Percy in his destestable Treason published by our former Proclamations, in their assembling together to move our people to Rebellion, Although perhaps many of them did never understand the secret and depth of his abhominable purpose; and that amongst those which do flee for feare of our power, and for the guiltinesse of their offence, we are informed that the said Percy is: wee have thought it good to make knowen to all men, both that wee put great odds betweene his part of the Treason and other mens; And also, that forasmuch as it importeth greatly that hee should bee taken, to the end that by his confessions, the whole plot and the partners thereof might bee discovered, and from himself the horrible purpose opened, which it is likely that many whom hee hath seduced did never understand, And also that by the exemplary punishment of him, others be terrified from such Treasons, as tend not onely to Our destruction, but to the confusion and utter dissolution of the State:

If any person shall apprehend the sayd Percy, and bring him to Us or any Our Officers alive; if that person be an offendour and partner with him in his Treason in whatsoever degree, We will not onely give him pardon of his Life, Lands, and Goods, but also bestow on him a reward of the value of one Thousand pounds at the least. And if hee be no offendor, yet shall he have that or a greater reward. And for their assurance wee do hereby give Our Princely Word.

Given at our Palace of Westminster the eighth day of November, in the third yeare of our Reigne of Great Brittaine, France, and Ireland.

God save the King.

-Imprinted at London by Robert Barker,

Printer to the Kings most Excellent Maiestie.

Anno Dom. 1605

Observations

Diary, Sir Roger Wilbraham, The 5 of Nov. 1605

The Lords & Commons attended to expect the King's coming the begynning of this parliament then to be held by prorogation: A week before, the Lord Mountegle imparted to the King & Council, a letter sent to his hands by one unknowen & fled: wherein he was advised to be absent from the parliament, for that undoutedlie, some great calamitie wold happen soddainlie by unknowen accident, which wold be as soddaine as the fyring of the letter: wherupon the king after one serch about Parliament Howse grew so ielouse he caused a secrett watch, & discovered one Johnson practizing about midnight to make a traine to fyre 34 barrels powder, hidden under billettz in a vault iust under the Upper Howse of Parliament, confessed by one Johnson servant to Thomas Percy, a pentioner, to have ben preparing 8 moneth to blow up the King, his Queen, children, nobles, bishops, iudges & all the commons assembled, if it had not been so happelie discovered. Wilbraham, 70-1

-:The Oxford Companion to the Year., Bonnie Blackburn, Leofranc Holford-Strevens; Oxford University Press, 1999.p.449.

To Sir Thomas Edwards, Ambassador at Brussells, Sir Edward Hoby, Gentleman of the Bedchamber, 1605

On the 5th of November we began our Parliament, to which the King should have come in person, but refrained through a practise but that morning discovered. The plot was to have blown up the King at such time as he should have been set on his Royal Throne, accompanied with all his Children, Nobility and Commoners and assisted with all Bishops, Judges and Doctors; at one instant and blast to have ruin'd the whole State and Kingdom of England. And for the effecting of this, there was placed under the Parliament House, where the king should sit, some 30 barrels of powder, with good store of wood, faggots, pieces and bars of iron.

-Nichols, John, <u>The Progresses, Processions, and Magnificent Festivities of King James the First, His Royal Consort, Family, and Court,</u> London: J. B. Nichols, 1828, p.584.

Letter, John Chamberlain, November 5, 1605

"great ringing and as great store of bonfires as ever I thincke was seene."

- McClure, Norman, Egbert, <u>The Letters of John Chamberlain, I</u>, 1939, p.213.

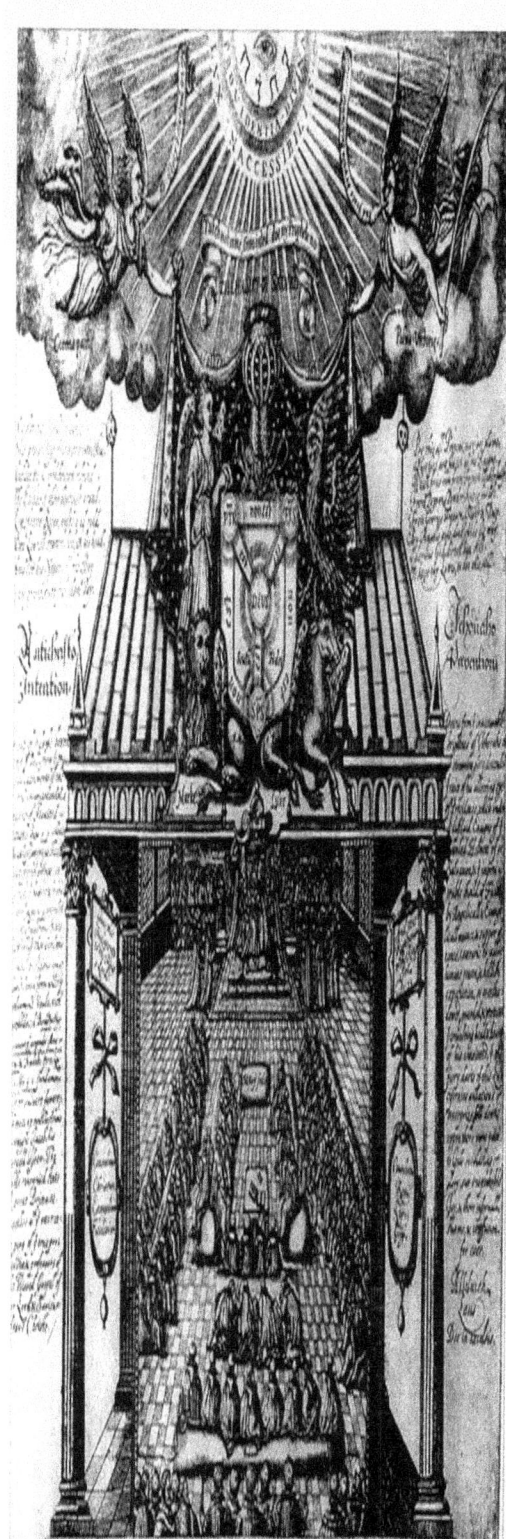

The matter that is now to be offered to you, my Lords the Commissioners, and to the Trial of you the Knights and Gentlemen of the Jury, is matter of Treason; but of such horrour, and monstrous

nature,

that before now,

The Tongue of Man never delivered,

The Ear of Man never heard,

The Heart of Man never conceived,

Nor the Malice of Hellish or Earthly Devil ever practised.

For, if it be abominable to murder the least; If to touch Gods Anointed, be to oppose themselves against God;

If (by blood) to subvert Princes, States, and Kingdoms, be hateful to God and Man, as all true Christians must acknowledge;

Then, how much more than too, too monstrous shall all Christian hearts judge the horror of this Treason, to murder and subvert,

Such a King, Such a Queen, Such a Prince,

Such a Progeny, Such a State,

Such a Government,

So compleat and absolute;

That God approves:

The World admires:

All true English Hearts honour and reverence:

The Pope and his Disciples onely envies and maligns. ~Sir Edward Philips Knight, his Majesties Sergeant at Law, The King's Book, "Trial of the Conspirators." Image left, Michael Droeshout, "The Powder Treason".

The King's Speech

On the very day of the discovery of the plot, King James created the Official assessment of the Plot and, believing himself to be guided by God and his all Seeing Eye, provided the first Paradigm for both official and public reaction.

A SPEECH Made by King JAMES to both Houses of Parliament, upon occasion of the discovery of the Gunpowder PLOT; designed to be executed on the 5 Nov. 1605, James I.

MY Lords Spiritual and Temporal, and you the Knights and Burgesses of this Parliament; It was far from my thoughts, till very lately, before my coming to this place, that this Subject should have been ministred unto me, whereupon I am now to speak. But now it so falleth out, That whereas in the preceding Session of this Parliament, the principal occasion of my Speech was, to thank and congratulate all you of this House, and in you, all the whole Commonwealth (as being the representative Body of the State) for your so willing, and loving receiving, and embracing of me in that place, which God and Nature by descent of Bloud, had in his own time provided for me:

So now my subject is, to speak of a far greater Thanksgiving than before I gave to you, being to a far greater person, which is to GOD, for the great and miraculous Delivery he hath at this time granted to me, and to you all, and consequently to the whole Body of this Estate,

I must therefore begin with this old and most approved Sentence of Divinity, Misericordia Dei supra omnia opera ejus. For Almighty GOD did not furnish so great matter to his Glory, by the Creation of this great World, as he did by the

Redemption of the same. Neither did his Generation of the little World, in our old and first ADAM, so much set forth the praises of GOD in his Justice and Mercy, as did our Regeneration in the last and second ADAM.

And now I must crave a little pardon of you, That since Kings are in the word of GOD itself called Gods, as being his Lieutenants and Vicegerents on earth, and so adorned and furnished with some sparkles of the Divinity; to compare some of the Works of GOD the Great King, towards the whole and general World, to some of his Works towards Me, and this little world of my Dominions, compassed and severed by the Sea from the rest of the Earth. For as GOD for the just punishment of the first great Sinner in the original world, when the Sons of GOD went in to the Daughters of Men, and the cup of their iniquities of all sorts was filled, and heaped up to the full, did by a general deluge and overflowing of waters, baptize the World to a general destruction, and not to general purgation (only excepted Noah and his family, who did repent and believe the threatenings of God's judgement:) So now, when the World shall wax old as a Garment, and that all the impieties and sins that can be devised against both the first and second Table, have, and shall be committed to the full measure; GOD is to punish the World the second time by Fire, to the general destruction and not purgation thereof. Although as it was done in the former to Noah and his Family by the waters; So shall all we that believe be likewise purged, and not destroyed by the Fire. In the like sort, I say, I may justly compare these two great and fearful Dooms-days, wherewith GOD threatened to destroy me, and all you of this little World that have interest in me. For although I confess, as all mankind, so chiefly Kings, as being in the higher places like the high Trees, or stayest Mountains, and steepest Rocks, are most subject to the daily tempests of innumerable dangers; and I amongst all other Kings, have ever been subject unto them, not only ever since my birth, but even as I may justly say, before my birth, and while I was yet in my Mothers belly: yet have I been exposed to two more special and greater dangers than all the rest.

The first of them, in the Kingdom where I was born, and passed the first part of my life: And the last of them here, which is the greatest. In the former, I should have been baptized in bloud, and in my destruction, not only the Kingdom, wherein I then was, but ye also by your future interest, should have tasted of my ruine. Yet it pleased GOD to deliver me, as it were, from the very brink of death, from the point of the dagger, and so to purge me by my thankful acknowledgement of so great a benefit. But in this which did so lately fall out, and which was a destruction prepared not for me alone, but for you all that are here present, and wherein no rank, age, or sex should have been spared; This was not a crying sin of bloud as the former, but it may well be called a roaring, nay, a thundering sin of Fire and Brimstone, from the which, God hath so miraculously delivered us all. What I can speak of this, I know not: Nay rather, what can I not speak of it? And therefore I must for horror say with the Poet. Vox faucibus haeret.

In this great and horrible attempt, whereof the like was never either heard or read, I observe three wonderful, or rather miraculous events.

First, in the cruelty of the Plot itself, wherein cannot be enough admired the horrible and fearful cruelty of their Device, which was not only for the destruction of my Person, nor of my Wife and Posterity only, but of the whole Body of the State in general; wherein should neither have been spared, or distinction made of young nor of old, of great nor of small, of man nor of woman: The whole Nobility, the whole Reverend Clergy, Bishops, and most part of the good Preachers, the most part of the Knights and Gentry; yea, and if that any in this Society were favourers of their Profession, they should all have gone one way: The whole Judges of the Land, with the most of the Lawyers and the whole Clerks: And as the wretch himself that is in the Tower, doth confess, it was purposely devised by them, and concluded to be done in this house; That where the cruel Laws (as they say) were made against their Religion, both place and persons should all be destroyed and blown up at once. And then consider therewithal the cruel form of that practice: for by three different sorts in general may mankind be put to death.

The First, by other men, and reasonable creatures, which is least cruel: for then both defence of men against men may be expected, and likewise who knoweth what pity GOD may stirr up in the hearts of the Actors at the very instant? besides the many ways and means, whereby men may escape in such a present fury.

And the Second way more cruel than that, is by Animal and unreasonable creatures: for as they have less pity then men, so is it a greater horror, and more unnatural for men to deal with them: But yet with them both resistance may avail, and also some pity may be had, as was in the Lyons, in whose Den Daniel was thrown; or that thankful Lyon, that had the Roman slave in his mercy.

But the Third, which is most cruel and unmerciful of all, is the destruction by insensible and inanimate things; and amongst them all, the most cruel are the two Elements of Water and Fire; and of those two the Fire most raging and merciless.

Secondly, How wonderful it is when you shall think upon the small, or rather no ground, whereupon the Practisers were enticed to invent this Tragedy. For if these Conspirators had only been bankrupt persons, or discontented upon occasion of any disgraces done unto them; this might have seemed to have been but a work of revenge. But for my own part, as I scarcely ever knew any of them, So cannot they allege so much as a pretended cause of grief: And the wretch himself in hands doth confess, That there was no cause moving him or them, but meerly, and only Religion. And specially, that Christian men, at least so called, Englishmen, born within the Countrey, and one of the specials of them, my sworn Servant, in an Honorable place, should Practise the destruction of their King, his Posterity, their Countrey and all: wherein their following obstinacy is so joyned to their former malice, as the fellow himself that is in hand, cannot be moved to discover any signes or notes of repentance, except only, that he doth not yet stand to avow, that he repents for not being able to perform his intent.

Thirdly, The discovery hereof is not a little wonderful, which would be thought the more miraculous by you all, if you were as well acquainted with my natural disposition, as those are who be near about me. For as I ever did hold suspition to be the sickness of a Tyrant, so was I so far upon the other extremity, as I rather contemned all advertisements, or apprehensions of practises. And yet now at this time was I so far contrary to my self, as when the Letter was shewed to me by my Secretary, wherein a general obscure adveriesment was given of some dangerous blow at this time, I did upon the instant interpret and apprehend some dark phrases therein, contrary to the ordinary Grammer construction of them, (and in another sort then I am sure any Divine, or Lawyer in any University would have taken them) to be meant by this horrible form of blowing us up all by Powder; and thereupon ordered, that search to be made, whereby the matter was discovered, and the man apprehended: whereas if I had apprehended or interpreted it to any other sort of danger, no worldly provision or prevention could have made us escape our utter destruction.

And in that also, was there a wonderful providence of God, that when the party himself was taken, he was but new come out of his house from working, having his Firework for kindling ready in his pocket, wherewith as he confesseth, if he had been taken but immediately before, when he was in the House, he was resolved to have blown up himself with his Takers.

One thing for my own part have I cause to thank GOD in, That if GOD for our sins had suffered their wicked intents to have prevailed, it should never have been spoken nor written in ages succeeding, that I had died ingloriously in an Ale-house, a Stews, or such vile place, but mine end should have been with the most Honourable and best company, and in that most Honourable and fittest place for a King to be in, for doing the turns most proper to his Office; And the more have We all cause to thank and magnifie GOD for this his merciful Delivery. And specially I for my part, that he hath given me yet once leave, whatsoever should come of me hereafter, to assemble you in this Honourable place; And here in this place, where our general destruction should have been, to magnifie and praise him for Our general delivery; That I may justly now say of mine enemies and yours, as David doth often say in the Psalm, Inciderunt in foveam, quam fecerunt. And since Scipio an Ethnick, led only by the light of Nature, That day when he was accused by the Tribunes of the people of Rome, for mispending and wasting in his Punick wars the Cities Treasure, even upon the sudden brake out with that diversion of them from that matter, calling them to remembrance how that day, was the day of the year, wherein GOD hath given them so great a victory against Hannibal, and therefore it was fitter for them all, leaving other matters, to run to the Temple to praise GOD for that so great delivery, which the people did all follow with one applause: How much more cause have we that are Christians to bestow this time in this place for Thansgiving to GOD for his great Mercy, tho we had had no other errand of assembling here at this time; wherein if I have spoken more like a Divine, than would seem to belong to this place, the matter it self must plead for mine excuse: for being here come to thank God for a Divine work of his Mercy, how can I speak of this deliverance of us from so hellish a practise, so well, as in language of Divinity, which is the direct opposite to so damnable an intention? And therefore may I justly end this purpose, as I did begin it with this Sentence, The mercy of God is above all his works.

It resteth now, that I should shortly inform you what is to be done hereafter upon the occasion of this horrible and strange accident. As for your part that are my faithful and loving Subjects of all degrees, I know that your hearts are so burnt up with zeal in this errand, and your tongues so ready to utter your dutiful affections, and your hands and feet so bent to concurr in the execution thereof, (for which as I need not to spurr you, so can I not but praise you for the same:) As it may very well be possible, that the zeal of your hearts shall make some of you in your speeches, rashly to blame such as may be innocent of this attempt;

But upon the other part I wish you to consider, That I would be sorry that any being innocent of this practise, either domestical or forrain, should receive blame or harm, for the same. For although it cannot be denied, That it was the only blind superstition of their errors in Religion, that led them to this desperate device; yet doth it not follow, That all professing that Romish Religion were guilty of the same. For as it is true, That no other sect of Heretiques, not excepting Turk Jew, nor Pagan, no not even those of Calicute who adore the Devil, did ever maintain by the grounds of their Religion, That it was lawful, or rather meritorious (as the Romish Catholicks call it) to murther Princes or people for quarrel of Religion. And although particular men of all professions of Religion have been some Thieves, some Murtherers, some Traitors, yet ever when they came to their end and just punishment, they confessed their fault to be in their nature, and not in their profession, (These Romish Catholicks only excepted:) Yet it is true on the other side, That many honest men blinded peradventure with some opinions of Popery, as if they be not found in the questions of the Real presence, or in the number of the Sacraments, or some such School-question: yet do they either not know, or at least, not believe all the true grounds of Popery, which is indeed, The mistery of iniquity. And therefore do we justly confess, that many Papists, especially our fore-fathers, laying their only trust upon Christ and his Merits at their last breath, may be, and oftentimes are saved; detesting in that point, and thinking the cruelty of Puritans worthy of Fire, that will admit no salvation to any Papist. I therefore thus do conclude this point, That as upon the one part many honest men, seduced with some errors of Popery, may yet remain good and faithful Subjects: So upon the other part, none of those that truly know and believe the whole grounds, and School-conclusions of their Doctrine, can ever prove either good Christians, or faithful Subjects. And for the part of forrain Princes and States, I may so much the more acquite them, and their Ministers, of their knowledge and consent to any such villany, as I may justly say, that in that point I better know all Christian Kings by my self, that no King nor Prince of Honor will ever abase himself so much, as to think a good thought of so base and dishonourable a Treachery: wishing you therefore, that as GOD hath given me an happy peace and amity, with all other Christian Princes my neighbors (as was even now very gravely told you by my L. Chancellor) that so you will reverently judge and speak of them in this case. And for my part I would wish with those antient Philosophers, that there were a Christal window in my breast, wherein all my people might see the secretest thoughts of my heart, for then might you all see no alteration in my mind for this accident, further than in those two points. The first, caution and wariness in government:

to discover and search out the mysteries of this wickedness as far as may be: The other, after due trial, Severity of punishment upon those that shall be found guilty of so detestable and unheard of villany. And now in this matter, if I have troubled your ears with an abrupt Speech, undisgested in any good method or order; you have to consider that an abrupt, and unadvised Speech doth best become in the relation of so abrupt and unorderly an accident.

And although I have ordained the Proroguing of this Parliament until after Christmass upon two necessary respects: whereof the first is, that neither I nor my Council can have leasure at this time both to take order for the apprehension and trial of these Conspirators, and also to wait upon the daily affairs of the Parliament, as the Council must do. And the other reason is, the necessity at this time of divers of your presences in your Shires that have Charges and Commandements there. For as these wretches thought to have blown up in a manner the whole world of this Island, every man being now come up here, either for publick causes of Parliament, or else for their own private causes in Law, or otherwise: So these Rebels that now wander through the Countrey, could never have gotten so fit a time of safety in their passage, or whatsoever unlawful Actions, as now when the countrey by the foresaid occasions is in a manner left desolate, and waste unto them. Besides that, It may be that I shall desire you at your next Session, to take upon you the Judgment of this Crime: for as so extraordinary a Fact deserves extraordinary Judgment, So can there not I think (following even their own Rule) be a fitter Judgement for them, then that they should be measured with the same measure wherewith they thought to measure us: and that the same place and persons, whom they thought to destroy, should be the just avengers of their so unnatural a Parricide: Yet not knowing that I will have occasion to meet with you my self in this place at the beginning of the next Session of this Parliament (because if it had not been for delivering of the Articles agreed upon by the Commissioners of the Union, which was thought most convenient to be done in my presence, where both Head and Members of the Parliament were met together, my presence had not otherwise been requisite here at this time:) I have therefore thought good for conclusion of this Meeting, to discourse to you somewhat anent the true nature and definition of a Parliament, which I will remit to your memories, till your next sitting down; that you may then make use of it as occasion shall be ministred.

For albeit it be true, that at the first Session of my first Parliament, which was not long after mine Entry into this Kingdome, It could not become me to informe you of any thing belonging to Law or State here: (for all knowledge must either be infused, or acquired, and seeing the former sort thereof is now with Prophesie, ceased in the World, it could not be possible for me, at my first Entry here, before Experience had taught it me, to be able to understand the particular Mysteries of this State:) yet now that I have reigned almost three years amongst you, and have been careful to observe those things that belong to the Office of a King, albeit that Time be but a short time for experience in others, yet in a King may it be thought a reasonable long time, especially in me, who, although I be but in a manner a new King here, yet have been long acquainted with the office of a King in such another Kingdom, as doth nearest of all others agree with the Lawes and Customes of this State. Remitting to your consideration to judge of that which hath been concluded by the Commissioners of the Union, wherein I am at this time to signifie unto you, That as I can bear witness to the foresaid Commissioners, that they have not agreed nor concluded therein any thing, wherein they have not foreseen as well the Weale and Commodity of the one Countrey, as of the other; So can they all bear me record, that I was so far from pressing them to agree to any thing, which might bring with it any prejudice to this People; as by the contrary I did ever admonish them, never to conclude upon any such Union, as might carry hurt or grudge with it to either of the said Nations: for the leaving of any such thing, could not but be the greatest hinderance that might be to such an Action, which GOD by the Laws of nature had provided to be in his own time, and hath now in effect perfected in my Person; to which purpose my Lord Chancellor hath better spoken, then I am able to relate.

And as to the nature of this high Court of Parliament, It is nothing else but the Kings great Council, which the King doth assemble, either upon occasion of interpreting, or abrogating old Lawes, or making of new, according as ill manners shall deserve, or for the publick punishment of notorious evil doers, or the praise and reward of the vertuous and well deservers; wherein these four things are to be considered.

First, Whereof this Court is composed.

Secondly, What Matters are proper for it.

Thirdly, To what end it is ordained.

And Fourthly, What are the meanes and wayes whereby this end should be brought to pass.

As for the thing it self, It is composed of a Head and a Body: The Head is the King, the Body are the members of the Parliament. This Body again is subdivided into two parts; The Upper and Lower House: The Upper compounded partly of Nobility, Temporal men, who are heritable Councellors to to the high Court of Parliament by the honor of their Creation and Lands: And partly of Bishops, Spiritual men, who are likewise by the vertue of their place and dignity Counsellors, Life-Renters, or Ad vitam of this Court. The other House is composed of Knights for the Shire; and Gentry, and Burgesses for the Towns. But because the number would be infinite for all the Gentlemen and Burgesses to be present at every Parliament, Therefore a certain number is selected and chosen out of that great Body, serving onely for that Parliament, where their persons are the representation of that Body.

Now the Matters whereof they are to treat ought therefore to be general, and rather of such matters as cannot well be performed without the assembling of that general Body, and no more of these generals neither, then necessity shall require: for as in Corruptissima Republica sunt plurimae leges: So doth the life and strength of the Law consist not in heaping up infinite and confused numbers of Lawes, but in the right interpretation and good execution of good and wholsome Laws. If this be so then, neither is this a place on the one side for every rash and harebrain fellow to propone new Laws of his own invention: nay rather I could wish these busie heads to remember that Law of the Lacedemonians, That whosoever came to propone a new Law to the People, behoved publickly to present himself with a Rope about his neck, that in case the Law were not allowed, he should be hanged therewith. So wary should men be of proponing Novelties, but most of all, not to propone any bitter or seditious Laws, which can produce nothing but grudges and discontentment between the Prince and his people: nor yet is it on the other side a convenient place for private men under the colour of general Laws, to propone nothing but their own particular gain, either to the hurt of their private neighbours, or to the hurt of the whole State in general, which many times under fair and pleasing Titles, are smoothly passed over, and so by stealth procure without consideration, that the private meaning of them tendeth to nothing but either to the wreck of a particular party, or else under colour of publique benefit to pill the poor people, and serve as it were for a general Impost upon them for filling the purses of some private persons.

And as to the end for which the Parliament is ordained, being only for the advancement of Gods glory, and the establishment and wealth of the King and his people: It is no place then for particular men to utter there their private conceipts, nor for satisfaction of their curiosities, and least of all to make shew of their eloquence, by tyning the time with long studied and eloquent Orations. No, the reverence of GOD, their King, and their Countrey being well setled in their hearts, will make them ashamed of such toyes, and remember that they are there as sworn Councellors to their King, to give their best advice for the furtherance of his Service, and the flourishing Weale of his Estate.

And lastly, if you will rightly consider the means and wayes how to bring all your labors to a good end, you must remember, That you are here assembled by your lawful King to give him your best advices, in the matters proposed by him unto you, being of that nature, which I have already told, wherein you are gravely to deliberate, and upon your consciences plainly to determine how far those things propounded do agree with the Weale, both of your King, and of your Country, whose weales cannot be separated. And as for my self, the world shall ever bear me witness, That I never shall propone any thing unto you, which shall not as well tend to the Weale publick, as to any benefit for me: So shall I never oppone my self to that, which may tend to the good of the Common-wealth, for the which I am ordained, as I have often said. And as you are to give your advice in such things, as shall by your King be proposed: So is it on your part your duties to propone any thing that you can, after mature deliberation judge to be needful, either for these ends already spoken of, or otherwise for the discovery of any latent evil in the Kingdom, which peradventure may not have come to the Kings eare. If this then ought to be your grave manner of proceeding in this place, Men should be ashamed to make shew of the quickness of their wits here, either in taunting, scoffing, or detracting the Prince or State in any point, or yet in breaking jests upon their fellowes, for which the Ordinaries or Alehouses are fitter places, than this Honourable and high Court of Parliament.

In conclusion then, since you are to break up, for the Reasons I have already told you, I wish such of you as have any charges in your Countreys, to hasten you home for the repressing of the insolencies of these Rebels, and apprehension of their persons, wherein, as I heartily pray to the Almighty for your prosperous success: So do I not doubt, but we shall shortly hear the good newes of the same; And that you shall have an happy return, and meeting here to all our comforts.

Here the Lord Chancellor spake touching the Proroguing of the Parliament. And hauing done, his Majesty rose again, and said.

Since it pleased GOD to grant me two such notable Deliveries upon one day of the week, which was Tuesday, and likewise one day of the Moneth, which was the fifth; thereby to teach me, That as it was the same Devil that still persecuted me: So it was one and the same GOD that still mightily delivered me; I thought it therefore not amiss, that the one and twentieth day of Ianuary, which fell to be upon Tuesday, should be the day of meeting of this next Session of Parliament, hoping and assuring my Self, that the same GOD who hath now granted me and you all so notable and gracious a Delivery, shall prosper all our affairs at that next Session, and bring them to a happy conclusion. And now I consider God hath well provided it that the ending of this Parliament hath been so long continued; For as for mine own part, I never had any other intention, but only to seek so far my weale, and prosperity, as might conjunctly stand with the flourishing State of the whole Common-wealth, as I have often told you: So on the other part I confess, if I had been in your places at the beginning of this Parliament (which was so soon after mine entry into this Kingdom, wherein ye could not possibly have so perfect a knowledge of mine inclination, as experience since hath taught you) I could not but have suspected, and misinterpreted divers things, In the trying whereof, now I hope, by your experience of my behaviour and form of government, you are well enough cleared, and resolved.

Arrest of Fawkes

John Moyr Smith c.1870 Minton Decorative Tile

The Official Account

English School, King James I in the Houses of Parliament, 1624

The King's Book, James I, 1605.

King James I in the King's Book creates the foundation for all that is to come. Regardless of historical fact, this account informed the construction of Artifacts of Celebrations and the building of relationships between the people, the country and the Celebration.

The King's Book

THE GUNPOWDER-TREASON: WITH A DISCOURSE OF THE MANNER OF ITS DISCOVERY;

AND

A PERFECT RELATION OF THE

Proceedings against those horrid Conspirators;

Wherein is Contained their Examinations, Tryals, and Condemnations:

LIKEWISE KING IAMES's SPEECH

To Both Houses of PARLIAMENT,

On that Occasion; Now Re-printed.

London, Printed by Tho. Newcomb, and H. Hills, and are to be Sold by Walter Kettilby, at the Bishops Head in St. Pauls Churchyard. 1679.

KING JAMES HIS SPEECH TO BOTH HOUSES OF PARLIAMENT, ON OCCASION OF THE

GUNPOWDER-TREASON:

With a Discourse of the manner of its Discovery, and a perfect Relation of the whole Proceedings against those horrid Conspirators.

LONDON, Re-printed by His Majesties Printers.

M.DC.LXXIX.

White-hall, Decemb. 12. 1678.

By License from the Right Honourable Mr. Secretary Coventry, this Book, containing King James his Speech to both Houses of Parliament, on occasion of the Gun-powder Treason; with a Discourse of the manner of its Discovery, and a perfect Relation of the whole Proceedings against those horrid Conspirators: May be Reprinted.

IO. COOKE.

(The King's Speech of Nov. 5 is relocated above)

A DISCOURSE OF THE MANNER OF THE DISCOVERY OF THE GUNPOWDER-PLOT, TOGETHER WITH THE EXAMINATIONS AND CONFESSIONS OF SOME OF THE MOST NOTORIOUS CONSPIRATORS CONCERN'D IN IT.

There is a time when no man ought to keep silence. For it hath ever been held as a general rule, and undoubted Maxime, in all well governed Common-wealths, (whether Christian, and so guided by the Divine Light of GOD'S Word; or Ethnick, and so led by the glimmering twi-light of Nature) yet howsoever their profession was, upon this ground have they all agreed, That when either their Religion, their King, or their Countrey was in any extreme hazard; no good Countreyman ought then to withhold either his tongue or his hand, according to his calling and faculty, from aiding to repel the Injury, repress the Violence, and avenge the Guilt upon the Authors thereof. But if ever any people had such an occasion ministred unto them, It is surely this People now, nay this whole Isle, and all the rest belonging to this great and glorious Monarchy. For if in any Heathenish Republick, no private man could think his life more happily and gloriously bestowed, then in the defence of any one of these three, That is, either pro Aris, pro Focis, or pro Patre patrioe; And that the endangering of any one of these, would at once stir the whole body of the Common-wealth, not any more as divided members, but as a solid and individual lump: How much more ought we, the truely Christian People, that inhabit this United, and truely happy Isle, under the wings of our gracious and religious Monarch? Nay, how infinitely greater cause have we to feel, and resent our selves of the smart of that wound, not onely intended and execrated (not consecrated) for the utter extinguishing of our true Christian profession, nor joyntly therewith onely for the cutting off of our Head and Father Politick, Sed ut nefas istud & sacrilegiosum parricidium omnibus modis absolutum reddi possit? And that nothing might be wanting for making this sacrilegious Parricide a pattern of mischief, and a crime (nay, a Mother or Storehouse of all crimes) without example, they should have joyned the destruction of the body to the head, so as Grex cum Rege, Arae cum focis,

Lares cum Penatibus, should all at one thunderclap have been sent to Heaven together: The King our Head, the Queen our fertile Mother, and those young and hopeful Olive plants, not theirs but ours: Our reverend Clergy, our honorable Nobility, the faithful Counsellors, the grave Judges, the greatest part of the worthy Knights and Gentry, as well as of the wisest Burgesses; The whole Clerks of the Crown, Council, Signet, Seals, or of any other principal Judgement seat. All the learned Lawyers, together with an infinite number of the Common people: Nay, their furious rage should not onely have lighted upon reasonable and sensible creatures without distinction, either of degree, sexe, or age; But even the insensible stocks and stones should not have been free of their fury. The Hall of Justice; The House of Parliament; the Church used for the Coronation of our Kings; The Monuments of our former Princes; The Crown, and other marks of Royalty; all the Records, as well of Parliament, as of every particular mans right, with a great number of Charters and such like, should all have been comprehended under that fearful Chaos. And so the earth as it were opened, should have sent forth of the bottom of the Stygian Lake such sulphured smoke, furious flames, and fearful thunder, as should have, by their diabolical Domesday destroyed and defaced, in the twinckling of an eye, not onely our present living Princes, and People, but even our insensible Monuments reserved for future ages. So as not only our selves that are mortal, but the immortal Monuments of our antient Princes and Nobility, that have been so preciously preserved from age to age, as the remaining Trophees of their eternal glory, and have so long triumphed over envious time, should now have been all consumed together; And so not onely we, but the memory of us and ours, should have been thus extinguished in an instant. The true horror therefore of this detestable devise, hath stirred me up to bethink my self, wherein I may best discharge my conscience in a cause so general and common, if it were to bring but one stone to the building, or rather with the Widow, one mite to the common Box. But since to so hateful and unheard of invention, there can be no greater enemy then the self, the simple truth thereof being once publickly known and divulged; and that there needs no stronger argument to bring such a Plot in universal detestation, then the certainty that so monstrous a thing could once be devised, nay concluded upon, wrought in, in full readiness, and within twelve hours of the execution: My threefold zeal to those blessings, whereof they would have so violently made us all Widows, hath made me resolve to set down here the true Narration of that monstrous and unnatural intended Tragedy, having better occasion by the means of my service, and continual attendance in Court, to know the truth thereof, than others that peradventure have it only by relation at the third or fourth hand.

So that whereas those worse than Catalines, thought to have extirpated us, and our memories; their infamous memory shall by these means remain to the end of the world, upon the one part; and upon the other, Gods great and merciful deliverance of his Anointed, and us all, shall remain in never-dying Records. And GOD grant that it may be in Marble Tables of Thankfulness engraven in our hearts.

While this Land and whole Monarchy flourished in a most happy and plentiful Peace, as well at home as abroad, sustained and conducted by those two main pillars of all good Government, Piety and Justice, no forreign grudge, nor inward whispering of discontentment any way appearing; The King being upon his return from his Hunting exercise at Royston, upon occasion of the drawing near of the Parliament time, which had been twice Prorogued already, partly in regard of the season of the year, and partly of the Term; As the winds are ever stillest immediately before a storm; and as the Sun blenks often hottest to foretell a following shower: So at that time of greatest calm, did this secretly hatched thunder begin to cast forth the first flashes, and flaming lightnings of the approaching tempest. For the Saturday of the week, immediately preceding the King's return, which was upon a Thursday (being but ten days before the Parliament) The Lord Mountegle, Son and Heir to the Lord Morley, being in his own Lodging, ready to goe to supper, at seven of the clock at night, one of his Footmen (whom he had sent of an errand over the street) was met by an unknown man, of a reasonable tall personage, who delivered him a Letter, charging him to put it in my Lord his Masters hands: which my Lord no sooner received, but that having broken it up, and perceiving the same to be of an unknown, and somewhat unlegible hand, and without either Date or Subscription; did call one of his men unto him for helping him to read it. But no sooner did he conceive the strange contents thereof, although he was somewhat perplexed what construction to make of it (as whether of a matter of consequence, as indeed it was, or whether some foolish devised Pasquil, by some of his enemies to scare him from his attendance at the Parliament) yet did he, as a most dutiful and loyal Subject, conclude not to conceal it,

Image: <u>Mischeefes Mysterie or Treasons Master-peece, The Powdeer-Plot</u>, John Vickers, 1617.

whatever might come of it. Whereupon, notwithstanding the lateness and darkness of the night in that season of the year, he presently repaired to His Majesties Palace at Whitehal, and there delivered the same to the Earl of Salisbury, His Majesties Principal Secretary. Whereupon the said Earl of Salisbury having read the Letter, and heard the manner of the coming of it to his hands, did greatly encourage, and commend my Lord for his discretion, telling him plainly, that whatsoever the purpose of the Letter might prove hereafter, yet did this accident put him in mind of divers advertisements he had received from beyond the Seas, wherewith he had acquainted, as well the King himself, as divers of His Privy Counsellors, concerning some business the Papists were in, both at home and abroad, making preparations for some combination amongst them against this Parliament time, for enabling them to deliver at that time to the King, some petition for toleration of Religion: which should be delivered in some such order and so well backed, as the King should be loth to refuse their requests; like the sturdy beggars craving alms with one open hand, but carrying a stone in the other, in case of refusal. And therefore did the Earl of Salisbury conclude with the Lord Mountegle, that he would, in regard of the Kings absence, impart the same Letter to some more of His Majesties Council; whereof my L. Mountegle liked well: only adding this request by way of protestation, That whatsoever the event hereof might prove, it should not be imputed to him, as proceeding from too light, and too suddain an apprehension, that he delivered this Letter, being only moved thereunto for demonstration of his ready devotion, and care for preservation of His Majesty and the State. And thus did the Earl of Salisbury presently acquaint rhe L. Chamberlain with the said Letter. Whereupon they two, in presence of the Lord Mountegle; calling to mind the former intelligence already mentioned, which seemed to have some relation with this Letter: The tender care which they ever carried to the preservation of His

Majesties Person, made them apprehend, that some perilous attempt did thereby appear to be intended against the same, which did the more neerly concern the said Lord Chamberlain to have a care of, in regard that it doth belong to the charge of his Office to oversee as well all places of Assembly where His Majesty is to repair, as his Highness own private Houses. And therefore did the said two Counsellors conclude, That they should joyn unto themselves Three more of the Counsel, to wit, the Lord Admiral, the Earls of Worcester and Northampton, to be also particularly acquainted with this accident, who having all of them concurred together to the re-examination of the Con tents of the said Letter, they did conclude That how slight a matter it might at the first appear to be, yet was it not absolutely to be contemned, in respect of the care which it behoved them to have of the preservation of His Majesties Person: But yet resolved for two reasons, First, To acquaint the King himself with the same, before they proceeded to any further Inquisition in the matter, as well for the expectation and experience they had of His Majesties fortunate Judgement in cleering and solving of obscure Riddles and doubtful Mysteries; as also, because the more time would in the mean while be given for the Practise to ripen, if any was, whereby the Discovery might be the more clear and evident, and the ground of proceeding thereupon more safe, just, and easie. And so according to their determination, did the said Earl of Salisbury, repair to the King in His Gallery upon Friday, being Alhallow day, in the afternoon, which was the day after His Majesties arrival, and none but himself being present with His Highness at that time, where without any other Speech or Judgement giving of the Letter, but only relating simply the form of the delivery thereof, he presented it to His Majesty. The Contents whereof follow.

My Lord, out of the love I bear to some of your friends, I have a care of your preservation. Therefore I would advise you, as you tender your life, to devise some excuse to shift off your attendance at this Parliament. For God and Man have concurred to punish the wickedness of this Time. And think not slightly of this Advertisement, but retire your self into your Countrey, where you may expect the event in safety. For though there be no appearance of any stir, yet I say, they shall receive a terrible Blow this Parliament, and yet they shall not see who hurts them. This Counsel is not to be contemned, because it may do you good, and can do you no harm; for the danger is past, so soon as you have burnt the Letter. And I hope God will give you the grace to make good use of it: To whose Holy protection I commend you.

The King no sooner read the Letter, but after a little pause, and then reading it over again, he delivered his judgement of it in such sort, as he thought it was not to be contemned, for that the Stile of it seemed to be more quick and pithy, than is usual to be in any Pasquil or Libel (the superfluities of idle brains:) But the Earl of Salisbury perceiving the King to apprehend it deeplier than he looked for, knowing his Nature, told him that he thougt by one sentence in it, that it was like to be written by some fool or mad man, reading to him this Sentence in it. For the danger is past, as soon as you have burnt the Letter; which he said, was likely to be the saying of a fool: for if the danger was past so soon as the Letter was burnt, then the warning behoved to be of a little avail, when the burning of the Letter might make the danger to be eschewed. But the King by the contrary, considering the former sentence In the Letter. That they should receive a terrible Blow at this Parliament, and yet should not see who hurt them, joyning it to the sentence immediately following, already alledged, did thereupon conjecture, That the danger mentioned should be some suddain danger by blowing up of Powder, For no other Insurrection, Rebellion, or whatsoever other private and desperate Attempt could be committed or attempted in time of Parliament, and the Authors thereof unseen, except only if it were by a blowing up of Powder, which might be performed by one base knave in a dark corner; whereupon he was moved to interpret, and construe the latter Sentence in the Letter (alledged by the Earl of Salisbury) against all ordinary sense and construction in Grammar, as if by these words, For the danger is past, as soon as you have burned the Letter, should be closely understood the suddainty and quickness of the danger, which should be as quickly performed, and at an end, as that paper should be of blazing up in the fire; turning that word of as soon, to the sense of, as quickly. And therefore wished, that before His going to the Parliament, the under rooms of the Parliament-house, (might be well and narrowly searched. But the Earl of Salisbury wondring at this His Majesties Commentary, which he knew to be so far contrary to His ordinary and natural disposition, who did rather ever sin upon the other side, in not apprehending nor trusting due Advertisements of Practises and Perils when he was truly enformed of them, whereby he had many times drawn himself into many desperate dangers: and interpreting rightly, this extraordinary Caution at this time, to proceed from the vigilant care he had of the whole State, more than of His own Person, which could not but have all perished together, if this designment had succeeded: He thought good to dissemble still unto the King, that there had been any just cause of such apprehensions. And ending the purpose with some merry jest upon this subject, as his custom is, took his leave for that time. But though he seemed so to neglect it to His Majesty; yet his customable and watchful care of the King, and the State still boyling within him. And having with the Blessed Virgin Mary laid up in his heart, the Kings so strange judgement and construction of it; He could not be at rest till he acquainted the foresaid Lords what had passed between the King and him in private. Whereupon they were all so earnest to renew again the memory of the same purpose to His Majesty, as it was agreed that he should the next day, being Saturday, repair to His Highness: which he did in the same Privy Gallery, and renewed the memory thereof, the L. Chamberlain then being present with the King. At what time it was determined; that the said Lord Chamberlain should, according to his custom and Office, view all the Parliament Houses, both above and below, and consider what likelyhood or appearance of any such danger might possibly be gathered by the sight of them: but yet, as well for staying of idle rumours, as for being the more able to discern any mystery, the nearer that things were in readiness, his journey thither was ordained to be deferred till the afternoon, before the sitting down of the

Parliament, which was upon the Munday following. At what time he (according to this conclusion) went to the Parliament house, accompanied with my Lord Mountegle, being in zeal to the Kings service, earnest and curious to see the event of that accident, whereof he had the fortune to be the first discoverer: where having viewed all the lower rooms, he found in the Vault, under the Upper House, great store and Provisions of Billets, Faggots and Coals: And enquiring of Whyneard, Keeper of the Wardrobe, to what use he had put those lower Rooms and Cellars: he told him,, That Thomas Percy had hired both the House, and part of the Cellar or Vault under the same, and that the Wood and Coal therein was the said Gentlemans own provision. Whereupon the Lord Chamberlain, casting his eye aside, perceived a fellow standing in a corner there, calling himself the said Percy's man, and keeper of that house for him, but indeed was Guido Fawkes, the owner of that hand, which should have acted that monstrous Tragedy

From: Mischeefes Mysterie or Treasons Master-peece,

The Powder-Plot, John Vickers, 1617

The Lord Chamberlain looking upon all things with a heedful indeed, yet in outward appearance with but a careless and rackless eye (as became so wise and diligent a minister) he presently addressed himself to the King in the said Privy Gallery, where in the presence of the Lord Treasurer, the Lord Admiral, the Earls of Worcester, Northampton, and Salisbury, he made his report, what he had seen and observed there: noting, that Mountegle had told him; That he no sooner heard Thomas Percy named to be the possessor of that house, but considering both his backwardness in Religion, and the old dearness in friendship, between himself, and the said Percy, he did greatly suspect the matter, and that the Letter should come from him. The said Lord Chamberlain also told, That he did not wonder a little at the extraordinary great provision of Wood and Coal in that house, where Thomas Percy had so seldom occasion to remain: As likewise it gave him in his mind, that his man looked like a very tall and desperate fellow.

Anon., A Plot with Powder, 1605, engraving. Burnet, vol. I, pt. 1, facing p. 11

This could not but increase the Kings former apprehension and jealousie: whereupon he insisted (as before) that the House was narrowly to be searched, and that those Billets and Coals should be searched to the bottom, it being most suspitious that they were laid there only for covering of the Powder. Of the same mind also, were all the Counselors then present. But upon the fashion of making of the search, was it long debated: for upon the one side they were all so jealous of the Kings safety, that they all agreed, that there could not be too much caution used for preventing his danger. And yet upon the other part, they were all extream loth and dainty, that in case this Letter should prove to be nothing but the evapouration of an idle brain; then a curious search being made, and nothing found, should not only turn to the general scandal of the King and the State, as being so suspicious of every light and frivolous toy, but likewise lay an ill savoured imputation upon the Earl of Northumberland, one of His Majesties greatest Subjects and Counselors; this Thomas Percy being his kinsman, and most confident familiar. And the rather were they curious upon this point, knowing how far the King detested to be thought suspicious or jealous of any of His good Subjects, though of the meanest degree. And therefore, though they all agreed upon the main ground, which was to provide for the security of the Kings Person, yet did they much differ in the circumstances, by which this action might be best carried with least dinne and occasion of slander. But the King himself still persisting that there were divers shrewd appearances, and that a narrow search of those places could pre-judge no man that was innocent, he at last plainly resolved them, That either must all the parts of those rooms be narrowly searched, and no possibility of danger left unexamined, or else he and they all must resolve not to meddle in it at all, but plainly to go the next day to the Parliament, and leave the success to Fortune, which he believed they would be loth to take upon their consciences: for in such a case as this, an half doing was worse than no doing at all. Whereupon it was at last concluded, That nothing should be left unsearched in those Houses: And yet for the better colour and stay of rumour, in case nothing were found, it was thought meet, that upon a pretence of Whyneards missing some of the Kings stuff or Hangings which he had in keeping, all those rooms should be narrowly ripped for them. And to this purpose was Sir Thomas Knevet, (a Gentleman of His Majesties Privy Chamber) employed, being a Justice of Peace in Westminster, and one, of whose antient fidelity, both the late Queen, and our now Sovereign have had large proof: who according to the trust committed unto him, went about the midnight next after to the Parliament house, accompanied with such a small number, as was fit for that errand. But before his entry into the house, finding Thomas Percy's alledged man standing without the doors, his Cloaths and Boots on, at so dead a time of the night, he resolved to apprehend him, as he did, and thereafter went forward to the searching of the house, where after he had caused to be overturned some of the Billets and Coals, he first found one of the small Barrels of Powder, and after all the rest, to the number of thirty six Barrels, great and small: And thereafter searching the fellow, whom he had taken, found three Matches, and all other instruments fit for blowing up the Powder, ready upon him, which made him instantly confess his own guiltiness, declaring also unto him, That if he had happened to be within the house when he took him, as he was immediately before (at the ending of his work) he would not have failed to have blown him up, house and all.

VAULT BENEATH THE OLD HOUSE OF LORDS (FROM AN OLD DRAWING).

The Vault Beneath the Old House of Lords, The Pictorial World, November 4, 1882, p. 294

Thus after Sir Thomas had caused the wretch to be surely bound, and well guarded, by the company he had brought with him, he himself returned back to the Kings Palace, and gave warning of his succese to the Lord Chamberlain, and Earl of Salisbury, who immediately warning the rest of the Council that lay in the house, as soon as they could get themselves ready, came, with their fellow-Counselors, to the Kings Bed-chamber, being at that time near four of the clock in the morning. And at the first entry of the Kings Chamber door, the Lord Chamberlain; being not any longer able to conceal his joy, for the preventing of so great a danger, told the King in a confused haste, that all was found and discovered, and the Traitor in hands, and fast bound.

Then, Order being first taken for sending for the rest of the Counsel, that lay in the Town, The prisoner himself was brought into the House, where in respect of the strangeness of the accident, no man was stayed from the [...]ight, or speaking with him. And within a while after, the Council did examine him; Who seeming to put on a Roman resolution, did both to the Council, and to every other person that spake with him that day, appear so constant and setled upon his grounds, as we all thought we had found some new Mutius Scaevola, born in England. For notwithstanding the horror of the Fact, the guilt of his conscience, his suddain surprising, the terror which should have been strucken in him, by coming into the presence of so grave a Council, and the restless, and confused questions that every man all that day did vex him with, yet was his countenance so far from being dejected, at he often smiled in scornful manner, not only avowing the Fact, but repenting only, with the said Scaevola, his failing in the execution thereof, whereof (he said) the Devil and not GOD was the Discoverer: answering quickly to every mans objection, scoffing at any idle questions, which were propounded unto him, and jesting with such as he thought had no authority to examine him- All that day could the Counsel get nothing out of him touching his Complices, refusing to answer to any such questions which he thought might discover the Plot, and laying all the blame upon himself; Whereunto he said, he was moved only for Religion and conscience sake, denying the King to be his lawful Sovereign, or the Anointed of GOD in respect he was an Heretick, and giving himself no other name than Iohn Iohnson, servant to Thomas Percy. But the next morning being carried to the Tower he did not there remain above two or three days, being twice or thrice in that space re-examined, and the Rack only offered and shewed unto him, when the masque of his Roman fortitude did visibly begin to wear and slide off his face; And then did he begin to confess part of the truth, and thereafter to open the whole matter, as doth appear by his depositions immediately following.

A TRUE COPY Of the Declaration of Guido Fawkes, taken in the presence of the Counselors, whose Names are under-written.

I Confess, that a practice in general was first broken unto me, against His Majesty for relief of the Catholique Cause, and not invented or propounded by my self. And this was first propounded unto me about Easter last was Twelve moneth, beyond the Seas, in the Low Countreys of the Arch-Dukes obeysance, by Thomas Winter, who came thereupon with me into England, and there we imparted our purpose to three other Gentlemen more, namely, Robert Catesby, Thomas Percy, and Iohn Wright, who all five consulting together of the means how to execute the same, and taking a vow among our selves for secresie; Catesby propounded to have it performed by Gunpowder, and by making a Myne under the upper House of Parliament: which place we made choice of the rather, because Religion having been unjustly suppressed there, it was fittest that Justice and Punishment should be executed there.

Fawkes Signatures on confessions-

[signature]

Fawkes signing as Johnson

[signature: Guido Fawkes]

After inteerogaion Nov. 8

Signature November 10 Subscribed

-Jardine, David, <u>Criminal Trials,</u> Vol.1, 1847.

This being resolved amongst us, Thomas Percy hired an house at Westminster for that purpose, near adjoyning to the Parliament House, and there we begun to make our Myne about the 11 of December 1604.

The five that first entred into the work, were Thomas Percy, Robert Catesby, Thomas Winter, Iohn Wright, and my self: and soon after we took another unto us, Christopher Wright, having sworn him also, and taken the Sacrament for Secrecy.

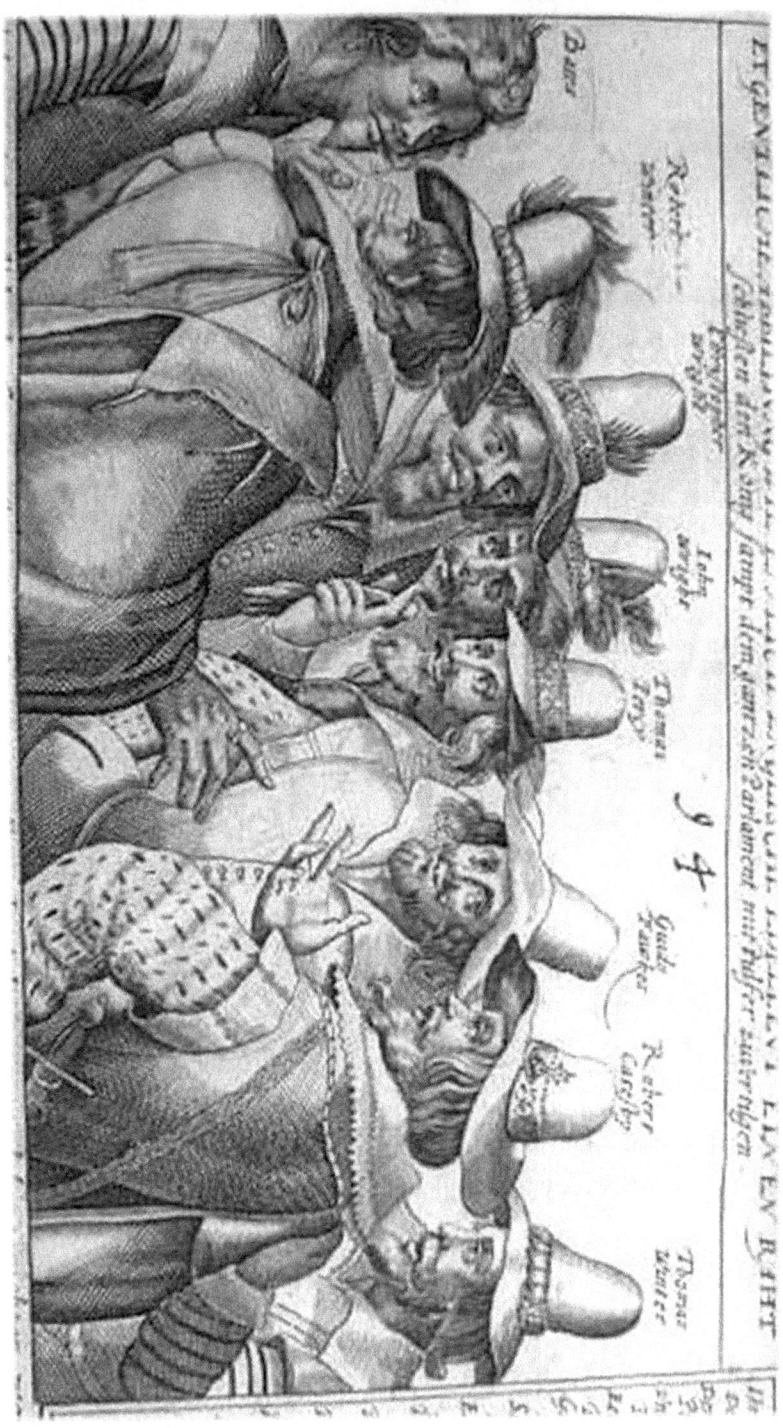

This portrait of the plotters by Franz Hogenberg dates from 1605. Although based in Holland Hogenberg traveled to England, to London during the period. The presentation of this work is not that of a stylized icon but as a broadside portrait. It is most likely that Hogenberg would haave been able, either from personal experience or through research to accurately depict the plotters. Many have discounted this and, related images because they were produced in Holland;, however, at the time Holland was a center for the arts of great importance for the English market.

When we came to the very foundation of the Wall of the House, which was about three yards thick, and found it a matter of great difficulty, we took unto us another Gentleman, Robert Winter, in like manner with Oath and Sacrament as aforesaid.

It was about Christmass when we brought our Myne unto the Wall, and about Candlemas we had wrought the Wall half through: And whilest they were in working, I stood as Sentinel, to descrie any Man that came near, whereof I gave them warning, and so they ceased until I gave notice again to proceed.

All we seven lay in the House, and had Shot and Powder, being resolved to die in that place, before we should yield or be taken.

As they were working upon the Wall, they heard a rushing in a Cellar of removing of Coales, whereupon we feared we had been discovered: and they sent me to go to the Cellar, who finding that the Coales were a selling, and that the Cellar was to be let, viewing the commodity thereof for our purpose, Percy went and hired the same for yearly rent.

We had before this provided and brought into the House Twenty Barrels of Powder, which we removed into the Cellar, and covered the same with Billets and Faggots, which were provided for that purpose.

About Easter, the Parliament being Prorogued till October next, we dispersed our selves, and I retired into the Low-Countreys, by advise and direction of the rest, as well to acquaint Owen with the particulars of the Plot, as also least by my longer stay I might have grown suspicious, and so have come in question.

In the mean time Percy having the key of the Cellar, laid in more Powder and Wood into it. I returned about the beginning of September next, and then receiving the key again of Percy, we brought in more Powder and Billets to cover the same again, and so I went for a time into the Countrey till the 30 of October.

It was further resolved amongst us, that the same day that this Act should have been performed, some other of our Confederates should have surprised the person of the Lady ELIZABETH, the Kings eldest Daughter, who was kept in Warwickshire at the Lord Haringtons House, and presently have proclaimed her Queen, having a Project of a Proclamation ready for that purpose; wherein we made no mention of altering of Religion, nor would have avowed the deed to be ours, until we should have had power enough to make our Party good, and then we would have avowed both.

Princess Elizabeth, Robert Peake the Elder, c. 1606

Concerning Duke CHARLES the Kings second Son, we had sundry Consultations how to seise on his Person.

Prince Charles, Robert Peake the Elder, c. 1611

But because we found no means how to compass it (the Duke being kept near London, where we had not Forces enough) we resolved to serve our turn with the Lady ELIZABETH.

The Names of other Principal Persons, that were made privy afterwards to this horrible Conspiracy.

Everard Digby Knight

Ambrose Rookwood

Francis Tresham

Iohn Grant

Robert Keyes

Commiss

Nottingham

Suffolke

Northampton

Marre

Popham.

Worcester

Devonshire

Salisbury

Dunbar.

Edw. Coke. W. Waad

And in regard that before this discourse could be ready to go to the Press, Thomas Winter being apprehended, and brought to the Tower, made a Confession in substance agreeing with this former of Fawkes, onely larger in some circumstances: I have thought good to insert the same likewise in this place, for the further clearing of the matter, and greater benefit of the Reader.

Thomas Winters Confession, taken the xxiii. of November 1605. in the presence of the Counsellors, whose Names are under-written.

My most Honorable Lords,

Not out of hope to Obtain Pardon: for, speaking of my temporal part, I may say, The Fault is Greater than can be forgiven; nor affecting hereby the Title of a good Subject: for I must redeem my Countrey from as great a danger, as I have hazarded the bringing of Her into, before I can purchase any such opinion; Only at your Honors command I will briefly set down mine own Accusation, and how farr I have proceeded in this business; which I shall the faithfuller do, since I see such courses are not pleasing to Almighty God, and that all, or the most material parts have been already confessed.

I remained with my brother in the Countrey from Alhallow tide until the beginning of Lent, in the year of our Lord 1603. the first year of the Kings Reign: about which time Master Catesby sent thither, intreating me to come to London, where he and other my friends would be glad to see me. I desired him to excuse me: for I found my self not very well disposed; and (which had happened never to me before) returned the Messenger without my company. Shortly I received another Letter, in any wise to come. At the second summons I presently came up, and found him with Master Iohn Wright at Lambeth, where he brake with me, how necessary it was not to forsake our Countrey (for he knew I had then a resolution to go over) but to deliver her from the servitude in which she remain'd, or at least to assist her with our uttermost endevours. I answered, That I had often hazarded my life upon far lighter termes, and now would not refuse any good occasion, wherein I might do service to the Catholick Cause; but for my self I knew no mean probable to succeed. He said that he had bethought him of a way at one instant to deliver us from all our Bonds, and without any forreign help to replant again the Catholick Religion; and withal told me in a word, It was to blow up the Parliament-House with Gunpowder; for, said he, in that place have they done us all the mischiefe, and perchance GOD hath designed that place for their punishment. I wondred at the strangeness of the conceipt, and told him, That true it was, this strake at the Root, and would breed a confusion fit to beget new alterations; But if it should not take effect (as most of this nature miscarried) the Scandal would be so great which Catholique Religion might hereby sustain, as not only our Enemies, but our Friends also would with good reason condemn us. He told me, The nature of the disease required so sharp a remedy, and asked me if I would give my consent. I told him, yes, in this or what else soever, if he resolved upon it, I would venture my life. But I proposed many difficulties, As want of an House, and of one to carry the Myne, noise in the working, and such like. His answer was, Let us give an attempt, and where it faileth pass no farther. But first, quoth he, Because we will leave no peaceable and quiet way untryed, you shall go over, and informe the Constable of the state of the Catholicks here in England, intreating him to sollicite His Majesty at his coming hither, that the Penal Lawes may be recalled, and we admitted into the rank of his other Subjects: withal, you may bring over some confident Gentleman, such as you shall understand best able for this business, and named unto me Mr. Fawkes. Shortly after, I passed the Sea, and found the Constable at Bergen near Dunkirke, where, by help of Mr. Owen I delivered my message, Whose answer was, That he had strict command from his Master, to do all good Offices for the Catholicks, and for his own part, he thought himself bound in Conscience so to do, and that no good occasion should be omitted, but spake to him nothing of this matter.

Returning to Dunkirck with Mr. Owen, we had speech whether he thought the Constable would faithfully help us, or no. He said he believed nothing less, and that they sought onely their own ends, holding small account of Catholicks. I told him, that there were many Gentlemen in England, who would not forsake their Countrey, until they had tried the uttermost, and rather venture their lives, than forsake her in this misery. And, to add one more to our number, as a sit man both for counsel and execution of whatsoever we should resolve, wished for M Fawkes, whom I had heard good commendations of: he told me the Gentleman deserved no less, but was at Brussels, and that if he came not, as happily he might, before my departure, he would send him shortly after into England. I went soon after to Ostend, where Sir William Stanley as then was not, but came two dayes after. I remained with him three or four dayes, in which time I asked him, if the Catholiques in England should do any thing to help themselves, whether he thought the Archduke would second them? He answered, No, for all those parts were so desirous of peace with England, as they would endure no speech of other enterprise: neither were it fit, said he, to set any project afoot now the Peace is upon concluding. I told him there was no such resolution, and so fell to discourse of other matters, until I came to speak of M. Fawkes, whose company I wished over into England. I asked of his sufficiency in the Wars, and told him we should need such as he if occasion required; he gave very good commendations of him. And as we were thus discoursing, and I ready to depart for Newport, and taking my leave of Sir William, Master Fawkes came into our company, newly returned, and saluted us. This is the Gentleman, said Sir William, that you wished for, and so we embraced again. I told him, Some good friends of his wished his company in England, and that if he pleased to come to Dunkirck, we would have further conference, whither I was then going: so taking my leave of them both, I departed. About two dayes after came Mr. Fawkes to Dunkirck, where I told him, That we were upon a resolution to do something in England, if the Peace with Spain helped us not, but had as yet resolved upon nothing; such, or the like talke we passed at Graveling, where I lay for a wind, and when it served came both in one Passage to Greenwich, near which place we took a pair of Oares, and so came up to London, and came to Mr. Catesby, whom we found in his lodging; he welcomed us into England, and asked me what newes from the Constable. I told him, good words, but I feared the deeds would not answer. This was the beginning of Easter Terme, and about the midst of the same Terme, (whether sent for by Master Catesby, or upon some business of his own) up came Mr. Thomas Percy. The first word he spake (after he came into our company) was, Shall we alwayes (Gentlemen) talke, and never do any thing? Mr. Catesby took him aside, and had speech about somewhat to be done, so as first we might all take an oath of secrecy, which we resolved within two or three dayes to do: so as there we met behind St. Clements, Mr. Catesby, Mr. Percy, Mr. Wright, Mr. Guy Fawkes, and my self; and having upon a Primer given each other the Oath of secrecy, in a chamber where no other body was, we went after into the next Room and heard Mass, and received the blessed Sacrament upon the same. Then did Mr. Catesby disclose to Mr. Percy, and I together with Iack Wright, tell to Mr. Fawkes the business for which we took this Oath, which they both approved. And then was Mr. Percy sent to take the House, which Mr. Catesby in mine absence had learned did belong to one Ferris, which with some difficulty in the end he obtained, and became as Ferris before was, Tenant to Whynniard. Mr. Fawkes underwent the name of Mr. Percies Man, calling himself Iohnson, because his face was the most unknown, and received the keyes of the house, until we heard that the Parliament was Adjourned to the seventh of February. At which time we all departed several wayes into the Countrey, to meet again at the beginning of Michaelmas-Terme. Before this time also it was thought convenient to have a house that might answer to Mr. Percies, where we might make provision of Powder and Wood for the Myne, which being there made ready, should in a night be conveyed by boat to the House by the Parliament, because we were loath to soyle that with often going in and out. There was none that we could devise so fit as Lambeth, where Mr. Catesby often lay, and to be keeper thereof (by Mr. Catesbies choice) we received into the number, Keyes, as a trusty honest Man: this was about a Month before Michaelmas.

HOUSE OF THE CONSPIRATORS AT LAMBETH (FROM AN OLD PRINT.)

-The Conspirator's House in Lambeth, The Pictorial World, November 4, 1882, p.294.

Some fortnight after, towards the beginning of the Terme, Mr. Fawkes and I came to Mr. Catesby at Morecrofts, where we agreed, That now was time to begin and set things in order for the Myne. So as Mr. Fawkes went to London, and the next day sent for me to come over to him: when I came, the cause was, for that the Scottish Lords were appointed to sit in conference of the Union in Mr. Percies house. This hindered our beginning until a fortnight before Christmass, by which time both Mr. Percy and Mr. Wright were come to London, and we against their coming had provided a good part of the Powder: so as we all five entred with tooles fit to begin our work, having provided our selves of Baked-meates, the less to need sending abroad. We entred late in the night, and were never seen, save onely Mr. Percy's Man, until Christmas-Eve. In which time we wrought under a little Entry to the Wall of the Parliament-House, and underpropped it as we went with Wood.

Whilest we were together, we began to fashion our business, and discoursed what we should do after this deed was done. The first question was, How we might surprise the next heir, the Prince haply would be at the Parliament with the King his Father, how should we then be able to seize on the Duke? This burthen Mr. Percy undertook, that by his acquaintance, he, with another Gentleman would enter the Chamber without suspition, and having some dozen others at several doors to expect his comming, and two or three on horseback at the Court-Gate to receive him, he would undertake (the Blow being given, until which he would attend in the Dukes Chamber) to carry him safe away: for he supposed most of the Court would be absent, and such as were there not suspecting, or unprovided for any such matter. For the Lady ELIZABETH, it were easie to surprise her in the Countrey, by drawing Friends together at an hunting near the Lord Haringtons, and Ashby, Mr. Catesbyes house, being not far off was a fit place for preparation. The next was for Money and Horses, which if we could provide in any reasonable measure (having the Heir apparent) and the first knowledge by four or five dayes, was odds sufficient.

Then what Lords we should save from the Parliament, which was first agreed in general as many as we could that were Catholicks, or so disposed: but after we descended to speak of particulars.

Next what Forreign Princes we should acquaint with this before, or joyn with after. For this point we agreed, that first we could not enjoyn Princes to that secrecie, nor oblige them by Oath, so to be secure of their promise: besides, we knew not, whether they will approve the Project, or dislike it. And if they do allow thereof, to prepare before might beget suspition; and not to provide until the business were acted, the same Letter that carried newes of the thing done, might as well intreate their help and furtherance. Spain is too slow in his preparations, to hope any good from in the first extremities, and France too near and too dangerous, who with the shipping of Holland we feared of all the world might make away with us.

But while we were in the middle of these discourses, we heard that the Parliament should be anew Adjourned until after Michaelmas, upon which tidings we broke off both discourse and working until after Christmas. About Candlemas we brought [...]ver in a boat the Powder, which we had provided at Lambeth, and laid it in Mr. Percies house, because we were willing to have all our danger in one place.

We wrought also another fortnight in the Myne against the stone Wall, which was very hard to beate thorough; at which time we called in Kit Wright, and near to Easter, as we wrought the third time, opportunity was given to hire the Cellar, in which we resolved to lay the Powder, and leave the Myne.

Now, by reason that the charge of maintaining us all so long together, besides the number of several Houses, which for several uses had been hired, and buying of Powder, &c. had layn heavy on Mr. Catesby alone to support; it was necessary for him to call in some others to ease his charge, and to that end desired leave, that he, with Mr. Percy, and a third, whom they should call, might acquaint whom they thought fit and willing to the business: for many, said he, may be content that I should know, who would not therefore that all the company should be acquainted with their names: to this we all agreed.

After this Master Fawkes laid into the Cellar (which he had newly taken) a thousand of Billets, and Five hundred of Faggots, and with that covered the Powder, because we might have the House free, to suffer any one to enter that would. Mr. Catesby wished us to consider, whether it were not now necessary to send Mr. Fawkes over, both to absent himself for a time, as also to acquaint Sir Wil. Stanly and Mr. Owen with this matter. We agreed, that he should (provided that he gave it them with the same oath that we had taken it fore) videlicet, to keep it secret from all the world. The reason why we desired Sir William Stanley should be acquainted herewith, was, to have him with us so soon as he could:

And for Mr Owen, he might hold good correspondency after with forreign Princes.

So Mr. Fawkes departed about Easter for Flanders, and returned the latter end of August. He told me, that when he arrived at Brussels, Sir William Stanley was not returned from Spain, so as he uttered the matter only to Owen, who seemed well pleased with the business, but told him, that surely Sir William would not be acquainted with any Plot, as having business now afoot in the Court of England: but he himself would be always ready to tell it him, and send him away so soon as it were done.

About this time did Mr. Percy, and Mr. Catesby meet at the Bath, where they agreed that the company being yet but few, Mr. Catesby should have the others authority to call in whom he thought best; By which authority he called in after, Sir Everard Digby, though at what time I know not, and last of all Mr. Francis Tresham. The first promised, as I heard Master Catesby say, Fifteen hundred pounds; The second Two thousand pounds; Mr. Percy himself promised all that he could g[...]t [...] the Earl of Northumberland's Rents, which was about four thousand pounds, and to provide many galloping Horses, to the number of ten.

Mean while Mr. Fawkes and my self alone bought some new Powder, as suspecting the first to be damp, and conveyed it into the Cellar, and set it in order, as we resolved it should stand. Then was the Parliament anew prorogued until the Fifth of November, so as we all went down, until some ten days before, when Mr. Catesby came up with Mr. Fawkes, to an house by Enfield-Chace, called White-Webbs, whither I came to them, and Mr. Catesby willed me to enquire, whither the young Prince came to the Parliament: I told him, that I heard that his Grace thought not to be there. Then must we have our Horses, said Mr. Catesby, beyond the water, and provision of more company to surprize the Prince, and leave the Duke alone.

Two days after, being Sunday at night, in came one to my chamber, and told me that a Letter had been given to my Lord Mountegle to this effect, That he wished his Lordships absence from the Parliament, because a Blow would there be given; which Letter he presently carried to my Lord of Salisbury.

On the morrow I went to White-webbes, and told it to Mr. Catesby, assuring him withal, that the matter was disclosed: and wishing him in any case to forsake his Countrey. He told me, he would see further as yet, and resolved to send Mr. Fawkes to try the uttermost, protesting, if the part belonged to himself, he would try the same adventure.

On Wednesday Mr. Fawkes went, and returned at night, of which we were very glad.

Thursday I came to London, and Friday Mr. Catesby, Mr. Tresham and I met at Barnet, where we questioned how this Letter should be sent to my Lord

Mountegle, but could not conceive, for Mr. Tresham forsware it, whom we only suspected.

On Saturday night I met Mr. Tresham again in Lincolns-Inn Walks. Wherein he told such speeches, that my Lord of Salisbury should use to the King, that I gave it lost the second time, and repeated the same to Mr. Catesby, who hereupon was resolved to be gone, but staid to have Mr. Percy come up, whose consent herein we wanted. On Sunday Mr. Percy being dealt with to that end, would needs abide the uttermost trial.

This suspition of all hands, put us into such confusion, as Mr. Catesby resolved to go down into the Countrey, the Munday that Mr. Percy went to Sion, and Mr. Percy resolved to follow the same night, or early the next morning. About five of the clock being Tuesday, came the younger Wright to my Chamber, and told me, that a Nobleman, called the Lord Mountegle, saying, Arise, and come along to Essex-house, for I am going to call up my Lord of Northumberland, saying withal, The matter is discovered. Go back Mr. Wright (quoth I) and learn what you can about Essex Gate. Shortly he returned and said, surely all is lost: for Lepton is got on horseback at Essex door, and as he parted, he asked if their Lordships would have any more with him: and being answered No, is rode fast up Fleetstreet as he can ride. Goe you then (quoth I) to Mr. Percy, for sure it is for him they seek, and bid him be gone, I will stay and see the uttermost. Then I went to the Court-Gates, and found them straightly guarded, so as no body could enter. From thence I went down towards the Parliament-house, and in the middle of King-street found the Guard standing, that would not let me pass, And as I returned, I heard one say, There is a Treason discovered, in which the King and the Lords should have been blown up. So then I was fully satisfied that all was known, and went to the Stable where my Gelding stood, and rode into the Countrey. Mr. Catesby had appointed our meeting at Dunchurch, but I could not overtake them, untill I came to my brothers, which was Wednesday night. On Thursday we took the Armor at my Lord Windsors, and went that night to one Stephen Littleton's house, where the next day (being Friday) as I was early abroad to discover, my man came to me, and said, That an heavy mischance had severed all the company, for that Mr. Catesby, Mr. Rookwood, and Mr. Grant, were burned with Gunpowder, upon which sight, the rest dispersed. Mr. Littleton wished me to flie, and so would he. I told him, I would first see the Body of my friend, and bury him, whatsoever befel me. When I came, I found Mr. Catesby reasonable well, Mr. Percy, both the Wrights, Mr. Rookwood, and Mr. Grant. I asked them what they resolved to do: they answered, we mean here to die. I said again, I would take such part as they did. About eleven of the clock came the company to beset the house, and as I walked into the Court, I was shot into the shoulder, which lost me the use of mine arm: with the next shot was the elder Wright strucken dead, after him the younger Mr. Wright, and fourthly Ambrose Rookwood. Then said Mr. Catesby to me (standing before the door they were to enter) Stand by me Tom, and we will die together. Sir (quoth I) I have lost the use of my right arm, and I fear that will cause me to be taken. So as we stood close together, Mr. Catesby, Mr. Percy, and my self, they two were shot (as far as I could guess with one Bullet) and then the company entred upon me, hurt me in the belly with a Pike, and gave me other wounds, until one came behind, and caught hold of both mine arms.

And so I remain yours, &c.

Commiss.

Nottingham,

Suffolk,

Worcester,

Devonshire,

Northapmton

Salisbury,

Marr,

Dunbar,

Popham.

Edw. Coke. W. Waad.

The Names of those that were first in the Treason, and laboured in the Myne.

Robert Catesby,

Esquires.

Robert Winter.

Thomas Percy,

Gentlem.

Thomas Winter,

Iohn Wright,

Christopher Wright.

Guido Fawkes.

And Bates Catesbies man.

Those that were made acquainted with it, though not personally labouring in the Myne, nor in the Cellar.

Everard Digby, Kt

Ambrose Rookwood.

Esquires.

Francis Tresham.

John Graunt, Gent.

Robert Keys.

But here let us leave Fawks in a Lodging fit for such a Guest, and taking time to advise upon his conscience; and turn our selves to that part of History, which concerns the fortune of the rest of his partakers in that abominable Treason. The news was no sooner spread abroad that morning, which was upon a Tuesday, the Fifth of November, and the First day designed for that Session of Parliament; The news (I say) of this so strange and unlooked for accident, was no sooner divulged, but some of those Conspirators, namely, Winter, and the two Brothers of Wrights thought it high time for them to hasten out of the Town (for Catesby was gone the night before, and Percy at four of the clock in the morning the same day of the Discovery) and all of them held their course, with more haste than good speed, to Warwick-shire, toward Coventry, where the next day morning, being Wednesday, and about the same hour that Fawkes was taken in Westminster, one Graunt, a Gentleman having associated unto him some others of his opinion, all violent Papists, and strong Recusants, came to a Stable of one Benock, a Rider of Great Horses, and having violently broken up the same, carried along with them all the great Horses that were therein, to the number of seven or eight, belonging to divers Noblemen and Gentlemen of that Country, who had put them into the Riders hands to be made fit for theire service. And so both that company of them which fled out of London, as also Graunt and his complices met all together at Dunchurch at Sir Everard Digby his lodging the Wednesday at night after the discovery of this treacherous Attempt: The which Digby had likewise for his part appointed a match of hunting to have been hunted the next day, which was Wednesday, though his mind was Nimrod-like, upon a farr other manner of hunting, more bent upon the bloud of reasonable men, than brute beasts.

This company, and hellish society thus convened, finding their purpose discovered, and their treachery prevented, did resolve to run a desperate course, and since they could not prevail by so private a Blow, to practise by a publick Rebellion, either to attain to their Intents, or at least to save themselves in the throng of others. And therefore gathering all the company they could unto them and pretending the quarrel of Religion, having intercepted such provision of Armour, Horses, and Powder, as the time could permit, thought by running up and down the Countrey both to augment peece and peece their number (dreaming to themselves that they had the vertue of a Snow-ball, which being little at the first, and tumbling down from a great hill groweth to a great quantity, by encreasing it self with the Snow that it meeteth by the way) and also that they beginning first this brave shew in one part of the Countrey, should by their Sympathy and example stir up and incourage the rest of their Religion in other parts of England to rise, as they had done there. But when they had gathered their Force to the greatest, they came not to the number of Fourscore, and yet were they troubled all the hours of the day to keep and contain their own servants from stealing from them; who (notwithstanding of all their care) dayly left them, being far inferior to Gedeons Hoste in number, but far more in faith, or justness of Quarrel.

And so after that this Catholique Troop had wandered a while through Warwick-shire to Worcester-shire, and from thence to the edge and borders of Stafford-shire, this gallantly armed Band had not the honor at the last, to be beaten with a Kings Lieutenant, or extraordinary Commissioner sent down for the purpose, but only by the ordinary Sheriff of Worcester-shire, were they all beaten, killed, taken and dispersed. Wherein ye have to note this following circumstance so admirable, and so lively displaying the greatness of Gods justice, as it could not be concealed without betraying in a manner the glory due to the Almighty for the same.

Although divers of the Kings Proclamations were posted down after these Traitors, with all the speed possible, declaring the odiousness of that bloudy attempt, the necessity to have Percy preserved alive, if it had been possible, and the assembly together of that rightly damned crew, now no more darkened Conspirators, but open and avowed Rebels: yet the far distance of the way (which was above an hundred miles) together with the extreme deepness thereof, joyned also with the shortness of the day, was the cause that the hearty and loving affections of the Kings good Subjects in those parts prevented the speed of His Proclamations. For upon the third day after the flying down of these Rebels, which was upon the Friday next after the discovery of their Plot, they were most of them all surprized by the Sheriff of Worcester-shire at Holbeach, about the noon of the day, and that in manner following.

Graunt, of whom I have made mention before for taking the great Horses, who had not all the preceding time stirred from his own house till the next morning after the attempt should have been put in execution, he then laying his account without his Host (as the proverb is) that their Plot had, without failing, received the day before, their hoped for success; took, or rather stole out those horses (as I said before) for enabling him, and so many of that soulless society that had still remained in the Countrey near about him, to make a suddain surprize upon the Kings elder Daughter, the Lady ELIZABETH, having her residence near by that place, whom they thought to have used for the colour of their treacherous designe (His Majesty her Father, her Mother, and male Children being all destroyed above) And to this purpose also [...]ad that Nimrod Digby, provided his hunt[...]ng match against that same time, that numbers of people being flocked together upon the pretence thereof, they might the easilier have brought to pass the suddain surprize of her Person.

Now the violent taking away of those horses long before day, did seem to be so great a riot in the eyes of the Common people, that knew of no greater Mystery:

And the bold attempting thereof, did ingender such a suspition of some following Rebellion in the hearts of the wiser sort, as both great and small began to stirr and arm themselves, upon this unlooked for accident. Among whom, Sir Fulke Grevil the elder, Knight, as became one both so antient in years, and good reputation, and by his Office being Deputy-Lieutenant of Warwick-shire tho unable in his Body, yet by the zeal and true fervency of his mind, did first apprehend this foresaid Riot, to be nothing but the sparkles and sure indices of a following Rebellion; whereupon both stoutly and honestly he took order to get into his own hands, the Munition and Armor of all such Gentlemen about him, as were either absent from their own houses, or in doubtful guard; And also sent such direction to the Towns about him, as thereupon did follow the striking of Winter by a poor Smith, who had likewise been taken by those vulgar people, but that he was rescued by the rest of his company, who perceiving that the Countrey before them, had notice of them, hastened away with the loss in their own sight, Sixteen of their followers being taken by the Townsmen, and sent presently to the Sheriff at Warwick, and from thence to London.

But before Twelve or Sixteen hours past, Catesby, Percy the Winters, Wrights, Rookwood, and the rest, bringing then the assurance, that their main Plot was failed and bewrayed, whereupon they had builded the golden Mountains of their glorious hopes: They then took their last desperate resolution to flock together in a Troop and wander, as they did, for the reasons aforetold. But as upon the one part, the zealous duty to their God and their Sovereigne was so deeply imprinted in the hearts of all the meanest and poorest sort of the people (although then knowing of no further mystery than such publick misbehaviours, as their own eyes taught them) as notwithstanding of their fair shews and pretence of their Catholick cause, no creature, Man or Woman through all the Countrey, would once so much as give them willingly a cup of drink, or any sort of comfort or support, but with execrations detested them: So on the other part, the Sheriffs of the Shires, where through they wandred, convening their people with all speed possible, hunted as hotly after them, as the evilness of the way, and the unprovidedness of their people upon that sudden could permit them. And so at last after Sir Richard Verney, Sheriff of Warwick-shire, had carefully and straightly been in chase of them to the confines of his County, part of the meaner sort being also apprehended by him: Sir Richard W[...]lsh Sheriff of Worcester-shire did likewis[...] dutifully and hotly pursue them thorow his Shire; and having gotten sure trial of their taking harbor at the house above named, he did send Trumpeters and Messengers to them, commanding them in the Kings name to render unto him, His Majesties Minister; and knowing no more at that time of their guilt, than was publickly visible, did promise, upon their dutiful and obedient rendring unto him to intercede at the Kings hands, for the sparing of their lives: Who received only from them this scornful answer (they being better witnesses to themselves of their inward evil consciences) That he had need of better assistance, than of those few numbers that were with him, before he could be able to command or controul them.

But here fell the wondrous work of Gods Justice, That while this message passed between the Sheriff and them, The Sheriff's and his people's zeal being justly kindled and augmented by their arrogant answer, and so they preparing themselves to give a furious assault; and the other party making themselves ready within the house to perform their promise by a defence as resolute; It pleased GOD, that in the mending of the fire in their chamber, one small sparkle should flie out, and light among less than two pound weight of Powder, which was drying a little from the chimney; which being thereby blown up, so maimed the faces of some of the principal Rebels, and the hands and sides of others of them (blowing up with it also a great bag full of Powder, which notwithstanding never took fire) as they were not only disabled, and discouraged hereby from any further resistance, in respect Catesby himself, Rookwood, Grant, and divers others of greatest account, among them were thereby made unable for defence: but also wonderfully strucken with amazement in their guilty consciences, calling to memory, how GOD had justly punished them with that same Instrument, which they should have used for the effectuating of so great a sin, according to the old Latine saying, In quo peccamus, in eodem plectimur, as they presently (see the wonderful power of Gods [...]justice upon guilty consciences) did all fall down upon their knees, praying GOD to pardon them for their bloudy enterprize; And thereafter giving over any further debate, opened the Gate, suffered the Sheriffs people to rush in furiously among them, and desperately sought their own present destruction; The three specials of them joyning backs together, Catesby, Percy, and Winter, whereof two with one shot, Catesby, and Percy were slain, and the third, Winter, taken and saved alive.

And thus these resolute and high aspiring Catholicks, who dreamed of no less than the destruction of Kings and Kingdomes, and promised to themselves no lower estate than the Government of great and antient Monarchies; were miserably defeated, and quite overthrown in an instant, falling in the pit which they had prepared for others; and so fulfilling that sentence which his Majesty did in a manner prophesie of them, In his Oration to the Parliament: some presently slain, others deadly wounded, stripped of their Clothes, left lying miserably naked, and so dying rather of cold, then of the danger of their wounds; and the rest that either were whole, or but lightly hurt, taken and led prisoners by the Sheriff, the ordinary Minister of Justice, to the Gaole, the ordinary place even of the basest Malefactors, where they remained till their sending up to London, being met with a huge confluence of people of all sorts, desirous to see them, as the rarest sort of Monsters; fools to laugh at them, women and children to wonder, all the common people to gaze, the wiser sort to satisfie their curiosity, in seeing the outward cases of so unheard of a villany: and generally all sorts of people, to satiate and fill their eyes with the sight of them, whom in their hearts they so far admired and detested: Serving so for a fearful and publick spectacle of Gods fierce wrath and just indignation.

What hereafter will be done with them, is to be left to the Justice of His Majesty and the State. Which as no good Subject needs to doubt will be performed in the own due time by a publick and an exemplary punishment: So have we all that are faithful and humble subjects, great cause to pray earnestly to the Almighty, that it will please him who hath the hearts of all Princes in his hands, to put it in his Majesties heart to make such a conclusion of this Tragedy to the Traytors, but Tragicomedy to the King and all his true Subjects; as thereby the glory of God and his true Religion may be advanced, the future security of the King and his estate procured and provided for, all hollow and unhonest hearts discovered and prevented, and this horrible attempt (lacking due Epithites) to be so justly avenged, That where they thought by one Catholick indeed, and Universal blow, to accomplish the wish of that Roman Tyrant, who wished all the bodies in Rome to have but one neck, and so by the violent force of Powder to break up as with a Pettard our triple locked peaceful Gates of Ianus, which (God be thanked) they could not compass by any other meanes; they may justly be so recompensed for their truely viperous intended Parricide, as the shame and infamy that otherwise would light upon this whole Nation, for having unfortunately hatched such Cockatrice egges, may be repaired by the execution of famous and honorable Justice upon the Offendors, and so the Kingdom purged of them, may hereafter perpetually flourish in peace and prosperity, by the happy conjunction of the hearts of all honest and true Subjects, with their just and Religious Soveraign.

And thus, whereas they thought to have effaced our memories, the memory of them shall remain (but to their Perpetual Infamy) and we (as I said in the beginning) shall, with all thankfulness, eternally preserve the memory of so great a benefit. To which let every good Subject say,

AMEN.

The Brief of the Matters whereupon Robert Winter, Esq. Thomas Winter, Gent. Guy Fawkes, Gent. Iohn Graunt, Esq. Ambrose Rookwood, Esq. Robert Keyes, Gent. Thomas Bates, were Indicted, and whereupon they were Arraigned.

That whereas our Sovereign Lord the King had, by the advise and assent of his Council, for divers weighty and urgent occasions, concerning his Majesty, the State, and defence of the Church and Kingdom of England, appointed a Parliament to be holden at his City of Westminister: That Henry Garnet, Superior of the Iesuits

Henry Garnet by Adriaen Lommelin mid 17th century.

within the Realm of England, (called also by the several names of Wally, Darcy, Roberts, Farmer, and Henry Philips) Oswald Tesmond Iesuit, otherwise called Oswald Greenwel; John Gerrard Iesuit, (called also by the several names of Lee and Brook) Robert Winter, Thomas Winter, Gentlemen, Guy Fawkes, Gent. otherwise called Guy Johnson; Robert Keyes Gent. and Thomas Bates Yeoman, late Servant to Robert Catesby Esq. together with the said Robert Catesby and Thomas Piercy, Esquires; John Wright and Christopher Wright, Gent. in open Rebellion and Insurrection against his Majesty, lately slain, and Francis Tresham Esq. lately dead, as false Traitors against our said Sovereign Lord the King, did Traiterously meet and assemble themselves together; and being so met, the said Henry Garnet, Oswald Tesmond, John Gerrard, and other Iesuits, did maliciously, falsly, and traiterously move and perswade as well the said Thomas Winter, Guy Fawkes, Robert Keyes, and Thomas Bates; as the said Robert Catesby, Thomas Percy, John Wright, Christopher Wright, and Francis Tresham; That our said Sovereign Lord the King, the Nobility, Clergy, and the whole Commonalty of the Realm of England (Papists excepted) were Hereticks, and that all Hereticks were accursed and Excommunicate; and that no Heretick could be a King, but that it was lawful and meritorious to kill our said Sovereign Lord the King, and all other Hereticks within this Realm of England, for the advancing and enlargement of the pretended and usurped Authority and Iurisdiction of the Bishop of Rome, and for the restoring of the Superstitious Romish Religion within this Realm of England. To which Traiterous perswasions, the said Thomas Winter, Guy Fawkes, Robert Keyes, Thomas Bates, Robert Catesby, Thomas Percy, John Wright, Christopher Wright, and Francis Tresham, traiterously did yield their assents: And that thereupon the said Henry Garnet, Oswald Tesmond, John Gerrard, and divers other Iesuits; Thomas

Winter, Guy Fawkes, Robert Keys, and Thomas Bates; as also the said Robert Catesby, Thomas Percy, John Wright, Christopher Wright, and Francis Tresham, traiterously among themselves did conclude and agree, with Gun-powder, as it were with one blast, suddenly, traiterously, and barbarously to blow up and tear in pieces our said Sovereign Lord the King, the Excellent, Virtuous, and Gracious Queen Anne his dearest Wife,

Anne of Denmark, De Critz, c. 1605

the most Noble Prince Henry their Eldest Son, the future Hope and Ioy of England,

and the Lords Spiritual and Temporal; the Reverend Iudges of the Realm, the Knights, Citizens, and Burgesses of Parliament, and divers other faithful Subjects and Servants of the King in the said Parliament, for the causes aforesaid, to be assembled in the House of Parliament; and all of them, without any respect of Majesty, Dignity, Degree, Sex, Age, or Place, most barbarously, and more than beastly, traiterously and suddenly, to destroy and swallow up. And further did most traiterously conspire and conclude among themselves, That not onely the whole Royal Issue Male of our said Sovereign Lord the King should be destroyed and rooted out, but that the Persons aforesaid, together with divers other false Traitors, traiterously with them to be assembled, should surprise [...] Persons of the Noble Ladies, Elizabeth and Mary, Daughters of our said Sovereign Lord the King, and falsly and traiterously should Proclaim said Lady Elizabeth to be the Queen of this Realm of England; and thereupon should publish a certain traiterous Proclamation in the Name of the said Lady Elizabeth, wherein it was especially agreed, by and between the said Conspirators, That no mention should be made at the first of the alteration of Religion established within this Realm of England; neither would the said false Traitors therein acknowledge themselves to be Authors, or Actors, or Devisors of the foresaid most wicked and horrible Treasons, until they had got sufficient power and strength for the assured execution and accomplishment of their said Conspiracy and Treason, and that then they would avow and justifie the said most wicked and horrible Treasons, as Actions that were in the number of those, *Quae non laudantur nisi peracta*, which be not to be commended before they be done. But by the said feigned and traiterous Proclamation they would publish, That all and singular abuses and grievances within this Realm of England, should, for satisfying of the People, be reformed. And that as well for the better concealing, as for the more effectual accomplishing of the said horrible Treasons, as well the said Thomas Winter, Guy Fawkes, Robert Keyes, and Thomas Bates; as the said Robert Catesby, Thomas Piercy, John Wright, Christopher Wright, and Francis Tresham, by the traiterous advice and procurement of the said Henry Garnet, Oswald Tesmond, John Gerrard, and other Iesuits, traiterously did further conclude and agree, That as well the said Thomas Winter, Guy Fawkes, Robert Keyes, and Thomas Bates, as the said Robert Catesby, Thomas Piercy, John Wright, Christopher Wright, and Francis Tresham, thereupon severally and traiterously should receive several corporal Oathes upon the holy Evangelists, and the Sacrament of the Eucharist, That they the Treasons aforesaid would traiterously conceal and keep secret, and would not reveal them directly nor indirectly, by words nor circumstances; nor ever would desist from the execution and final accomplishment of the said Treasons, without the consent of some three of the foresaid false Traitors first in that behalf Traiterously had. And that thereupon, as well the said Thomas Winter, Guy Fawkes, Robert Keyes, and Thomas Bates, as the said Robert Catesby, Thomas Piercy, John Wright, Christopher Wright, and Francis Tresham, did traiterously take the said several corporal Oathes severally, and did receive the Sacrament of the Eucharist aforesaid by the hands of the said Henry Garnet, John Gerrard, Oswald Tesmond, and other Iesuits. And further, that the said Thomas Winter, Guy Fawkes, Robert Keyes, and Thomas Bates; together with the said Robert Catesby, Thomas Piercy, John Wright, Christopher Wright, and Francis Tresham, by the like traiterous advise and counsel of the said Henry Garnet, John Gerrard, Oswald Tesmond, and other Iesuits, for the more effectual compassing and final execution of the said Treasons, did traiterously amongst them selves conclude and agree, to dig a certain Mine under the said House of Parliament, and there secretly under the said House to bestow and place a great quantity of Gun-powder; and that according to the said traiterous conclusion, the said Thomas Winter, Guy Fawkes, Robert Keyes, and Thomas Bates; together with the said Robert Catesby, Thomas Piercy, John Wright, and Christopher Wright, afterwards secretly, not without great labour and difficulty, did dig and make the said Mine unto the midst of the foundation of the wall of the said house of Parliament, the said foundation being of the thickness of three yards, with a traiterous intent to bestow and place a great quantity of Gunpowder in the Mine aforesaid, so as aforesaid traiterously to be made for the traiterous accomplishing of their traiterous purposes aforesaid, and that the said Thomas Winter, Guy Fawkes, Robert Keyes, and Thomas Bates, together with the said Robert Catesby, Thomas Percy, John Wright, and Christopher Wright, finding and perceiving the said work to be of great difficulty by reason of the hardness and thickness of the said wall, and understanding a certain Cellar under the said house of Paliament, and adjoyning to a certain house of the said Thomas Percy then to be letten to farm for a yearly Rent, the said Thomas Percy, by the traiterous procurement as well of the said Henry Garnet, Oswald Tesmond, John John Gerrard and other Iesuits, Thomas Winter, Guy Fawkes, Robert Keyes, and Thomas Bates, as of the said Robert Catesby, John Wright and Christopher Wright, traiterously did hire the Cellar aforesaid for a certain yeerly Rent and term; & then those Traitors did remove twenty barrels full of gunpowder out of the said house of the said Thomas Percy, and secretly and traiterously did bestow and place them in the Cellar aforesaid under the said House of Parliament, for the traiterous effecting of the Treason, and traiterous purposes aforesaid. And that afterwards the said Henry Garnet, Oswald Tesmond, John Gerrard, and other Iesuits, Thomas Winter, Guy Fawkes, Robert Keyes and Thomas Bates, together with the said Robert Catesby, Thomas Percy, John Wright and Christopher Wright, traiterously did meet with Robert Winter, John Grant, and Ambrose Rookwood and Francis Tresham Esquires, and traiterously did impart to the said Robert Winter, John Grant, and Ambrose Rookwood and Francis Tresham, the Treasons, traiterous intentions and purposes aforesaid, and did require the said Robert Winter, John Grant, Ambrose Rookwood and Francis Tresham, to joyn themselves as well with the said Henry Garnet, Oswald Tesmond, John Gerrard, Thomas Winter, Guy Fawkes, Robert Keys and Thomas Bates, as with the said Robert Catesby, Thomas Percy, John Wright and Christopher Wright, and in the Treasons, traiterous intentions, and purposes aforesaid, and traiterously to provide horse, armour, and other necessaries, for the better accomplishment and effecting of the said Treasons; To which traiterous motion and request, the said Robert Winter, John Grant, Ambrose Rookwood and Francis Tresham, did traiterously yield their Assents, and as well with the said Henry Garnet, Oswald Tesmond, John Gerrard, Robert Winter, Thomas Winter, Guy Fawkes, Robert Keys, and Thomas Bates, as with the said Rob. Catesby, Thomas Percy, John Wright, Christopher Wright, and Francis Tresham, in the said Treasons, traiterous intentions and purposes aforesaid, traiterously did adhere and unite themselves; And thereupon several corporal Oathes in form abovesaid Traiterously did take, and the Sacrament of the Eucharist by the hand of the said Iesuits did receive, to such intent and purpose as is aforesaid; And horses, armour, and other necessaries, for the better effecting of the said Treasons, according to their traiterous assents aforesaid traiterously did provide; And that afterwards all the said false Traitors did traiterously provide and bring into the Cellar aforesaid, ten other barrels full of Gunpowder newly bought, fearing least the former Gunpowder so as aforesaid bestowed and placed there, was become Dankish, and the said several quantities of Gunpowder aforesaid, with Billets and Fagots, least they should be spied, secretly and traiterosly did cover; And that afterwards the said Traitors traiterously provided and brought into the Cellar aforesaid, four Hogsheads full of Gunpowder, and layed divers great Iron Bars, [...]nd stones upon the said four Hogsheads, and the other quanties of Gunpowder; And the said quanties of Gunpowder, Bars and stones, with Billets and Fagots, lest they should be espied, secretly and traiterously did likewise cover; And that the said Guy Fawkes afterwards for a full and final accomplishment of [...]he said Treasons, traiterous intentions and purposes aforesaid, by the traiterous procurement as well of the said Henry Garnet, Oswald Tesmond, John Gerrard, and other Iesuits, Robert Winter, Thomas Winter, Robert Keyes, Thomas Bates, John Grant, and Ambrose Rookwood, as of the said Robert Catesby, Thomas Percy, John Wright, Christopher Wright, and Francis Tresham, traiterously had prepared, and had upon his person Touchwood and Match, therewith traiterously to give fire to the several Barrels, Hogsheads and quantities of Gunpowder aforesaid, at the time appointed for the execution of the said horrible Treasons; And further, that after the said horrible Treasons were by the great favour and mercy of God in a wonderful manner discovered, not many hours before it should have been executed, as well the said Henry Garnet, Oswald Tesmond, John Gerard, Robert Winter, Thomas Winter, Robert Keyes, Thomas Bates, John Grant, and Ambrose Rookwood, as the said Robert Catesby, Thomas Percy, John Wright, and Christopher Wright, Traiterously did flie and withdraw themselves, to the intent Traiterously to stir up, and procure such Popish persons as they could, to joyn with them in actual, publick and open Rebellion, against our said Sovereign Lord the King, and to that end did publish divers fained and false rumors, that the Papists throats should have been cut: And that thereupon divers Papists were in Arms, and in open publick and Actual Rebellion against our said Sovereign Lord the King, in divers parts of this Realm of England.

To this Indictment, they all pleaded, Not Guilty; and put themselves upon God and the Countrey.

Then did Sir Edward Philips Knight, his Majesties Sergeant at Law, open the Indictment to this effect as followeth.

The matter that is now to be offered to you, my Lords the Commissioners, and to the Trial of you the Knights and Gentlemen of the Jury, is matter of Treason; but of such horrour, and monstrous nature, that before now,

The Tongue of Man never delivered,

The Ear of Man never heard,

The Heart of Man never conceited,

Nor the Malice of Hellish or Earthly Devil ever practised.

For, if it be abominable to murder the least;

If to touch Gods Anointed, be to oppose themselves against God;

If (by blood) to subvert Princes, States, and Kingdoms, be hateful to God and Man, as all true Christians must acknowledge;

Then, how much more than too too monstrous shall all Christian hearts judge the horror of this Treason, to murder and subvert,

Such a King,

Such a Queen,

Such a Prince,

Such a Progeny,

Such a State,

Such a Government,

So compleat and absolute;

That God approves:

The World admires:

All true English Hearts honour and reverence:

The Pope and his Disciples onely envies and maligns.

The Proceeding wherein is properly to be divided into three general Heads.

1. First, Matter of Declaration.

2. Secondly, Matter of Aggravation.

3. Thirdly, Matter of Probation.

My self am limited to deal onely with the matter of Declaration, and that is contained within the compass of the Indictment onely.

For the other two, I am to leave to him to whose place it belongeth.

The Substance of which Declaration consisteth in four parts.

1. First, in the Persons and Qualities of the Conspirators.

2. Secondly, in the Matter conspired.

3. Thirdly, in the mean and manner of the proceeding and execution of the Conspiracy.

4. And Fourthly, of the end and purpose why it was so conspired.

As concerning the first, being the Persons.

They were

Garnet,

Jesuits not then taken.

Gerrard,

Tesmond,

Thomas Winter,

At the Bar.

Guy Fawkes,

Robert Keyes,

Thomas Bates,

Everard Digby,

Ambrose Rookewood,

Iohn Graunt,

Robert Winter.

Robert Catesby,

Slain in Rebellion.

Thomas Piercy,

Iohn Wright,

Christopher Wright.

Francis Tresham, Lately dead.

All grounded Romanists, and corrupted Scholars of so Irreligious and Traiterous a School.

As concerning the second, which is the Matter Conspired, it was,

1. First, to deprive the King of his Crown.

2. Secondly, to murder the King, the Queen, and the Prince.

3. Thirdly, to stir Rebellion and Sedition in the Kingdom.

4. Fourthly, to bring a miserable destruction among the Subjects.

5. Fifthly, to change, alter, and subvert the Religion here established.

6. Sixthly, to ruinate the state of the Commonwealth, and to bring in Strangers to invade it.

As concerning the third, which is the mean and manner how to compass and execute the same.

They did all conclude,

1. First, that the King and his People (the Papists excepted) were Hereticks.

2. Secondly, that they were all cursed, and Excommunicate by the Pope.

3. Thirdly, that no Heretick could be King.

4. Fourthly, that it was lawful and meritorious to kill and destroy the King, and all the said Hereticks.

The mean to effect it, they concluded to be, That

1. The King, the Queen, the Prince, the Lords Spiritual and Temporal, the Knights and Burgesses of the Parliament, should be blown up with Powder.

2. That the whole Royal Issue Male should be destroyed.

3. That they would take into their custody Elizabeth and Mary, the Kings Daughters, and proclaim the Lady Elizabeth Queen.

4. That they should feign a Proclamation in the Name of Elizabeth, in which no mention should be made of alteration of Religion, nor that they were parties to the Treason, until they had raised power to perform the same, and then to proclaim, All grievances in the Kingdom should be reformed.

That they also took several Oathes, and received the Sacrament; first, for secresie: secondly, for prosecution, except they were discharged thereof by three of them.

That after the destruction of the King, the Queen, the Prince, the Royal Issue Male, the Lords Spiritual and Temporal, the Knights and Burgesses; they should notifie the same to Foreign States; and thereupon Sir Edmund Baynam, an attainted person of Treason, and stiling himself prime of the damned Crew, should be sent, and make the same known to the Pope, and crave his aid: An Ambassador fit, both for the Message and Persons, to be sent betwixt the Pope and the Devil.

That the Parliament being Prorogued till the 7th. of February, they in December made a Mine under the House of Parliament, purposing to place their Powder there: but the Parliament being then further Adjourned till the 3d. of October, they in Lent following hired the Vault, and placed therein twenty barrels of powder.

That they took to them Robert Winter, Graunt, and Rookwood, giving them the Oathes and Sacrament as aforesaid, as to provide Munition.

20 Iulii they laid in more ten Barrels of Powder, laying upon them divers great Bars of Iron, and pieces of Timber, and great massie Stones, and covered the same with Fagots, &c.

20 Septemb. they laid in more four Hogsheads of Powder, with other Stones and Bars of Iron thereupon.

4 Novemb. (the Parliament being Prorogued to the 5th.) at eleven a clock at night, Fawkes had prepared (by the procurement of the rest) Touch-wood and Match, to give fire to the Powder the next day.

That the Treason being miraculously discovered, they put themselves, and procured others to enter into open Rebellion; and gave out most untruly, It was, for that the Papists throats were to be cut.

The Effect of that which Sir Edward Coke, Knight, his Majesties Attorney General, said at the former Arraignment, so near to his own words as it could be taken.

It appeareth to your Lordships, and the rest of this most Honourable and Grave Assembly, even by that which Mr. Sergeant hath already opened, that these are the greatest Treasons that ever were plotted in England, and concern the greatest King that ever was of England. But when this Assembly shall further hear, and see discovered the Roots and Branches of the same, not hitherto published, they will say indeed: Quis haec posteris sic narrare poterit, ut facta non ficta esse videantur? That when these things shall be related to Posterity, they will be reputed matters feigned, not done. And therefore in this so great a cause, upon the carriage and event whereof the eye of all Christendom is at this day bent, I shall desire that I may with your patience be somewhat more copious, and not so succinct as my usual manner hath been, and yet will I be no longer than the very matter it self shall necessarily require. But before I enter into the particular Narration of this cause, I hold it fit to give satisfaction to some, and those well-affected amongst us, who have not only marvelled, but grieved, that no speedier expedition hath been used in these proceedings, considering the monstrousness and continual horror of this so desperate a cause.

1. It is Ordo Naturae, agreeable to the order of Nature, that things of great weight and magnitude should slowly proceed, according to that of the Poet, Tarda solet magnis rebus adesse fides. And surely of these things we may truly say, Nunquam ante dies nostros talia acciderunt, Neither hath the eye of man seen, nor the ear of man heard the like things to these.

2. Veritas Temporis filia, Truth is the daughter of Time, especially in this case; wherein by timely and often Examinations, First, matters of greatest moment have been lately found out. Secondly, some known Offenders, and those capital, but lately apprehended. Thirdly, sundry of the principal and Arch-traytors before unknown, now manifested, as the Jesuits. Fourthly, Heretical, Treasonable, and damnable Books lately found out, one of Equivocation, and another De officio Principis Christiani, of Francis Tresham's.

3. There have been already twenty and three several days spent in Examinations.

4. We should otherwise have hanged a man unattainted, for Guy Fawkes passed for a time under the name of Iohn Iohnson: So that if by that name greater expedition had been made, and he hanged, though we had not missed of the man, yet the proceeding would not have been so orderly or justifiable.

5. The King out of his wisdom and great moderation, was pleased to appoint this Trial in time of Assembly in Parliament, for that it concerned especially those of the Parliament.

Now touching the offences themselves, they are so exorbitant and transcendent, and aggregated of so many bloody and fearful crimes, as they cannot be aggravated by any inference, argument or circumstance whatsoever, and that in three respects: First, because this offence is Primae impressionis, and therefore sine Nomine, without any name which might be adaequatum, sufficient to express it, given by any Legist, that ever made or writ of any Laws. For the highest Treason that all they could imagine, they called it only Crimen laesae Majestatis, the violating of the Majesty of the Prince. But this Treason doth want an apt name, as tending not only to the hurt, but to the death of the King; and not the death of the King only, but of his whole Kingdom, Non Regis, sed Regni, that is, to the destruction and dissolution of the frame and Fabrick of this Ancient, Famous, and ever-flourishing Monarchy, even the deletion of our whole Name and Nation: And therefore hold not thy tongue, O God, keep not still silence, refrain not thy self, O God: for loe thine enemies make a murmuring, and they that hate thee have lift up their heads; They have said, Come, and let us root them out, that they be no more a people, and that the Name of Israel may be no more in remembrance. Secondly, it is Sine exemplo, beyond all examples, whether in fact or fiction, even of the Tragick Poets, who did beat their wits to represent the most fearful and horrible murthers. Thirdly, it is Sine modo, without all measure or stint of iniquity, like a Mathematical line, which is Divisibilis in semper divisibilia, infinitely divisible: It is Treason to imagine or intend the the death of the King, Queen, or Prince.

For Treason is like a Tree, whose root is full of poyson, and lyeth secret and hid within the earth, resembling the imagination of the heart of man, which is so secret as God only knoweth it. Now the wisdom of the Law provideth for the blasting and nipping both of the leaves, blossoms and buds which proceed from this root of Treason, either by words which are like to leaves, or by some overt Act, which may be resembled to buds or blossoms, before it cometh to such fruit and ripeness as would bring utter destruction and desolation upon the whole State.

It is likewise Treason to kill the Lord Chancellor, Lord Treasurer, or any Justice of the one Bench or other, Justices of Assise, or any other Judge mentioned in the Statute of 25 Edw. 3. sitting in their Judicial places, and exercising their Offices. And the reason is, for that every Judge so sitting by the King's Authority, representeth the Majesty and Person of the King, and therefore it is

Crimen laesae Majestatis, to kill him, the King being always in Judgment of Law present in Court. But in the High Court of Parliament, every man by vertue of the King's Authority by Writ under the Great Seal, hath a Judicial place, and so consequently the killing of every of them had been a several Treason, and Crimen laesae Majestatis. Besides, that to their Treasons were added open Rebellion, Burglary, Robbery, Horse-stealing, &c. So that this offence is such as no man can express it, no example pattern it, no measure contain it.

Concerning Forreign Princes, there was here a protestation made for the clearing of them from all imputation or aspersion whatsoever. First, for that whilst Kingdoms stood in hostility, hostile Actions are holden honourable and just. Secondly, it is not the King's Serjeant, Attorney, or Solicitor, that in any sort touch or mention them: for we know that great Princes and Personages are reverently and respectively to be spoken of, and that there is Lex in Sermone tenenda. But it is Faux, Winter, and the rest of the Offenders, that have confessed so much as hath been said; and therefore the Kings Councel learned doth but repeat the Offenders Confession, and charge or touch no other person. They have also slandered unjustly our great Master King Iames, which we onely repeat, to shew the wickedness and malice of the Offenders. Thirdly, so much as is said concerning Foreign Princes, is so woven into the matter of the charge of these Offenders, as it cannot be severed or singled from the rest of the matter. So as it is inevitable, and cannot be pretermitted.

Now as this Powder Treason is in it self prodigious and unnatural, so is it in the Conception and Birth most monstrous, as arising out of the dead ashes of former Treasons. For it had three Roots, all planted and watered by Jesuits, and English Romish Catholicks: The first Root in England, in December and March; the second in Flanders, in Iune; the third in Spain, in Iuly. In England it had two Branches; One in December was twelve moneths, before the death of the late Queen of blessed memory: Another in March, wherein she died.

First, in December, Anno Dom. 1601. do Henry Garnet, Superior of the Jesuits in England; Robert Tesmond, Jesuit; Robert Catesby, who was (homo subacto & versuto ingenio, & profunda perfidia) together with Francis Tresham, and others; in the names, and for the behalf of all the English Romish Catholicks, employ Thomas Winter into Spain, as for the general good of the Romish Catholick cause: And by him doth Garnet write his Letters to Father Creswel, Jesuit, residing in Spain, in that behalf. With Thomas Winter doth Tesmond, alias Greeneway the Jesuit go, as an Associate and Confederate in that Conspiracy. The Message (which was principally committed unto the said Winter) was, that he should make a proposition and request to the King of Spain, in the behalf and names of the English Catholicks, that the King would send an Army hither into England, and that the Forces of the Catholicks in England should be prepared to joyn with him, and do him service. And further, that he should move the King of Spain to bestow some Pensions here in England, upon sundry Persons Catholicks, and devoted to his service: And moreover to give advertisement, that the said King of Spain, making use of the general discontentment that young

Gentlemen and Soldiers were in, might, no doubt, by relieving their necessities, have them all at his devotion. And because that in all attempts upon England, the greatest difficulty was ever found to be the transportation of Horses; the Catholicks in England would assure the King of Spain, to have always in readiness for his use and service 1500 or 2000 Horses, against any occasion or enterprise. Now Thomas Winter undertaking this Negotiation, and with Tesmond the Jesuit coming into Spain, by means of Father Creswel the Legier Jesuit there, as hath been said, had readily speech with Don Pedro Francesa, second Secretary of State, to whom he imparted his Message, as also to the Duke of Lerma; who assured him, that it would be an office very grateful to his Master, and that it should not want his best furtherance.

Concerning the place for landing of the King of Spain's Army, which from the English Romish Catholicks he desired might be sent to invade the Land, it was resolved, That if the Army were great, that Essex and Kent were judged fittest. (Where note by the way, who was then Lord Warden of the Cinque Ports) If the Army were small, and trusted upon succour in England, then Milford-Haven was thought more convenient.

Now there being at that time Hostility betwixt both Kingdoms, the King of Spain willingly embraced the motion, saying, That he took the message from the Catholicks very kindly, and that in all things he would respect them with as great care as his proper Castilians. But for his further Answer, and full dispatch, Thomas Winter was appointed to attend the Progress. In the end whereof, being in Summer-time, Count Miranda gave him this Answer in the behalf of his Master, That the King would bestow a hundred thousand Crowns to that use, half to be paid that year, and the rest the next Spring following. And withall required, that we should be as good as our promise; for the next Spring he meant to be with us, and set foot in England. And lastly, he desired on the Kings behalf of Winter, that he might have certain advertisement and intelligence, if so it should in the mean time happen that the Queen did die. Thomas Winter, laden with these hopes, returns into England about a month before Christmas, and delivered answer of all that had passed to Henry Garnet, Robert Catesby, and Francis Tresham. But soon after Set that Glorious Light, her Majesty died. Mira cano: Soloccubuit, Nox nulla secuta est.

Presently after whose death was Christopher Wright, another Messenger, sent over into Spain by Garnet, (who likewise did write by him to Creswel for the furtherance of the Negotiation) Catesby and Tresham, in the name and behalf of all the Romish Catholicks in England, as well to carry news of her Majesties death, as also to continue the aforesaid Negotiation for an Invasion and Pensions, which, by Thomas Winter, had before been dealt in. And in the Spanish Court, about two moneths after his arrival there, doth Christopher Wright meet with Guy Fawkes, who upon the two and twentieth of Iune was employed out of Flanders from Bruxels, by Sir W[...]lliam Stanley, Hugb Owen, (whose finger had been in every Treason which hath been of late years detected) and Baldwyn the Leger Jesuit in Flanders; from whom likewise the said Fawkes carried Letters to Creswel in Spain, for the countenancing and furtherance of his affairs.

Now the end of Fawkes his employment [...] to give advertisement to the King of [...], how the King of England was like to suceed rigorously with the Catholicks, and to run the same course which the late Queen did; and withall to entreat that it would please him to send an Army into England to Milford Haven where the Romish Catholicks would be ready to assist him, and then the Forces that should be transported in Spinola's Gallies, should be landed where they could most conveniently. And these their several messages did Christopher Wright and Guy Fawkes in the end intimate and propound to the King of Spain. But the King as then very honorably answered them both, that he would not in any wise further listen to any such motion, as having before dispatched an Ambassage into England to Treat concerning peace; Therefore this course by forreign forces fayling, they fell to the Powder plot, Catesby and Tresham being in at all, in the Treason of the Earl of Essex, in the Treason of Watson and Clarke, Seminary Priests, and also in this of the Jesuits, Such a greedy appetite had they to practise against the State.

The rest of that which Master Attorney then spake continuedly, was by himself divided into three general parts. The first containing certain considerations concerning this Treason. The second observations about the same. The third a comparison of this Treason of the Jesuits, with that of the Seminary Priests, and that other of Rawley and others. For the considerations concerning the Powder Treason, they were in number eight: That is to say, 1 The persons by whom, 2 The persons against whom, 3 The time when, 4 The place where, 5 The means, 6 The end, 7 The secret contriving, And lastly, The admirable discovery thereof.

1 For the persons offending, or by whom, they are of two sorts: either of the Clergy, or Laity, and for each of them there is a several objection made. Touching those of the Laity, it is by some given out, that they are such men as admit just exception, either desperate in estate, or ba[...]e, or not setled in their wits, such as are Sine Religione, Sine Sede, Sine Fide, Sine Re, & Sine Spe, without Religion, without habitation, without credit, without means, without hope; But (that no man, though never so wicked, may be wronged) true it is they were Gentlemen of good houses, of excellent parts, howsoever most perniciously seduced, abused, corrupted, and Jesuited, of very competent fortunes and States; Besides that Percy was of the house of Northumberland, Sir William Stanley, who principally imployed Fawkes into Spain, and Iohn Talbot of Grafton, who at the least is in case of misprision of High Treason, both of great and honorable families. Concerning those of the spiritualty, it is likewise falsly said, that there is never a Religious man in this action. For I never yet knew a Treason without a Romish Priest: but in this there are very many Jesuits, who are known to have dealt, and passed through the whole action: Three of them are Legiers and States men, as Henry Garnet, alias Walley, the Superiour of the Jesuits, Legier here in England, Father Creswell Legier Jesuit in Spain,

Father Baldwin Legier in Flaunders, as Parsons at Rome, besides their Cursory men, as Gerrard, Oswald Tesmonda alias Greenway, Hamond, Hall, and other Jesuits: So that the principal offendors are the seducing Jesuits, men that use the reverence of Religion, yea even the most Sacred and Blessed name of JESUS as a mantle to cover their impiety, blasphemy, treason, and rebellion, and all manner of wickedness, as by the help of Christ shall be made most apparent to the glory of God, and the honour of our Religion. Concerning this Sect, their Studies and practises principally consist in two Degrees, to wit, in Deposing of Kings, and Disposing of Kingdoms: their profession and doctrine is a Religion of distinctions, the greatest part of them being without the text, and therefore in very deed, idle and vain conceits of their own brains, not having Membra dividentia, that is all the parts of the division warranted by the word of God, and Ubi lex non distinguit, nec nos distinguere debemus. And albeit that Princes hold their Crowns immediately of and from God, by right of lawful Succession and inheritance inherent by Royal Blood, yet think these Jesuits with a Goose quill, within four distinctions to remove the Crown from the head of any King christened, and to deal with them as the old Romans are said to have done with their Viceroys, or petty Kings, who in effect were but Lieutenants unto them, to crown and uncrown them at their pleasures. Neither so onely, but they will proscribe and expose them to be butchered by vassals, which is against their own Canons, for Priests to meddle in cause of blood. And by this means they would make the condition of a King far worse than that of the poorest creature that breatheth. First saith Simanca. Haeretici omnes ipso Iure sunt excommunicati, & à Communione fidelium diris proscriptionibus separati, & quotannis in coena Domini excommunicantur à Papa: So then every Heretick stands and is reputed with them as excommunicated and accursed, if not de Facto, yet de Iure, in law and right to all their intents and purposes, therefore may he be deposed, proscribed and murdered. I but suppose he be not a professed Heretick, but dealeth reservedly, and keepeth his conscience to himself, how stands he then? Simanca answers, Quaeri autem solet, An Haereticus occultus excommunicatus sit ipso Iure, & in alias etiam poenas incidat contra Haereticos statutas? Cui quaestioni simpliciter Iurisperiti respondent, Quòd etsi haeresis occulta sit, nihilominus occultus Haereticus incidit in illas poenas. Whether he be a known or a secret Heretick all is one, they thunder out the same Judgment and Curse for both: Whereas Christ saith, Nolite Iudicare, Judge not, which is, saith Augustine, Nolite Iudicare de occultis, of those things which are secret. But suppose that a Prince thus accursed and deposed, will eftsoons return and conform himself to their Romish Church, shall he then be restored to his State, and again receive his Kingdom? Nothing less: For saith Simanca, Si Reges aut alij Principes Christiani facti sint Haeretici, protinus subjecti & vasalli ab eorum dominio liberantur. Nec Ius hoc recuperabunt, quamvis postea reconcilientur Ecclesiae. O But Sancta Mater Ecclesia nunquam claudit gremium redeunti, Our holy Mother the Church never shuts her bosom to any Convert. It is true, say they, but with a distinction, Quoad Animam: Therefore so he may, and shall be restored, that is, spiritually, in respect of his souls health. Quoad Animam he shall again be taken into the

Holy Church, but not Quoad Regnum, in respect of his Kingdom or State temporal he must not be restored. The reason is, Because all hold only thus far, Modò non sit ad damnum Ecclesiae: So that the Church receive thereby no detriment. I but suppose that such an unhappy deposed Prince have a Son, or lawful and right heir, and he also not to be touched or spotted with his Fathers crime, shall not he at the least succeed and be invested into that Princely estate? Neither will this down with them: Heresie is a leprosie, an hereditary disease. Et ex leprosis parentibus leprosi generantur filij. Of leprous parents come leprous children. So that saith Simanca: Propter Haeresim Regis, non solum Rex Regno privatur, sed et ejus filij à Regni successione pelluntur, ut noster Lupus, (who is indeed Vir secundùm Nomen ejus, a Wolf as well in nature as name,) luculenter probat. Now if any man doubt whom they here mean by an Heretick, Creswell in his book called Philopater gives a plain resolution, Regnandi Ius amittit (saith he) qui Religionem Romanam deserit, He is the Heretick we speak of, even whosoever forsakes the Religion of the Church of Rome, he is accursed, deprived, proscribed, never to be absolved but by the Pope himself, never to be restored either in himself or his posterity.

One place amongst many out of Creswells Philopater shall serve to give a taste of the Jesuitical spirits and doctrine, which is Sect. 2. pag. 109. Hinc etiam infert universa Theologorum ac Iurisconsultorum Ecclesiasticorum schola, (& est certum & de fide) quemcunque Principem Christianum, si à Religione Catholica manifestò diflexerit, & alios avocare voluerit, excidere statim omni potestate ac dignitate, ex ipsa vi Iuris tum humani tum divini, hoc que ante dictam sententiam Supremi Pastoris ac Iudicis contra ipsum prolatam, & subditos quoscunque liberos esse ab omni Iuramenti obligatione, quod de obedientia tanquam Principi legittimo praestitissent: posseque & debere, (si vires habeant) istius modi hominem tanquam Apostatam, hereticum, ac Christi Domini desertorem, & reipub. suae Inimicum hostemque ex hominum Christianorum dominatu ejicere, nè alios inficiat, vel suo exemplo aut Imperio à fide avertat; atque haec certa, definita & indubitata virorum doctissimorum sententia. That is, this inference also doth the whole School both of Divines and Lawyers make, (and it is a Position certain, and to be undoubtedly believed) that if any Christian Prince whatsoever, shall manifestly turn from the Catholick Religion, and desire or seek to reclaim other men from the same, he presently falleth from all Princely Power and Dignity, and that also by vertue and force of the Law it self, both Divine and Humane, even before any Sentence pronounced against him by the Supreme Pastor and Judge. And that his Subjects, of what estate or condition soever, are freed from all Bond of Oath of Allegiance, which at any time they had made unto him, as to their lawful Prince. Nay, that they both may and ought (provided they have competent strength and force) cast out such a man from bearing rule amongst Christians, as an Apostate, an Heretick, a backslider and revolter from our Lord Christ, and an enemy to his own State and Common-Wealth, lest perhaps he might infect others, or by his example or command turn them from the Faith. And this is the certain, resolute, and undoubted Judgment of the best learned men. But Tresham in his Book De Officio Principis

Christiani, goeth beyond all the rest; for he plainly concludeth and determineth, that if any Prince shall but favour, or shew countenance to an Heretick, he presently loseth his Kingdom. In his fifth Chapter he propoundeth this Problem, An aliqua possit secundum Conscientiam Subditis esse Ratio, cur legitimo suo Regi, bellum sine scelere moveant? Whether there may be any lawful cause, justifiable in Conscience, for Subjects to take Arms, without sin, against their lawful Prince and Sovereign? The resolution is, Si Princeps haereticus sit, & obstinatè ac pertinaciter intolerabilis, summi Pastoris divina potestate deponatur, & aliud caput constituatur, cui Subditi se jungant, & legitimo ordine & authoritate tyrannidem amoveant. Princeps indulgendo haereticos non solùm Deum offendit, sed perdit & Regnum, & gentem. Their conclusion therefore is; That for heresy, as above is understood, a Prince is to be deposed, and his Kingdom bestowed by the Pope at pleasure; and that the people, upon pain of damnation, are to take part with him whom the Pope shall so Constitute over them. And thus whilst they imagine with the wings of their light-feathered distinctions to mount above the Clouds and level of vulgar conceits, they desperately fall into a Sea of gross absurdities, blasphemy and impiety. And surely the Jesuits were so far engaged in this Treason, as that some of them stick not to say, that if it should miscarry, that they were utterly undone, and that it would overthrow the State of the whole Society of the Jesuits: And I pray God that in this they may prove true Prophets, that they may become like the Order of Templarii, so called, for that they kept near the Sepulcher at Ierusalem, who were by a general and universal Edict in one day throughout Christendom quite extinguished, as being Ordo impietatis, an Order of impiety. And so, from all Sedition and privy Conspiracy; from all false Doctrine and Heresie; from hardness of heart, and contempt of thy Word and Commandment, Good Lord deliver us. Their protestations and pretences, are to win souls to God, their proofs weak, light, and of no value; their conclusions false, damnable, and damned heresies: The first mentioneth God, the second savoureth of weak and frail Man, the last of the Devil, and their practise easily appeareth out of the dealing of their holy Father.

Henry the Third of France, for killing a Cardinal, was Excommunicated, and after murdered by Iames Clement a Monk: That Fact doth Sixtus Quintus, then Pope, instead of orderly censuring thereof, not only approve, but commend in a long Consistory Oration: That a Monk, a Religious man, saith he, hath slain the unhappy French King in the midst of his Host; It is rarum, insigne, memorabile facinus; a rare, a notable, and a memorable Act; yea further, It is Facinus non sine Dei Optimi Maximi particulari providentia & dispositione, &c. A Fact done not without the special Providence and appointment of our good God, and the suggestion and assistance of his holy Spirit; yea, a far greater work than was the slaying of Holofernes by holy Iudith.

Verus Monachus fictum occiderat, A true Monk had killed the false Monk, for that, as was reported, Henry the Third sometimes would use that habit when he went in Procession. And for France, even that part thereof which entertaineth the Popish Religion, yet never could of ancient time brook this usurped Authority of the Sea of Rome: Namely, that the Pope had power to Excommunicate Kings, and Absolve Subjects from their Oath of Allegiance. Which Position is so directly opposite to all the Canons of the Church of France, and to all the Decrees of the King's Parliament there, as that the very Body of Sorbone, and the whole University of Paris condemned it as a most schismatical, pestilent, and pernicious Doctrine of the Jesuits, as may appear in a Treatise made to the French King, and set out 1602. Entituled Le Franc Discours. But to return to the Jesuits, Catesby was resolved by the Jesuits, that the Fact was both lawful and meritorious, and herewith he perswaded and setled the rest, as any seemed to make doubt.

Concerning Thomas Bates, who was Catesby's man, as he was wound into this Treason by his Master, so was he resolved, when he doubted of the lawfulness thereof, by the Doctrine of the Jesuits. For the manner, it was after this sort; Catesby noting that his man observed him extraordinarily, as suspecting somewhat of that which he the said Catesby went about, called him to him at his Lodging in Puddle-Wharf, and in the presence of Thomas Winter, asked him what he thought the business was they went about, for that he of late had so suspiciously and strangely mark'd them. Bates answered, that he thought they went about some dangerous matter, whatsoever the particular were: whereupon they asked him again, what he thought the business might be? and he answered, that he thought they intended some dangerous matter about the Parliament-House, because he had been sent to get a Lodging near unto that place. Then did they make the said Bates take an Oath to be secret in the Action, which being taken by him, they then told him that it was true, that they were to execute a great matter; namely, to lay Powder under the Parliament-House to blow it up. Then they also told him that he was to receive the Sacrament for the more assurance, and thereupon he went to Confession to the said Tesmond the Jesuit; and in his Confession told him, that he was to conceal a very dangerous piece of work, that his Master Catesby and Thomas Winter had imparted unto him, and said he much feared the matter to be utterly unlawful, and therefore therein desired the counsel of the Jesuit, and revealed unto him the whole intent and purpose of blowing up the Parliament-House upon the first day of the Assembly, at what time the King, the Queen, the Prince, the Lords Spiritual and Temporal, the Judges, the Knights, Citizens, and Burgesses, should all have been there Convented, and met together. But the Jesuit being a Confederate therein before, resolved and encouraged him in the Action, and said that he should be secret in that which his Master had imparted unto him, for that it was for a good cause. Adding moreover, that it was not dangerous unto him, nor any offence to conceal it: And thereupon the Jesuit gave him Absolution, and Bates received the Sacrament of him, in the company of his Master Robert Catesby, and Thomas Winter. Also when Rookwood, in the presence of sundry of the Traitors, (having first received the Oath of Secresie) had, by Catesby, imparted unto him the Plot of the blowing up of the King and State; the said Rookwood being greatly amazed thereat, answered, That it was a matter of Conscience to take away so much blood. But Catesby replied, That he was resolved, and that by good Authority, (as coming from the Superiour of the Jesuits) that in Conscience it might be done, yea, though it were with the destruction of many Innocents, rather than the Action should quail. Likewise Father Hammond absolved all the Traitors at Robert Winters house, upon Thursday after the Discovery of the Plot, they being then in open Rebellion: And therefore, Hos, O Rex, magne caveto, and let all Kings take heed how they either favour, or give allowance or connivance unto them.

2. The second Consideration respecteth the Persons against whom this Treason was intended, which are, 1. The King, who is Gods Anointed; nay, it hath pleased God to communicate unto him his own name, Dixi Dii estis, not Substantially or Essentially so; neither yet on the other side Usurpativè, by unjust Usurpation, as the Devil and the Pope; but Potestativè, as having his Power derived from God within his Territories. 2. Their Natural Liege Lord and Dread Sovereign, whose just Interest and Title to his Crown may be drawn from before the Conquest; and if he were not a King by Descent, yet deserved he to be made one for his rare and excellent Endowments and Ornaments both of Body and Mind. Look into his true and constant Religion and Piety, his Justice, his Learning above all Kings Christned, his Acumen, his Judgment, his Memory; and you will say that he is indeed, Solus praeteritis major, meliorque futuris. But because I cannot speak what I would, I will forbear to speak what I could. Also against the Queen, a most gracious and graceful Lady, a most virtuous, fruitful, and blessed Vine, who hath happily brought forth such Olive Branches, as that in benedictione erit memoria ejus, her memory shall be blessed of all our posterity. Then against the Royal Issue Male, next under God, and after our Sovereign, the future hope, comfort, joy, and life of our State. And as for preserving the good Lady Elizabeth, the Kings Daughter, it should onely have been for a time to have served their purposes, as being thought a fit project to keep others in appetite for their own further advantage; and then, God knoweth what would have become of her. To conclude, against all the most Honourable and Prudent Counsellors, and all the true hearted and worthy Nobles, all the Reverend and Learned Bishops, all the grave Judges and Sages of the Law, all the principal Knights, Gentry, Citizens, and Burgesses of Parliament, the Flower of the whole Realm. Horret Animus, I tremble even to think of it. Miserable desolation!

No King, no Queen, no Prince, no Issue Male, no Counsellors of State, no Nobility, no Bishops, no Judges. O barbarous, and more than Scythian or Thracian cruelty! No Mantle of Holiness can cover it, no pretence of Religion can excuse it, no shadow of good intention can extenuate it; God and Heaven condemn it, Man and Earth detest it, the Offenders themselves were ashamed of it, wicked people exclaim against it, and the Souls of all true Christian Subjects abhor it. Miserable, but yet sudden had their ends been, who should have died in that fiery Tempest and storm of Gunpowder: but more miserable had they been that had escaped. And what horrible effects the blowing up of so much Powder and Stuff would have wrought, not onely amonst Men and Beasts, but even upon insensible Creatures, Churches and Houses, and all places near adjoyning, you who have been Martial men best know. For my self, Vox faucibus haeret: so that the King may say with the Kingly Prophet David, O Lord, the proud are risen against me, and the congregation, even Synagoga, the synagogue of naughty men have sought after my soul, and have not set thee before their eyes. And as it is, Psal. 140. 5. The proud have laid a snare for me, and spread a net abroad, yea, and set traps in my way. But let the ungodly fall into their own nets together, and let me ever escape them. We may say, If the Lord himself had not been on our side, yea, if the Lord himself had not been on our side when men rose up against us, they had swallowed us up quick, when they were so wrathfully displeased at us. But praised be the Lord, which hath not given us over for a prey unto their teeth. Our soul is escaped even as a bird out of the snare of the fowler; the snare is broken, and we are delivered. Our help standeth in the name of the Lord, which hath made heaven and earth.

3. The third Consideration respects the time when this Treason was conspired: wherein note, that it was primo Iacobi, even at that time when his Majesty used so great lenity towards Recusants, in that by the space of a whole year and four months, he took no Penalty by Statute of them. So far was his Majesty from severity, that besides the benefit and grace before specified, he also honoured all alike with advancement and favours; and all this was continued until the Priests Treason by Watson and Clark. But as there is Misericor dia puniens, so is there likewise Crudelitas parcens; for they were not onely by this not reclaimed, but (as plainly appeareth) became far worse. Nay, the Romish Catholiks did at that very time certifie, that it was very like, the King would deal rigorously with them; and the same do these Traitors now pretend as the chiefest motive: whereas indeed they had Treason on foot against the King before they see his face in England. Neither afterwards for all the lenity he used towards them, would any whit desist or relent from their wicked attempts. Nay (that which cometh next to be remembered in this part of their Arraignment) they would pick out the time of Parliament for the execution of their hideous Treasons, wherein the flour of the land being assembled, for the honour of God, the good of his Church, and this Commonwealth, they might, as it were, with one blow, not wound, but kill and destroy the whole State. So that with these men, Impunitas continuum affectum tribuit peccandi, Lenity having once bred a hope of Impunity, begat not onely Insolency, but Impenitency and increase of sin.

4. We are to consider the place, which was the Sacred Senate, the House of Parliament. And why there? For that, say they, unjust Laws had formerly been there made against Catholicks; therefore that was the fittest place of all others to revenge it, and to do Justice in. If any ask, who should have executed this their Justice, it was Justice Fawkes, a man like enough to do according to his name. If by what Law they meant to proceed? It was Gun-powder Law, fit for Justices of

Hell. But concerning those Laws which they so calumniate as unjust, it shall in few words plainly appear, that they were of the greatest, both moderation and equity that ever were any: For from the year 1 Eliz. unto 11. all Papists came to our Church and Service without scruple. I my self have seen Cornewallis, Beddingfield, and others, at Church. So that then, for the space of ten years, they made no conscience nor doubt to Communicate with us in Prayer: But when once the Bull of Pope Pius Quintus was come and published, wherein the Queen was accursed and deposed, and her Subjects discharged of their Obedience and Oath, yea, cursed if they did obey her; then did they all forthwith refrain the Church, then would they have no more society with us in Prayer. So that Recusancy in them is not for Religion, but in an acknowledgment of the Popes Power, and a plain manifestation what their judgment is concerning the right of the Prince in respect of Regal Power and Place. Two years after, viz. Anno 13 Eliz. was there a Law made against the bringing in of Bulls, &c. Anno 18. came M[...]yne a Priest to move sedition. Anno 20. came Campion the first Jesuit, who was sent to make a Party here in England, for the execution of the former Bull. Then follows Treasonable Books. Anno 23 Eliz. after so many years sufferance, there were Laws made against Recusants and seditious Books. The Penalty or Sanction for Recusancy was not loss of Life, or Limb, or whole Estate; but onely a pecuniary Mulct and Penalty, and that also until they would submit and conform themselves, and again come to Church, as they had done for ten years before the Bull. And yet afterwards the Jesuits and Romish Priests, both coming daily into, and swarming within the Realm, and infusing continually this poison into the Subjects hearts, that by reason of the said Bull of Pius Quintus, her Majesty stood Excommunicated and deprived of her Kingdom, and that her Subjects were discharged of all obedience to her, endeavouring by all means to draw them from their Duty and Allegiance to her Majesty, and to reconcile them to the Church of Rome. Then 27 Eliz. a Law was made, That it should be Treason for any (not to be a Priest and an Englishman, born the Queens Natural Subject) but for any being so born her Subject, and made a Romish Priest, to come into any of her Dominions, to infect any her Loyal Subjects with their treasonable and damnaable perswasions and practises: Yet so, that it concerned onely such as were made Priests sithence her Majesty came to the Crown, and not before.

Concerning the execution of these Laws, it is to be observed likewise, that whereas in the Quinquenny, the five years of Queen Mary, there were cruelly put to death about 300 persons for Religion; In all her Majesties time, by the space of 44 years and upwards, there were for treasonable practises executed in all not 30 Priests, nor above five receivers and harborers of them; and for Religion, not any one. And here by the way, I desire those of Parliament to observe, that it is now questioned and doubted, Whether the Law of Recusants and reconciled Persons do hold for Ireland also, and the parts beyond the Seas; that is, Whether such as were there reconciled, be within the compass of the Statute or not, to the end it may be cleared and provided for.

Now against the Usurped Power of the Sea of Rome, we have of former times about thirteen several Acts of Parliament: So that the Crown and King of England is no ways to be drawn under the Government of any Foreign Power whatsoever; neither oweth duty to any, but is immediately under God himself. Concerning the Popes, for thirty three of them, namely, unto Silvester, they were famous Martyrs; but, Quicunque desiderat primatum in terris, inveniet confusionem in coelis: He that desires Primacy upon Earth, shall surely find confusion in Heaven.

The fifth consideration is of the end, which was, to bring a final and fatal confusion upon the State. For howsoever they sought to shadow their Impiety with the Cloak of Religion, yet they intended to breed a confusion fit to get new Alterations; for they went to joyn with Romish Catholicks, and discontented persons.

Now the sixth point, which is the means to compass and work these designs, were damnable, by Mining, by six and thirty Barrels of Powder, having Crows of Iron, Stones, and Wood, laid upon the Barrels, to have made the Breach the greater. Lord, what a Wind, what a Fire, what a Motion and Commotion of Earth and Air would there have been! But, as it is in the Book of Kings, when Elias was in the Cave in Mount Horeb, and that he was called forth to stand before the Lord, behold a mighty strong Wind rent the Mountains, and brake the Rocks, sed non in vento Dominus, but the Lord was not in the Wind. And after the Wind came a Commotion of the Earth and Air: Et non in Commotione Dominus, the Lord was not in that Commotion. And after the Commotion came Fire, Et non in igne Dominus, the Lord was not in the Fire. So neither was God in any part of this monstrous Action. The Authors whereof were, in this respect, worse than the very damned Spirit of Dives, who, as it is in the Gospel, desired that others should not come in locum tormentorum.

7. The next consideration is the secret contriving and carriage of this Treason, to which purpose there were four means used. First, Catesby was commended to the Marquis for a Regiment of Horse in the Low-Countreys, (which is the same that the Lord Arundel now hath) that under that pretence he might have furnished this Treason with Horses without suspicion. The second means was an Oath, which they solemnly and severally took, as well for secresie, as perseverance and constancy in the execution of their Plot. The form of the Oath was as followeth,

Yoou shall swear by the Blessed Trinity, and by the Sacrament you now purpose to receive, never to disclose directly nor indirectly, by word or circumstance, the matter that shall be proposed to you to keep secret, nor desist from the execution thereof, until the rest shall give you leave.

This Oath was by Gerrard the Jesuit given to Catesby, Piercy, Christopher Wright, and Thomas Winter at once, and by Greenwel the Jesuit to Bates at another time, and so to the rest.

The third was the Sacrament, which they impiously and devillishly prophan'd to this end. But the last was their perfidious and perjurious equivocating, abetted, allowed, and justified by the Jesuits, not onely simply to conceal or deny an open truth, but Religiously to aver, to protest upon Savation, to swear that which themselves know to be most false; and all this, by reserving a secret and private sense inwardly to themselves, whereby they are by their Ghostly Fathers persuaded, that they may safely and lawfully delude any question whatsoever. And here was shewed a Book written not long before the Queens death, at what time Thomas Winter was employed into Spain, entituled, A Treatise of Equivocation; which Book being seen and allowed by Garnet, the Superior of the Jesuits, and Blackwel the Arch-priest of England, in the beginning thereof, Garnet, with his own hand, put out those words in the Title of Equivocation, and made it thus, A Treatise against Lying, and Fraudulent Dissimulation; whereas indeed and truth it makes for both, Speciosáque nomina Culpae Imponis Garnette tuae. And in the end thereof, Blackwel besprinkles it with his Blessing, saying, Tractatus iste, valde doctus & verè pius, & Catholicus est. Certe S. Scripturarum, Patrum, Doctorum, Scholasticorum, Canonistarum & optimarum Rationum praesidiis plenissimè firmat aequitatem aequivocationis. Ideoque dignissimus est qui Typis propagetur, ad consolationem afflictorum Catholicorum, & omnium piorum instructionem. That is, This Treatise is very Learned, Godly, and Catholick, and doth most fully confirm the Equity of Equivocation, by strong proofs out of holy Scriptures, Fathers, Doctors, School-men, Canonists, and soundest reasons; and therefore worthy to be published in Print, for the comfort of afflicted Catholicks, and instruction of all the godly.

Now in this Book there is, Propositio mentalis, verbalis, scripta, and mixta, distinguishing of a mental, a verbal, a written, and a mixt Proposition, a very labyrinth to lead men into error and falshood. For example, to give you a little taste of this Art of cozening.

A man is asked upon Oath this question, Did you see such an one to day? he may, by this Doctrine, answer No, though he did see him, viz. reserving this secret meaning, not with purpose to tell my Lord Chief Justice. Or, I see him not, Visione beatifica, or, not in Venice, &c. Likewise, to answer thus, I was in the company, reserving and intending secretly, as added, this word Not: As Strange the Jesuit did to my Lord Chief Justice and my self: Take one or two of these out of that very Book, as for purpose. A man cometh unto Coventry in time of a suspicion of Plague, and at the Gates the Officers meet him, and upon his Oath examine him, whether he came from London or no, where they think certainly the Plague to be: This man knowing for certain the Plague not to be at London, or at least knowing that the Air is not there infectious, and that he only rid through some secret place of London, not staying there, may safely swear he came not from London, answering to their final intention in their demand, that is, whether he came so from London, that he may endanger their City of the Plague, although their immediate intention were to know whether he came from

London or no. That man (saith the Book) the very light of nature would clear from Perjury. In like manner, one being Convented in the Bishop's Court, because he refuseth to take such a one to his Wife, as he had Contracted with per verba de praesenti, having Contracted with another privily before, so that he cannot be Husband to her that claimeth him, may answer, that he never Contracted with her per verba de praesenti, understanding that he did not so Contract that it was a Marriage, for that is the final intention of the Judge, to know whether there were a sufficient Marriage between them or no. Never did Father Cranmer, Father Latimer, Father Ridley, those blessed Martyrs know these shifts, neither would they have used them to have saved their lives. And surely let every good man take heed of such Jurors or Witnesses, there being no Faith, no bond of Religion or Civility, no Conscience of Truth in such men, and therefore the conclusion shall be that of the Prophet David: Domine, libera Animam meam à labiis iniquis & à lingua dolosa; Deliver me, O Lord, from lying lips, and from a deceitful tongue.

S. P. Q. R. Was sometimes taken for these words, Senatus Populusque Romanus, the Senate and People of Rome, but now they may truly be expressed thus, Stultus Populus quaerit Romam: A foolish people that runneth to Rome. And here was very aptly and delightfully inserted and related the Apologue or Tale of the Cat and the Mice. The Cat having a long time preyed upon the Mice, the poor creatures at last, for their safety, contained themselves within their holes; but the Cat finding his prey to cease, as being known to the Mice, that he was indeed their enemy, and a Cat, deviseth this course following, viz. changeth his hue, getteth on a Religious habit, shaveth his crown, walks gravely by their holes: And yet perceiving that the Mice kept their holes, and looking out, suspected the worst, he formally, and Father-like said unto them, Quod fueram non sum, frater, caput aspice tonsum: Oh Brother, I am not as you take me for, no more a Cat, see my habit, and shaven crown. Hereupon some of the more credulous and bold among them, were again by this deceit snatched up; and therefore when afterwards he came as before to entice them forth, they would come out no more, but answered, Cor tibi restat idem, vix tibi proesto fidem, Talk what you can, we will never believe you, you have still a Cats heart within you: you do not watch and pray, but you watch to prey. And so have the Jesuits, yea, and Priests too; for they are all joyned in the tails like Sampson's Foxes, Ephraim against Manasses, and Manasses against Ephraim, but both against Iuda.

8. The last Consideration is, concerning the admirable discovery of this Treason, which was by one of themselves, who had taken the Oath and Sacrament, as hath been said, against his own will: The means was, by a dark and doubtful Letter sent to my Lord Mountegle. And thus much as touching the Considerations; the Observations follow, to be considered in this Powder-Treason, and are briefly thus.

1. If the Cellar had not been hired, the Mine-work could hardly or not at all have been discovered; for the Mine was neither found, nor suspected, until the danger

was past, and the Capital Offenders apprehended, and by themselves, upon Examination, confessed.

2. How the King was Divinely illuminated by Almighty God, the only Ruler of Princes, like an Angel of God, to direct and point as it were to the very place, to cause a search to be made there, out of those dark words of the Letter concerning a terrible Blow.

3. Observe a miraculous accident which befel in Stephen Littleton's house, called Holbach in Staffordshire, after they had been two days in open Rebellion, immediately before the apprehension of these Traitors: For some of them standing by the fire-side, and having set 2l. and di. of Powder to drie in a Platter before the fire, and under-set the said Platter with a great linen bag, full of other Powder, containing some fifteen or sixteen pounds; it so fell out, that one coming to put more wood into the fire, and casting it on, there flew a coal into the Platter, by reason whereof, the Powder taking fire and blowing up, scorched those who were nearest, as Catesby, Graunt, and Rookewood, blew up the roof of the house, and the linnen bag which was set under the Platter being therewith suddenly carried out through the Breach, fell down in the Court-yard whole and unfired; which if it had took fire in the room, would have slain them all there, so that they never should have come to this Trial. And, Lex justior ulla est, Quàm necis artifices arte perire sua?

4. Note, That Gun-powder was the invention of a Friar, one of that Romish Rabble; as Printing was of a Soldier.

5. Observe the sending of Rainham, one of the damned Crew, to the High Priest of Rome, to give signification of this blow, and to crave his direction and aid.

6. That for all their stirring and rising in open Rebellion, and notwithstanding the false Rumors given out by them, that the throats of all Catholicks should be cut; such is his Majesties blessed Government, and the Loyalty of his Subjects, as they got not any one man to take their parts besides their own company.

7. Observe, the Sheriff, the ordinary Minister of Justice, according to the duty of his Office, with such power as he on a sudden by Law collected, suppressed them.

8. That God suffered their intended mischief to come so near the period, as not to be discovered but within few hours before it should have been executed.

9. That it was in the entring of the Sun into the Tropick of Capricorn, when they began their Mine; noting, that by Mineing they should descend, and by Hanging ascend.

10. That there never was any Protestant Minister in any Treason and Murder, as yet attempted within this Realm.

I am now come to the last part, which I proposed in the beginning of this discourse, and that is, touching certain Comparisons of this Powder Treason of the Jesuits, with that of Raleigh, and the other of the Priests, Watson and Clark. 1. They had all one end, and that was the Romish Catholick cause. 2. The same means, by Popish and discontented persons, Priests and Lay-men. 3. They all plaid at hazard; the Priests were at the By, Raleigh at the Main, but these in at all, as purposing to destroy all the Kings Royal Issue, and withall the whole Estate. 4. They were all alike obliged by the same Oath and Sacrament. 5. The same Proclamations were intended (after the fact) to be published for reformation of abuses. 6. The like Army provided for invading, to land at Milford-haven, or in Kent. 7. The same Pensions of Crowns promised. 8. The agreeing of the times of the Treason of Raleigh and these men, which was, when the Constable of Spain was coming hither, and Raleigh said, there could be no suspicion of any Invasion, seeing that the Constable of Spain was then expected for a Treaty of Peace; and the Navy might be brought to the Groine under pretence of the Service in the Low-Countreys. And Raleigh further said, That many more were hanged for words than for deeds. And before Raleigh's Treason was discovered, it was reported in Spain, That Don Raleigh and Don Cobham should cut the King of England's throat. I say not that we have any proofs, that these of the Powder-plot were acquainted with Raleigh, or Raleigh with them: but as before was spoken of the Jesuits and Priests, so they all were joyned in the ends, like Samson's Foxes in the tails, howsoever severed in their heads.

The Conclusion shall be, from the admirable clemency and moderation of the King, in that howsoever these Traitors have exceeded all others their Predecessors in mischief, and so Crescente malitia, crescere debuit & Poena; yet neither will the King exceed the usual punishment of Law, nor invent any new torture or torment for them, but is graciously pleased to afford them as well an ordinary course of Trial, as an ordinary punishment, much inferiour to their offence. And surely worthy of observation is the punishment by Law provided and appointed for High Treason, which we call Crimen laesae Majestatis.

For first, after a Traitor hath had his just Trial, and is convicted and attainted, he shall have his judgment to be drawn to the place of Execution from his Prison, as being not worthy any more to tread upon the face of the earth, whereof he was made. Also for that he hath been retrograde to Nature, therefore is he drawn backwards at a Horse-tail. And whereas God hath made the head of man the highest and most supreme part, as being his chief grace and ornament: Pronáque cum spectent Animalia caetera terram, Os homini sublime dedit; he must be drawn with his head declining downward, and lying so near the ground as may be, being thought unfit to take benefit of the common Air: For which cause also he shall be Strangled, being hanged up by the neck between Heaven and Earth, as deemed unworthy of both, or either; as likewise, that the eyes of men may behold, and their hearts contemn him. Then is he to be cut down alive, and to have his Privy parts cut off, and burnt before his face, as being unworthily begotten, and unfit to leave any generation after him. His bowels and inlayed parts taken out and burnt, who inwardly had conceived and harboured in his heart such horrible Treason. After, to have his head cut off, which had imagined the mischief. And lastly, his body to be quartered, and the quarters set up in some high and eminent place, to the view and detestation of men, and to become a prey for the Fouls of the Air. And this is a reward due to Traitors, whose hearts be hardned: for that it is Physick of State and Government, to let out corrupt blood from the heart. But, Poenitentia vera nunquam sera, sed paenitentia sera rarò vera. True repentance is indeed never too late, but late repentance is seldom found true; which yet I pray the merciful Lord to grant unto them, that having a sense of their offences, they may make a true and sincere Confession, both for their Souls health, and for the good and safety of the King and this State. And for the rest that are not yet apprehended, my prayer to God is, Ut aut convertantur ne pereant, aut confundantur ne noceant; that either they may be converted, to the end they perish not, or else confounded that they hurt not.

After this, by the direction of Master Attorney General, were their several Examinations (subscribed by themselves) shewed particularly unto them, and acknowledged by them to be their own, and true, wherein every one had confessed the Treason. Then did Master Attorney desire, that albeit that which had been already done and confessed at the Bar, might be all-sufficient for the Declaration and Justification of the course of Justice then held, especially seeing we have Reos confitentes, the Traitors own voluntary Confessions at the Bar; yet for further satisfaction to so great a Presence and Audience, and their better memory of the carriage of these Treasons, the voluntary and free Confessions of all the said several Traitors in writing, subscribed with their own proper hands, and acknowledged at the Bar by themselves to be true, were openly and distinctly read. By which, amongst other things, it appeared, that Bates was resolved for what he undertook concerning the Powder-Treason, and being therein warranted by the Jesuits. Also it appeared, that Hammond the Jesuit, after that he knew the Powder-Treason was discovered, and that these Traitors had been in actual Rebellion, Confessed them and gave them Absolution; and this was on Thursday the 7th. of November. Here also was mention made by Master Attorney, of the Confessions of Watson and Clark, Seminary Priests, upon their apprehension, who affirmed, That there was some Treason intended by the Jesuits, and then in hand, as might appear; First, by their continual negotiating at that time with Spain, which they assured themselves tended to nothing, but a preparation for a Foreign commotion.

2. By their collecting and gathering together such great sums of money, as then they had done, therewith to levy an Army when time should serve.

3. For that sundry of the Jesuits had been tampering with Catholicks, as well to disswade them from acceptance of the King at his first coming, saying, That they ought rather to die, than to admit of any Heretick (as they continually termed his Majesty) to the Crown: And that they might not, under pain of

Excommunication, accept of any but a Catholick for their Sovereign; as al[...] to disswade Catholicks from their Loyalty, after the State was setled.

Lastly, in that they had both bought up store of great Horses throughout the Countrey, and conveyed Powder, and Shot, and Artillery secretly to their Friends, wishing them not to stir, but keep themselves quiet until they heard from them.

After the reading of their several Examinations, Confessions, and voluntary Declarations, as well of themselves, as of some of their dead Confederates, they were all, by the Verdict of the Jury, found guilty of the Treasons contained in their Indictment; and then being severally asked what they could say, wherefore Judgment of Death should not be pronounced against them, there was not one of these (except Rookwood) who would make any continued Speech, either in defence or extenuation of the fact. Thomas Winter onely desired, that he might be Hanged both for his Brother and himself. Guy Fawkes being asked why he pleaded Not Guilty, having nothing to say for his excuse, answered, That he had so done in respect of certain conferences mentioned in the Indictment, which, he said, that he knew not of; which were answered to have been set down according to course of Law, as necessarily presupposed before the resolution of such a design. Keyes said, That his Estate and Fortunes were desperate, and as good now as another time, and for this cause rather than for another. Bates craved mercy. Robert Winter mercy. Iohn Grant was a good while mute, yet after submissly said, He was guilty of a Conspiracy intended, but never effected. But Ambrose Rookwood first excused his denial of the Indictment, for that he had rather lose his life than give it. Then did he acknowledge his offence to be so heinous, that he justly deserved the indignation of the King, and of the Lords, and the hatred of the whole Common-wealth; yet could he not despair of Mercy at the hands of a Prince, so abounding in Grace and Mercy: And the rather, because his Offence, though it were incapable of any excuse, yet not altogether incapable of some extenuation, in that he had been neither Author nor Actor, but onely perswaded and drawn in by Catesby, whom he loved above any worldly man: And that he had concealed it, not for any malice to the Person of the King, or to the State, or for any ambitious respect of his own, but onely drawn with the tender respect, and the faithful and dear affection he bare to Mr. Catesby his Friend, whom he esteemed more dear than any thing else in the world. And this mercy he desired not for any fear of the image of Death, but for grief that so shameful a Death should leave so perpetual a blemish and blot unto all Ages upon his Name and Blood. But howsoever that this was his first Offence, yet he humbly submitted himself to the Mercy of the King, and prayed, that the King would herein imitate God, who sometimes doth punish corporaliter, non mortaliter; corporally, yet not mortally.

Then was related, how that on Friday immediately before this Arraignment, Robert Winter having found opportunity to have conference with Fawkes in the Tower, in regard of the nearness of their Lodgings, should say to Fawkes, as Robert Winter and Fawkes confessed, That he and Catesby had Sons, and that

Boys would be men, and that he hoped they would revenge the cause: nay, that God would raise up Children to Abraham out of stones. Also that they were sorry, that no body did set forth a Defence or Apology of their Action; but yet they would maintain the cause at their deaths.

Here also was reported Robert Winters Dream, which he had before the blasting with Powder in Littletons house, and which he himself confessed, and first notified, viz. That he thought he saw Steeples stand awry, and within those Churches strange and unknown faces. And after, when the foresaid blast had, the day following, scorched divers of the Confederates, and much disfigured the faces and countenances of Grant, Rookwood, and others: Then did Winter call to mind his Dream, and to his remembrance thought, that the faces of his Associates so scorched, resembled those which he had seen in his Dream. And thus much concerning the former Indictment.

Then was Sir Everard Digby Arraigned, and after his Indictment was read, wherein he was charged, not onely to have been acquainted with the Powder-treason, and concealed it, and taken the double Oath of Secresie and Constancy therein, but likewise to have been an Actor in this Conspiracy. And lastly, to have exposed, and openly shewed himself in the Rebellion in the Countrey, amongst the rest of the Traitors. All which, after he had attentively heard and marked, knowing that he had freely confessed it, and the strength and evidence of the proofs against him, and convicted with the testimony of his own Conscience, shewed his disposition to confess the principal part of the said Indictment, and so began to enter into a Discourse. But being advertised, that he must first plead to the Indictment directly, either Guilty, or Not Guilty, and that afterwards he should be licensed to speak his pleasure, he forthwith confessed the Treason contained in the Indictment, and so fell into a Speech, whereof there were two parts, viz. Motives and Petitions. The first Motive which drew him into this action, was not ambition, nor discontentment of his estate, neither malice to any in Parliament, but the friendship and love he bare to Catesby, which prevailed so much, and was so powerful with him, as that for his sake he was ever contented and ready to hazard himself and his Estate. The next Motive was, the cause of Religion, which alone, seeing (as he said) it lay at the stake, he entred into resolution to neglect in that behalf, his Estate, his Life, his Name, his Memory, his Posterity, and all worldly and earthly felicity whatsoever, though he did utterly extirpate and extinguish all other hopes, for the restoring of the Catholick Religion in England. His third Motive was, That promises were broken with the Catholicks. And lastly, That they generally feared harder Laws from this Parliament against Recusants, as, That Recusants Wives, and Women, should be liable to the Mulct as well as their Husbands, and Men. And further, that it was supposed, that it should be made a Praemunire onely to be a Catholick.

His Petitions were, That sithens his offence was confined and contained within himself, that the punishment also of the same might extend onely to himself, and not be transferred either to his Wife, Children, Sisters, or others: and therefore for his Wife he humbly craved, that she might enjoy her Joynture, his Son the benefit of an Entail made long before any thought of this action; his Sisters, their just and due Portions which were in his hands; his Creditors, their rightful Debts; which that he might more justly set down under his hand, he requested, that before his death, his Man (who was better acquainted both with the men, and the particulars, than himself) might be licensed to come unto him. Then prayed he pardon of the King and Ll. for his guilt. And lastly, he entreated to be beheaded, desiring all men to forgive him, and that his death might satisfie them for his trespass.

To this Speech forthwith answered Sir Edw. Coke, Attorney General,

-Sir Edward Coke, C. Northcote Parkinson, <u>Gunpowder Treason and Plot</u>, St. Martins Press, Ny, 1976.

but in respect of the time (for it grew now dark) very briefly. 1. For his friendship with Catesby, that it was mere folly, and wicked Conspiracy. 2. His Religion, Error, and Heresie. 3. His promises, idle and vain presumptions: As also his fears, false alarms. Concerning Wives that were Recusants, if they were known so to be before their Husbands (though they were good Protestants) took them, and yet for outward and worldly respects whatsoever, any would match with such, great reason there is, that he or they should pay for it, as knowing the penalty and burthen before; for, Volenti & scienti non fit Injuria, No man receives injury in that, to which he willingly and knowingly agreeth and consenteth. But if she were no Recusant at the time of Marriage, and yet afterwards he suffer her to be corrupted and seduced, by admitting Priests and Romanists into his house, good reason likewise that he, be he Papist or Protestant, should pay for his negligence and misgovernment.

4. Concerning the Petitions for Wife, for Children, for Sisters, &c. O how he doth now put on the bowels of Nature and Compassion in the peril of his private and domestical estate! But before, when the publick state of his Countrey, when the King, the Queen, the tender Princes, the Nobles, the whole Kingdom, were designed to a perpetual destruction, Where was then this piety, this Religious affection, this care? All Nature, all Humanity, all respect of Laws both Divine and Humane, were quite abandoned; then was there no conscience made to extirpate the whole Nation, and all for a pretended zeal to the Catholick Religion, and the justification of so detestable and damnable a Fact.

Here did Sir Everard Digby interrupt Mr. Attorney, and said, that he did not justifie the fact, but confessed, that he deserved the vilest death, and most severe punishment that might be; but he was an humble Petitioner for mercy, and some moderation of Justice. Whereupon Mr. Attorney repli'd, that he should not look by the King to be honoured in the manner of his death, having so far abandoned all Religion and Humanity in his Action; but that he was rather to admire the great moderation and mercy of the King, in that, for so exorbitant a crime, no new torture answerable thereunto was devised to be inflicted upon him. And for his Wife and Children, whereas he said, that for the Catholik Cause he was content to neglect the ruine of himself, his Wife, his Estate, and all; he should have his desire as 'tis in the Psalm, Let his Wife be a widow, and his Children vagabonds; let his posterity be destroyed, and in the next generation let his name be quite put out. For the paying of your Creditors, it is equal and just, but yet fit the King be first satisfied and paid, to whom you owe so much, as that all you have is too little: yet these things must be left to the pleasure of his Majesty, and the course of Justice and Law.

My Lord of Northamptons Speech, as it was taken at the Arraignment of Sir Everard Digby, by T. S.

You must not hold it strange, Sir Everard Digby, though at this time, being pressed in Duty, Conscience and Truth, I do not suffer you to wander in the Laberinth of your own idle conceits without opposition, to seduce others, as your Self have been seduced, by false Principles; or to convey your self by charms of imputation, by clouds of errour, and by shifts of lately devised Equivocation, out of that streight wherein your late secure and happy fortune hath been unluckily entangled; but yet justly surprised, by the rage and revenge of your own rash humors. If in this crime (more horrible than any man is able to express) I could lament the estate of any person upon earth, I could pity you, but thank your Self and your bad Counsellours, for leading you into a Crime of such a kind; as no less benummeth in all faithfull, true and honest men, the tenderness of affection, than it did in you, the sense of all humanity.

That you were once well thought of, and esteemed by the late Queen, I can witness, having heard her speak of you with that grace which might have encouraged a true Gentleman to have run a better course: Nay I will add further, that there was a time, wherein you were as well affected to the King our Masters expectation, though perhaps upon false rumours and reports, that he would have yielded satisfaction to your unprobable and vast desires: but the seed that wanted moisture (as our Saviour himself reporteth) took no deep root: that zeal which hath no other end or object than the pleasing of it Self, is quickly spent: and Trajan that worthy and wise Emperour, had reason to hold himself discharged of all debts to those, that had offended more by prevarication, than they could deserve by industry.

The grace and goodness of his Majesty in giving honour at his first coming unto many men of your own affection, & (as I think) unto your self; his facility in admitting all without distinction of Trojan or of Tyrian, to his Royal presence, upon just occasions of access, his integrity in setting open the gate of civil Iustice unto all his Subjects equally and indifferently, with many other favours that succeeded by the progression of Peace, are so palpable and evident to all men, that have either eyes of understanding, or understanding of capacity, as your Self and many others, have been driven of late to excuse and countenance your execrable ingratitude, with a false and scandalous report of some further hope and comfort yielded to the Catholicks for Toleration or connivency, before his coming to the Crown, than since hath been performed, made good or satisfied.

I am not ignorant, that this seditious and false alarm hath awaked and incited many working spirits to the prejudice of the present State, that might otherwise have slept as before with silence and sufferance: it hath served for a shield of wax against a sword of power: it hath been used as an Instrument of Art to shadow false approches, till the Trojan horse might be brought within the walls of the Parliament, with a belly stuffed, not as in old time with armed Greeks, but with hellish Gunpowder. But howsoever God had blinded you and other in this Action, as he did the King of Egypt and his Instruments, for the brighter evidence of his own powerful glory; yet every man of understanding could discern, that a Prince whose Iudgment had been fixed by experience of so many years, upon the Poles of the North and the South, could not shrink upon the suddain: no nor since with fear of that combustion which Catesby that Archtraitor, like a second Phaeton, would have caused in an instant in all the Elements. His Majesty did never value fortunes of the world, in lesser matter than Religion, with the freedom of his thoughts: he thought it no safe policy, (professing as he did and ever will) to call up more spirits into the circle than he could put down again: he knew, that omne Regnum in se divisum desolabitur. Philosophy doth teach, that whatsoever any man may think in secret thought, that where one doth hold of Cephas, another of Apollo, openly dissension ensues, Quod insitum alieno solo est, in id quo alitu[...], natura vertente, degenerat: and the world will ever apprehend, that Quorum est commune symbolum, facilimus est transitus.

Touching the point it self of promising a kind of Toleration to Catholicks, as it was divulged by these two limbs of Lucifer, Watson and Percy, to raise a ground of practise and conspiracy against the State and Person of our Dear Soveraign: let the Kingdom of Scotland witness for the space of so many years before his coming hither, whether either flattery or fear, (no not upon that enterprise of the 17th of November, which would have put the patience of any Prince in Europe to his proof) could draw from the King the least inclination to this dispensative indifference, that was onely believed because it was eagerly desired.

Every man doth know how great art was used, what strong wits sublimed, and how many Ministers suborned and corrupted many years, both in Scotland and in Forein parts, to set the Kings teeth on edge, with fair promises of future helps and supplies, to that happy end of attaining his due right in England, when the Sun should set to rise more gloriously in the same Hemisphere, to the wonder both of this Island and of the world. But all in vain: for jacta erat alea, the Kings compass had been set before, and by a more certain rule: and they were commonly cast off as forlorn hopes in the Kings favour, that ran a course of ranking themselves in the foremost front of forein correspondency.

Upon notice given to his Majesty from hence, some years before the death of the late Queen, that many men were grown suspicious of his Religion, by rumors spread abroad, that some of those in forein part[...], that seemed to be well affected to his future expectation, had used his name more audaciously, and spoken of his favour to the Catholicks, more forwardly than the Kings own Conscience, and unchangeable Decree could acknowledge, or admit, (either with a purpose to prepare the minds of Forein Princes, or for a practise to estrange and alienate affections at home) not onely utterly renounced, and condemned these encrochments of blind zeal, and rash proceedings, by the voices of his own Ministers, but was careful also for a caution to succeeding hopes, so far as lay in him, that by the disgrace of the Delinquents in this kind, the minds of all English Subjects chiefly might be secured, and the world satisfied.

No man can speak in this case more confidently than my self, that received in the Queens time for the space of many years, directions and warnings to take heed, that neither any further comfort might be given to Catholicks concerning future favours, than he did intend, which was, to bind all Subjects in one Kingdom to one Law, concerning the Religion established, howsoever in Civil Matters he might extend his favour as he found just cause: nor any seeds of jealousie and diffidence sown in the minds of Protestants by Semeis and Achitophels, to make them doubtful of his constancy, to whom he would confirm with his dearest blood that faith which he had sucked from the breast of his Nurse, apprehended from the Cradle of his Infancy, and maintained with his uttermost endeavour, affection and strength, since he was more able out of reading and disputing to give a reason of those Principles which he had now digested, and turned to Nutriment.

He that wrote the Book of Titles before the late Queens death, declares abundantly, by seeking to possess some Forein Prince of the Kings Hereditary

Crowns, when the cause should come to the proof, and may witness in stead of many, what hope there was of the Kings favour or affection to Catholicks in the case of Toleration or Dispensation with exercise of Conscience. For every man may guess that it was no sleight or ordinary degree of despair, that made him and other of his Suit renounce their portion in the Son and Heir of that renowned and rare Lady, Mary Queen of Scotland, a Member of the Roman Church, as some did in David, Nulla nobis pars in David, nec haereditas in filio Isai. For hereof, by Letters intercepted in their passage into Scotland, the Records and Proofs are evident. His Majesty, so long as he was in expectation of that which by the work and grace of God he doth now possess, did ever seek to settle his establishment upon the Faith of Protestants in generality, as the most assured Shoot-Anchor. For though he found a number on the other side, as faithful and as well affected to his Person, Claim, and Interest, as any men alive, as well in respect of their dependency upon the Queen his Mother, as for the taste which they had of the sweetness of himself; yet finding with what strength of blood many have been over-carried out of a fervency in zeal in former times, observing to what censures they were subject, both in points of Faith, and limitation of Loyalty; And last of all, forecasting to what end their former Protestation would come, when present satisfaction should shrink, he was ever fearful to embark himself for any further voyage and adventure in this Streight, than his own Compass might stear him, and his Iudgment level him.

If any one green leaf for Catholicks could have been visibly discerned by the eye of Catesby, Winter, Garnet, Faux, &c. they would neither have entred into practise with Forein Princes during the Queens time, for prevention of the Kings Lawful and Hereditary Right, nor have renewed the same both abroad and at home, by Missions and Combinations, after his Majesty was both applauded and entred.

It is true, that by Confessions we find that false Priest Watson, and Arch-Traitor Percy, to have been the first devisers and divulgers of this scandalous report, as an accursed ground, whereon they might with some advantage, as it was conceived, build the Castles of their Conspiracy.

Touching the first, no man can speak more soundly to the point than my self; for being sent into the Prison by the King to charge him with this false Alarm, onely two days before his death, and upon his Soul to press him in the presence of God, and as he would answer it at another Bar, to confess directly, whether at either of both these times he had access unto his Majesty at Edinburgh, his Majesty did give him any promise, hope or comfort of encouragement to Catholicks concerning Toleration; he did there protest upon his Soul, that he could never win one inch of ground, or draw the smallest comfort from the King in those degrees, nor further than that he would have them apprehend, that as he was a Stranger to this State, so till he understood in all points how those matters stood, he would not promise favour any way, but did protest, that all the Crowns and Kingdoms in this world should not induce him to change any Iote of his Profession, which was the Pasture of his Soul, and earnest of his eternal

Inheritance. He did confess, that in very deed, to keep up the hearts of Catholicks in love and duty to their King, he had imparted the Kings words to many in a better tune, and a higher kind of descant, than his Book of Plainsong did direct; because he knew that others, like slie Barge-men, looked that way, when their stroke was bent another way. For this he craved pardon of the King in humble manner, and for his main Treasons of a higher nature than these Figures of Hypocrisie; and seemed penitent, as well for the horrour of his crime, as for the falshood of his whisperings.

It hindered not the satisfaction which may be given to Percy's shadow (the most desperate Boutefeu in the pack) that as he died impenitent, for any thing we know, so likewise he died silent in the particulars: For first, it is not strange, that such a Traitor should devise so scandalous a slander out of the malice of his heart, intending to destroy the King by any means, and to advance all means that might remove obstructions and impediments to the plot of Gun-powder. The more odious that he could make him to the Party Male-content, and the more sharply that he could set the Party Male-content upon the point and humour of revenge, the stronger was his hope at the giving of the last blow, to be glorifi'd and justifi'd. But touching the truth of the matters, it will be witnessed by many, that this Traitor Percy, after both the first and second return from the King, brought to the Catholicks no spark of comfort, of encouragement, of hope; whereof no stronger proof of argument doth need, than that Fawkes and others were employed both into Spain and other parts, for the reviving of a practise suspended and covered, after Percy's coming back, as in likelihood they should not have been, in case he had returned with a branch of Olive in his mouth, or yielded any ground of comfort to resolve upon.

Therefore I thought it thus far needful to proceed for the clearing of those scandals that were cast abroad by these forlorn Hopes and graceless Instruments. It onely remains, that I pray for your repentance in this world for the satisfaction of many, and forgiveness in the next world for the saving of your self; having had by the Kings favour so long a time to cast up your Accompt, before your appearance at the seat of the great Auditor.

H. Northampton.

Then spake the Earl of Salisbury, especially to that point of his Majesties breaking of promise with Recusants, which was used and urged by Sir Everard Digby, as a motive to draw him to participate in this so hideous a Treason: Wherein his Lordship, after acknowledgment, that Sir Everard Digby was his Ally; And having made a zealous and Religious protestation, concerning the sincerity and truth of that which he would deliver; shortly and clearly defended the honour of the King herein, and freed his Majesty from all imputation and scandal of Irresolution in Religion, and in the constant and perpetual maintaining thereof; as also from having at any time given the least hope, much less promise of Toleration. To which purpose he declared, how his Majesty, as well before his coming to this Crown, as at that very time, and always since, was so far from making of promise, or giving hope of Toleration, that he ever professed he should not endure the very notion thereof from any.

And here his Lordship shewed what was done at Hampton-Court at the time of Watson's Treason, where some of the greater Recusants were convented; and being found then not to have their fingers in Treason, were sent away again with encouragement to persist in their dutiful carriage, and with promise onely of thus much favour, That those mean profits which had occurred since the Kings time to his Majesty for their Recusancy, should be forgiven to the principal Gentlemen, who had both at his Entry shewed so much Loyalty, and had kept themselves so free since from all Conspiracies.

Then did his Lordship also (the rather to shew how little truth Sir Everard Digby's words did carry in any thing which he had spoken) plainly prove, That all his protestations, wherein he denied so constantly to be privy to the Plot of Powder, were utterly false, by the testimony of Fawkes (there present at the Bar) who had confessed, That certain moneths before that Session, the said Fawkes being with Digby at his house in the Countrey, about what time there had fallen much wet; Digby taking Fawkes aside after Supper, told him, That he was much afraid that the Powder in the Cellar was grown dank, and that some new must be provided, lest that should not take fire.

Next, the said Earl did justly and greatly commend the Lord Mounteagle, for his Loyal and honourable care of his Prince and Countrey, in the speedy bringing forth of the Letter sent unto him, wherein he said, That he had shewed both his discretion and fidelity. Which Speech being ended, Digby then acknowledged, That he spake not that of the breach of promise out of his own knowledge, but from their Relation whom he trusted, and namely from Sir Tho. Tresham.

Now were the Jury returned, who having returned their Verdict, whereby they joyntly found those seven Prisoners, Arraigned upon the former Indictment, Guilty, Serjeant Philips craved Judgment against those Seven upon their Conviction; and against Sir Everard Digby upon his own Confession.

Then the Lord Chief Justice of England, after a grave and prudent Relation and Defence of the Laws made by Queen Elizabeth against Recusants, Priests, and Receivers of Priests, together with the several occasions, progresses, and reasons of the same; and having plainly demonstrated and proved, that they were all necessary, mild, equal, moderate, and to be justified to all the world, pronounced Judgment.

Upon the rising of the Court, Sir Everard Digby bowing himself towards the Lords, said, If I may but hear any of your Lordships say, you forgive me, I shall go more chearfully to the Gallows. Whereunto the Lords said, God forgive you, and we do.

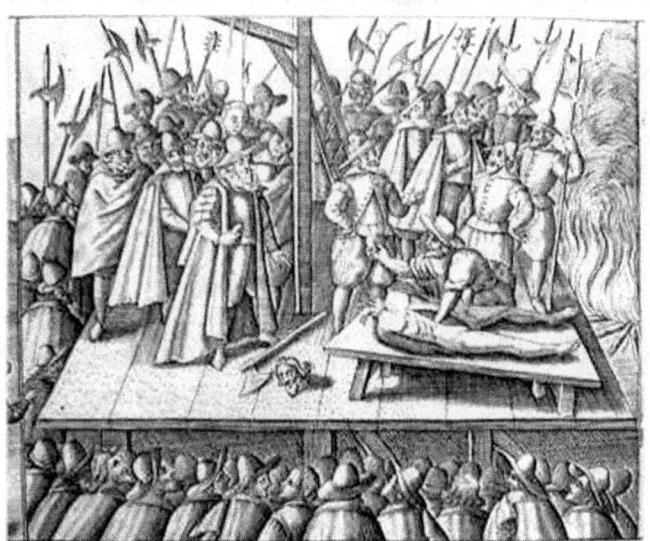

Franz Hogenberg, 1605, Executon of the Conspirators

And so according to the Sentence, on Thursday following, execution was done upon Sir Everard Digby, Robert Winter, Iohn Graunt, and Thomas Bates, at the West end of Pauls Church; and on the Friday following, upon Thomas Winter, Ambrose Rookwood, Robert Keyes, and G[...]y Fawkes, within the old Palace-yard at Westminster not far from the Parliament-house.

THE ARRAIGNMENT OF HENRY GARNET, Superiour of the Iesuits in England, on Friday the 28th day of March, 1606. at Guild-hall in the City of London, before the Lords Commissioners there present.

Sir Leonard Holiday, Lord Mayor.

The Earl of Nottingham.

The Earl of Suffolk.

The Earl of Worcester.

The Earl of Northampton.

The Earl of Salisbury.

The Lord Chief Justice of England.

The Lord Chief Baron of the Exchequer.

Sir Christopher Yelverton, Knight, one of His Majesties Justices of the Kings Bench.

The Substance and Effect of the Indictment of Henry Garnet Superior of the Jesuits in England, appeareth before in the Relation of the former Arraignment, and therefore unnecessary to be repeated again; which Indictment was summarily and effectually repeated by Sir Iohn Croke Knight, his Majesties Serjant at Law, in this manner.

THis Person and Prisoner here at the Bar, this place, and this present occasion and Action, do prove that true, which the Author of all Truth hath told us, That, Nihil est occultum quod non manifestabitur, & nihil est secretum, quod non revelabitur & in in palam veniet, There is nothing hid that shall not be made manifest, there is nothing secret that shall not be revealed and come in publick; and that God by whom Kings do raign, *Consilium pravorum dissipat*, doth scatter and bring to nought the counsel of the wicked.

That he spake with fear and trembling, and with horror and amazedness, against that rotten root of that hideous and hateful tree of Treason, and of that detestable, and unheard of wickedness, he did crave pardon for it; affirming that no flesh could mention without astonishment.

He shewed that Henry Garnet of the profession of the Iesuits, otherwise Walley, otherwise Darcy, otherwise Roberts, otherwise Farmer, otherwise Philips (for by all those names he called himself) stood indicted of the most barbarous and damnable Treasons, the like whereof were never heard of, that he was a man *Multorum Nominum*, but not *boni Nominis*, of many names, as appeared by the Indictment, but of no good Name; adorned by God and nature with many gifts and graces, if the Grace of God had been joyned with them; But that wanting, *quanto ornatior in other gifts, tanto nequior*.

That this Garnet (his Majesty summoning his Parliament to be holden at Westminister, the 19th of March, in the first year of his Reign, and by divers Prorogations continuing it till the third of October last,) together with Catesby, lately slain in open Rebellion, and with Oswald Tesmond a Iesuit, otherwise Oswald Greenwell, as a false Traitor against the most mighty, and most renowned King our Soveraign Lord King King James, the 9th of June last, traiterously did conspire and compass,

To depose the King, and to deprive him of his Government.

To destroy and kill the King, and the noble Prince Henry his eldest Son: Such a King, and such a Prince, Such a Son of Such a Father, whose vertues are rather with amazed silence to be wondred at, than able by any speech to be expressed.

To stir sedition and slaughter throughout the Kingdom.

To subvert the true Religion of God, and whole Government of the Kingdom.

To overthrow the whole State of the Common wealth.

The manner how to perform these horrible treasons, the Serjeant said *Horreo dicere*, his lips did tremble to speak it, but his heart praised God for his mighty deliverance. The practise so inhumane, so barbarous, so damnable, so detestable, as the like was never read nor heard of, or ever entred into the heart of the most wicked man to imagine. And here he said, he could not but mention that religious observation so religiously observed by his Religious Majesty, wishing it were ingraven in letters of gold in the hearts of all his people, The more hellish the Imagination, the more Divine the Preservation.

This Garnet, together with Catesby and Tesmond, had speech and conference together of these treasons, and concluded most traiterously, and devilishly.

That Catesby, Winter, Fawkes, with many other Traitors lately attainted of high treason, would blow up with Gun-powder in the Parliament house, the King, the Prince, the Lords Spiritual and Temporal, the Iudges of the Realm, the Knights, Citizens and Burgesses, and many other subjects and servants of the King assembled in Parliament, at one Blow traiterously and devilishly to destroy them all, and piece meal to tear them in sunder, without respect of Majesty, Dignity, Degree, Age or Place.

And for that purpose great quantity of Gun-powder was traiterously and secretly placed, and hid by these Conspirators under the Parliament house.

This being the substance and the effect of the Indictment, Garnet did plead Not guilty to it: and a very discreet and substantial Iury, with allowance of challenges unto the prisoner, were sworn at the Bar for the trial of him.

To whom the Serjeant shewed that they should have evidences to prove him guilty, that should be Luce clariores, that every man might read them running.

They should have Testimonia Rerum, and Loquentia signa, Witnesses and Testimonies of the things themselves.

Reum confitentem, or rather, Reos confitentes & accusantes invicem.

That every one may say unto him, Serve nequam, thou wicked subject, thou wicked servant, Ex ore tuo te judico, Of thine own mouth I judge thee, of thine own mouth I condemn thee.

And this shall be made so manifest by him that best can do it, as shall stop the mouth of all contradiction.

The effect of that which Sir Edward Coke, Knight, His Majesties Attorney General, said at the Arraignment of Henry Garnet, Superiour of the Iesuits in England, as near to his own words as the same could be taken.

Your Lordships may perceive by the parts of the Indictment, which have been succinctly opened, that this is but a latter Act of that heavy and woful Tragedy, which is commonly called the Powder-treason, wherein some have already played their parts, and, according to their demerits, suffered condign punishment and pains of death. We are now to proceed against this Prisoner for the same Treason; in which respect, the necessary repetition of some things before spoken, shall at the least seem tolerable: for that Nunquam nimis dicitur, quod nunquam satis dicitur, It is never said too often, that can never be said enough: Nay, it may be thought justifiable to repeat in this case, for that in respect of the confluence and access of people, at the former Arraignment, many could not hear at that time. And yet because I fear it would be tedious, for that most of all my Lords Commissioners, and of this Honourable and Great Assembly, were present at the Arraignment, and for that I am now to deal with a man of another quality, I will onely touch, and that very little, of the former Discourse or Evidence, and that little also shall be mingled with such new matter as shall be worth the hearing, as being indeed of weight and moment; and all this with very great brevity.

But before I further proceed to the opening of this so great a Cause, I hold it fit and necessary to give satisfaction to two divers and adverse sorts of men, who according to the divers affections of their hearts, have divined and conjectured diversly of the cause of the procrastination and delay of proceeding, especially against this person, the matter wherewith he stands charged being so transcendant and exorbitant as it is. The first sort of these, out of their hearty love and loyalty to their Natural Liege Lord and King, and to their dear Countrey, and this State, have feared the issue of this delay, lest that others might be animated by such protraction of Judgment, to perpetrate the like: For they say, (and it is most true) Quia non profertur citò contra malos sententia, absque timore ullo filii hominum perpetrant mala: Because speedy Justice is not executed against wicked men, the people without all fear commit wickedness. And pity it were that these good men should not be satisfied. The other sort are of those, who in respect no greater expedition hath been used against this Prisoner at the Bar, fall to excusing of him, as gathering these presumptions and conjectures: First, that if he, or any of the Iesuits, had indeed been justly to be touched with this most damnable and damned Treason, surely they should have been brought forth and tried before this time. Secondly, that there was a Bill exhibited in Parliament concerning this Treason, and this Traitor, but that it was deferred, and proceeded not for want of just and sufficient proofs. Nay, thirdly, there was a particular Apology spread abroad for this man, and another general for all Iesuits and Priests, together with this imputation, That King-killing, and Queen-killing was not indeed a Doctrine of theirs, but onely a Fiction and Policy of our State, thereby to make the Popish Religion to be despised, and in disgrace. Now for these men, pity it were, that the eye of their understanding should not be enlightned and cleared, that so being by demonstrative and luculent proofs convinced, they may be to their Prince and Countrey truly converted. First therefore concerning the delay, (though it be true, Quod flagellatur in corde, qui laudatur in ore) yet must I remember the great pains of my Lords the Commissioners of his Majesties Privy Council, in this cause for Garnet, being first examined upon the 13th. of the last moneth, hath sithence been again examined and interrogated above twenty several times, which lasted unto the 26th. of March, within two days of this Arraignment. Touching the Bill in Parliament, it was indeed exhibited before Garnet was apprehended: but his Majesties gracious pleasure was, That albeit this Treason be without all president and example, yet they should quietly and equally be Indicted, Arraigned, publickly heard, and proceeded withall in a moderate, ordinary, and just course of Law. Concerning their Apologies, and the Fictions of State (as they term them) answer shall be made, by Gods grace, in the proper place, when I come to lay open the plots and practises of the Jesuits, to the satisfaction of all this Honourable and Great Assembly. But first I have an humble Petition to present to your Lordships, and the rest of this grave Auditory, for my self, in respect that I am necessarily to name great Princes; yet with protestation and caution, that no blot is intended to be laid upon any of them. I know there is Lex in sermone tenenda, a Law and Rule to be observ'd in speaking, especially in this kind; and that Kings and great Princes, and the mighty Men of this earth, are to be reverently and respectfully dealt withall. And therefore I humbly recommend unto you these Considerations, concerning this point of mentioning these Forein States. First, That the Kingdoms were at those times in open enmity and hostility, and that might be honourable at one time which was not so at another; so that hostile actions were then justifiable and honourable, as being in times of Hostility and War. Secondly, in these things, it is not the Kings Attorney that speaks, but Garnet the Iesuit: as also, that it proceedeth from an inevitable necessity, for that the Examinations as well of this, as of the rest of the Traitors, cannot otherwise be opened and urged against them: so is the mention of great men by the impudency of these wicked Traitors, woven into their Confessions, as they cannot be severed.

And with this comfort I conclude the Preface, That I hope in God, this days work, in the judgment of so many as shall be attentive and well disposed, shall tend to the glory of Almighty God, the honour of our Religion, the safety of his most Excellent Majesty and his Royal Issue, and the security of the whole Common-wealth.

For Memory and Method, all that I shall speak may be contracted to two general Heads: First, I will consider the Offences, together with certain Circumstances,

Precedent before the offence.

Concurrent with the offence.

Subsequent after the offence.

Secondly, I will lay down some observations concerning the same.

For the proper name of this offence, because I must speak of several Treasons, for distinction and separation of this from the other, I will name it the Jesuits Treason, as belonging to them, both ex congruo & condigno, They were the Proprietaries, Plotters, and Procurers of it; and in such crimes, plus peccat Author quàm Actor, the Author or Procurer offendeth more, than the Actor or Executor, as may appear by Gods own judgment given against the first sin in Paradise, where the Serpent had three punishments inflicted upon him, as the Original Plotter; the Woman two, being as the immediate Procurer; and Adam but one, as the Party seduced.

Circumstances precedent and subsequent, so termed here, are indeed in their proper natures all high Treasons, but yet in respect of the magnitude, nay, monstrousness of this Treason, may comparatively, without any discountenance to them in this case, be used as Circumstances.

And because I am to deal with the Superior of the Jesuits, I will onely touch such Treasons, as have been plotted and wrought by the Jesuits, of whom this man was Superiour, and those Treasons also sithens this Garnet his coming into England, whereof he may truly say, Et quorum pars magna fui.

The coming of this Garnet into England, (which very act was a Treason) was about twenty years past, viz. in Iuly, 1586. in the 28th. year of the Reign of the late Queen of famous and blessed memory; whereas the year before, namely the 27th. year of Eliz. there was a Statute made, whereby it was Treason for any, who was made a Romish Priest by any Authority from the Sea of Rome, sithens the first year of her Reign, to come into her Dominions. Which Statute the Romanists calumniate as a bloody, cruel, unjust, and a new upstart Law; and abuse that place of our Saviour, O Ierusalem, Ierusalem, thou that killest the Prophets, and stonest them that are sent unto thee, &c. to that purpose. But indeed it is both mild, merciful, and just, and grounded upon the ancient fundamental Laws of England. For (as hath already in the former Arraignments been touched) before the Bull of Impious Pius Quintus, in the 11th. year of the Queen, wherein her Majesty was Excommunicated and Deposed, and all they accursed who should yield any obedience unto her, &c. there were no Recusants in England, all came to Church, (howsoever Popishly inclined, or persuaded in most points) to the same Divine Service we now use: but thereupon presently they refused to assemble in our Churches, or joyn with us in publick Service, not for conscience of any thing there done, against which they might justly except out of the Word of God, but because the Pope had Excommunicated and Deposed her Majesty, and cursed those who should obey her: and so upon this Bull ensued open Rebellion in the North, and many Garb[...]ils. But see the event: Now most miserable in respect of this Bull was the state of Romish Recusants, for either they must be hanged for Treason, in resisting their lawful Sovereign, or cursed for yielding the due obedience unto her Majesty. And therefore of this Pope it was said by some of his own favourits, that he was Homo pius & doctus, sed nimis credulus, A holy and a learned man, but over credulous; for that he was informed and believed, that the strength of the Catholicks in England was such, as was able to have resisted the Queen. But when the Bull was found to take such an effect, then was there a Dispensation given, both by Pius Quintus himself, and Gregory the 13th. That all Catholicks here might shew their outward obedience to the Queen, ad redimendam vexationem, & ad ostendendam externam obedientiam; but with these cautions and limitations: 1. Rebus sic stantibus, things so standing as they did. 2. Donec publica Bullae executio fieri posset; that is to say, They might grow into strength, until they were able to give the Queen a Mate, that the publick execution of the said Bull might take place. And all this was confessed by Garnet under his own hand, and now again openly confessed at the Bar.

In the 20th. year of Queen Elizabeth, came Campion the Jesuit, and many others of his Profession with him, purposely to make a Party in England for the Catholick cause, to the end that the Bull of Pius Quintus might be put in execution. And though all this while Recusancy being grounded upon such a disloyal Cause, were a very dangerous and disloyal thing; yet was there no Law made in that behalf until the 23d. year of her Majesties Reign. And that also imposing onely a Mulct or Penalty upon it, until conformity were offered and shewed. Anno 26 Eliz. came Parry with a resolution from Cardinal de Como and others, that it was lawful to kill her Majesty, as being Excommunicated and Deposed. Whereupon her Majesty entring into consultation how (together with her safety, and the protection of her Subjects) she might avoid the imminent dangers, and yet draw no blood from these Priests and Jesuits, found out this moderate and mild course, as the best means to prohibit their coming at all into her Land, there never being any King who would endure, or not execute any such persons within their Dominions, as should deny him to be lawful King, or go about to withdraw his Subjects from their Allegiance, or incite them to resist or rebel against him. Nay, the bringing in of a Bull by a Subject of this Realm against another, in the time of Edward the first, was adjudged Treason. But by the way, for that Garnet hath exclaimed, saying, Shew us where was your Church before Luther, design the place, name the persons, and so forth; it is answered, by a comparison of a Wedge of pure Gold, which coming into the hands of Impostors, is, by their sophistications and mixtures, for gain and worldly respects, increased and augmented into a huge body and mass, and retaining still an outward fair shew andtincture of Gold. Where is now the pure Gold, saith one? shew me the place. I answer, In that mass, but for the extracting thereof, and purifying it from dross, that must be done by the Art of the Workman, and the Trial of the Touchstone. So the true Religion and Service of Almighty God, being, for humane respects, and worldly pomp, mixed and over-laden with a number of superstitious Ceremonies and Inventions of man; yet ever had God his true Church holding his truth, which hath been by skilful Workmen, with the Touch-stone of the Word of God, refined and separate from the Dross of mans Inventions.

But to proceed. In the 28th. year of Queen Elizabeth, being the year of our Lord 86. in Iune, came Garnet into England, breaking through the Wall of Treason, being in truth, *Totus compositus ex proditione*. And this was at that time, when the great Armado of Spain, which the Pope blessed and Christened by the name of, The Invincible Navy, was, by the instigation of that high Priest of Rome, preparing and collecting together of many parcels, out of divers parts, where they could be bought, or hired, or borrowed, and therefore may be called, A compounded Navy, having in it 158 great Ships. The Purveyors and Fore-runners of this Navy and Invasion, were the Jesuits, and Garnet among them, being a Traitor even in his very entrance and footing in the Land. But the Queen, with her own Ships, and her own Subjects, did beat this Armado, God himself (whose cause indeed it was) fighting for us against them, by Fire, and Seas, and Winds, and Rocks, and Tempests, scattering all, and destroying most of them. For, *Offenso Creatore, offenditur omnis creatura*, the Creator being offended, every Creature is readily armed to revenge his quarrel; in which respect he is called, The Lord of Hosts. So that of 158, scarce 40 of their Ships returned to the Bar of their own Haven; and it is reported, most of them also perished. Insomuch that in this respect, we may say of Queen Elizabeth, as the Poet writeth of the Christian Emperor,

O nimium dilecta Deo, cui militat aether,

Et conjuratt veniunt ad classica venti.

Observe here, that about the time of this Invasion, there being in Spain met in consultation about that business, the Cardinal of Austria, the Duke of Medina, Count Fuentes, two Irish Bishops, with sundry Military men, and amongst others, Winslade an Englishman; The Irish Bishops perceiving that they expected a Party of Catholicks in England, resolved, that true it was, that it was not possible to do any good here in England, unless there were a Party of Catholicks made before-hand. But such, said they, was the policy of England, as that could never be effected; for if any suspicion or fear arose, the Catholicks should quickly be either shut up, or quite cut off. Oh, saith an old Soldier, there present, Hoc facit pro nobis, that makes for us; for by that means their Souls shall go to Heaven for their Religion, their Bodies to the Earth for their Treason, and their Lands and Goods to us as Conquerors: and this was that indeed they principally aimed at. Note here, that sithence the Jesuits set foot in this Land, there never passed four years without a most pestilent and pernicious Treason, tending to the subversion of the whole State. After that hostile Invasion in 88. the Jesuits fell again to secret and treasonable practises; for then, in the year 92, came Patrick Cullen, who was incited by Sir William Stanley, Hugh Owen, Iaques Fraunces, and Holt the Jesuit, and resolved by the said Holt to kill the Queen; to which purpose he received Absolution, and then the Sacrament at the hands of the said Jesuit, together with this ghostly counsel, That it was both lawful and meritorious to kill her. Nay, said Iaques, that base Landress Son, (who was a continual practiser both with this Cullen and others, to destroy her Majesty) The State of England is, and will be so setled, that unless Mistris Elizabeth be suddenly taken away, all the Devils in Hell will not be able to prevail against it, or shake it.

Now Cullen's Treason was accompanied with a Book called Philopater, written for the abetting and warranting of such a devilish act in general by Creswel the Legier Jesuit in Spain, under the name of Philopater. Anno 94. came Williams and York to the same end, viz. to kill the Queen, being wrought to undertake so vile and detestable a fact by Father H[...]lt the Jesuit, and other his complices; And thereupon the said Willams and York, in the Jesuits Colledge received the Sacrament together of father Holt, and other Iesuits, to execute the same. And that Treason likewise was accompanied with a Book written by the legier Iesuit and Rector at Rome, Parsons, under the name of Doleman, concerning Titles, or rather tittles: a lewd and a lying book, full of falshood, forgery and malediction. Anno 97. came Squire from Spain, to poyson her Majesty, incited, directed, and warranted by Walpole a Iesuit, then residing there: at whose hands likewise, after absolution, he received the Sacrament, as well to put the practise in execution, as to keep it secret. All these Treasons were freely and voluntarily confessed by the parties themselves, under their own hands, and yet remain extant to be seen.

In the year 1601. when practises failed, then was Force again attempted; For then (as in the former Arraignment hath been declared) was Thomas Winter imployed to the King of Spain, together with Tesmond the Jesuit, by this Garnet, who wrote his Letters to Arthur alias Ioseph Creswell, (the only man whom I have heard of to change his Christian name) the legier Jesuit in Spain, for the furtherance of that negotiation, which was, as hath been said, To offer the services of the English Catholicks to the King, and to deal further concerning an Invasion, with promise from the Catholicks here, of forces, both of men and horses, to be in a readiness to joyn with him. This negotiation by the means of Creswel, to whom Garnet wrote, [...]ook such effect, that the two kingdoms standing then in hostlity, the proposition of the English Romish Catholicks was accepted and entertained, an army to Invade (as hath been specified in the former Arraignment) promised, and 100000. Crowns to be distributed amongst Romanists and discontented persons, making of a party in England, and for the furtherance of the said service granted. In the mean time the King earnestly desired, That if the Queen of England should happen to die, he might receive present and certain Advertisemene thereof.

Now this Treason was accompanied with the Popes own writing. For now doth the Holy Father cause to be sent hither to Garnet two Briefs or Buls, one to the Clergy, and another to the Laity: wherein observe the Title, the Matter, the Time. The Title of the one was, Dilectis filijs, Principibus, & Nobilibus Catholicis Anglicanis, Salutem & Apostolicam benedictionem: that is, To our beloved sons the Nobles and Gentlemen of England, which are Catholicks, Greeting, and Apostolical benediction. The title of the other was, Dilectis filijs Archipresbytero, & reliquo Clero Anglicano, &c. To our beloved sons, the Archpriest, and the rest of the Catholik Clergy. The matter was, that after the death of her Majesty, whether by course of Nature or otherwise, whosoever should lay claim or Title to the Crown of England, though never so directly & neerly interested therein, by Descent and Blood Royal, yet unless he were such an one as would not onely tolerate the Catholick (Romish) Religion, but by all his best endeavours and force promote it, and according to the ancient custom, would by a solemn and sacred Oath religiously promise and undertake to perform the same, they should admit or receive none to be King of England· His words are these, Quantumcunque propinquitate sanguinis niterentur, nisi ejusmodi essent, qui fidem Catholicam non modò tolerarent, sed omni ope ac studio promoverent, & more Majorum Iurejurando se id praestituros susciperent, &c.

As for King Iames (at whom the Pope aimed) he hath indeed both Propinquitatem, and Antiquitatem Regalis sanguinis, Propinquity and Antiquity of blood Royal, for his just Claim and Title to this Crown both before and since the Conquest. To insist upon the declaration and deduction of this point, and pass along through the Series and course of so many Ages and Centuries, as it would be over long for this place, so further I might herein seem as it were to guild gold: Onely in a word, His Majesty is lineally descended from Margaret the Saint, daughter of Edward son of King Edmund Grandchild of Great Edgar the Britain Monarch: which Margaret, sole Heir of the English Saxon King, was maried to Malcolme King of Scotland, who by her had issue David the Holy their King, from whom that Race Royal at this day is deduced, and Maud the Good, wife of the first and learned Henry King of England, from whom his Majesty directly and lineally proceedeth, and of whom a Poet of that time wrote.

Nec decor effecit fragilem, non sceptra superbam,

Sola potens humilis, sola pudica decens.

And lastly his Majesty cometh of Margaret also the eldest daughter of Henry the 7th. who was descended of that famous Union of those two fair Roses, the White and the Red, York and Lancaster, the effecting of which union cost the effusion of much English blood, over and besides four-score or thereabouts of the Blood-Royal. But a more famous Union is, by the goodness of the Almighty, perfected in his Majesties person, of divers Lions, two Famous, Ancient, and Renowned Kingdoms, not onely without bloud, or any opposition, but with such an universal acclamation and applause of all sorts and degrees, (as it were with one voice) as never was seen or read of. And therefore, most Excellent King, for to him I will now speak,

Cum triplici fulvum conjunge Leone Leonem,

Ut varias Atavus junxerat antè Rosas.

Majus opus varios sine pugna unire Leones,

Sanguine quàm varias consociâsse Rosas.

These four Noble and Magnanimous Lions, so firmly and undividually united, are able, without any difficulty or great labour, to subdue and overthrow all the Letters and Bulls (and their Calves also) that have been, or can be sent into England.

Now for the time observe, that these Bulls or Briefs came upon the aforesaid Negociation of Thomas Winter into Spain, at what time an Army should shortly after have been sent to invade the Land: and this was to be put in execution, Quandocunque contingeret miseram illam foeminam ex hac vita excedere. Whensoever it should happen, that that miserable Woman (for so it pleased the High Priest of Rome to call Great Queen Elizabeth) should depart this life. Was Queen Elizabeth miserable? It is said, that Misera constat ex duobus contrarus, scilicet, Copia, & Inopia: Ex copia tribulationis, & inopia consolationis. Was she, I say, miserable, whom Almighty God so often and so miraculously protected, both from the arrow that flieth by day, their great Armado; and from the Pestilence that walketh in the darkness, their secret and treacherous Conspiracies? That did beat her most potent Enemy? That set up a King in his Kingdom? That defended Nations, and harboured and protected distressed People? That protected her Subjects in peace and plenty, and had the hearts of the most and the best of her Subjects? That Reigned Religiously and Gloriously, and died Christianly and in peace? Oh blessed Queen, our late dear Sovereign, Semper honos nomenque tuum laudesque manebunt. But Queen Elizabeth of famous memory, (for memoria ejus semper erit in benedictione) as a bright Morning-Star, in the fulness of time, lost her natural light, when the great and glorious Sun appeared in our Horizon. And now sithence the coming of great King Iames, there have not passed, I will not say four years, but not four, nay, not two months, without some Treason. First, in March 1603. upon the death of her Majesty, and before they had seen his Majesties face, was Christopher Wright employed into Spain by Garnet, Catesby, and Tresham, to give advertisement of the Queens death, and to continue the former Negotiation of Thomas Winter. And by him also doth this Garnet write to Creswel the Jesuit in commendation, and for assistance and furtherance of his business.

As also in the 22d. of Iune following, was Guy Fawkes sent out of Flanders, by Baldwin the Jesuit, by Sir William Stanley, and Hugh Owen, about the same Treason; and by Letters from Baldwin, directed and commended to Creswel the Legier Jesuit in Spain, for the procuring of his dispatch, as in the former Arraignment hath been declared. In the same Iune doth Garnet the Superiour, together with Gerrard and other Jesuits, and Jesuited Catholicks, labour, not onely in providing of Horses, which, by Thomas Winter and Christopher Wright, upon their several negotiations they, in the names of all the Catholicks in England, had promised the King of Spain to assist and do him service withall, at such time as the said King should send Forces to invade, either at Milford-haven, or in Kent, as hath before been shewed: But also did, by force of the said two Bulls or Briefs, disswade the Romish Catholicks from yielding their due obedience to his Majesty, for that he was not of the Roman Religion, contrary to the practise of the true Church and Churchmen, that undergo Wars, Ferendo, non feriendo, with patience, not with strokes, their Weapons being properly Orationes & Lachrymae, Prayers and Tears.

In the same Iune 9. which was 1603. Primo Iacobi, brake out likewise the Treason of the Romish Priests, Watson and Clark; as also that other of Sir Walter Raleigh and others. But the Jesuits seeing that the Peace was now in great forwardness; and having advertisement also, that the King of Spain did now distaste their Propositions, so that there was no further hope left for force, then fell they again to secret practise. As for the Bulls or Briefs before mentioned, when Catesby had informed Garnet, that King Iames was proclaimed, and the State setled; they were by Garnet, as himself hath affirmed, burnt. But to proceed. In March, 1603. Garnet and Catesby (a pestilent Traitor) confer together, and Catesby in general telleth him, (though most falsly) that the

King had broken promise with the Catholicks, and therefore assuredly there would be stirs in England before it were long. In September following meets Catesby and Thomas Piercy, and after an unjust, but a grievous complaint made by Catesby of the Kings proceedings, for that contrary to their expectations, his Majesty both did hold, and was like continually to run the same course which the Queen before had held; Piercy presently breaks forth into this devilish speech, That there was no way but to kill the King, which he the said Piercy would undertake to do. But Catesby, as being Versuto ingenio & profunda perfidia, a cunning, a wily, and a deep Traitor, intending to use this so furious and fiery a Spirit to a further purpose, doth, as it were, stroke him for his great forwardness; yet with sage and stayed counsel tells him, No, Tom, thou shalt not adventure thy self to so small purpose; If thou wilt be a Traitor, there is a Plot to greater advantage, and such a one as can never be discovered, viz. the Powder-Treason.

In Ianuary, in the first year of his Majesty, Garnet took out a General Pardon under the Great Seal of England, of all Treasons, which Pardon, his Majesty, of his Grace, granted to all men at his first entrance into his Kingdom, under the name of Henry Garnet of London, Gent. but therein he never used any of his alias dictus Walley, Farmer, or any other of his feigned names. But Catesby fearing lest any of those whom he had or should take into Confederacy, being touched in Conscience with the horrour of so damnable a fact, might give it over, and endanger the discovery of the Plot, seeks to Garnet (as being the Sup[...]riour of the Jesuits, and therefore of high estimation and authority amongst all those of the Romish Religion) to have his judgment and resolution in Conscience, concerning the lawfulness of the fact, that thereby he might be able to give satisfaction to any who should in that behalf make doubt or scruple to go forward in that Treason. And therefore Catesby coming to Garnet, propoundeth unto him the Case, and asketh whether for the good and promotion of the Catholick cause against Hereticks (the necessity of time and occasion so requiring) it be lawful or not, amongst many Nocents, to destroy and take away some Innocents also. To this question Garnet advisedly and resolvedly answered, That if the advantage were greater to the Catholick part by taking away some Innocents together with many Nocents, then doubtless it should be lawful to kill and destroy them all: And to this purpose he alledged a comparison of a Town or City which was possessed by an Enemy, If at the time of taking thereof there happen to be some few friends within the place, they must undergo the fortune of the Wars in the general and common destruction of the Enemy. And this resolution of Garnet the Superior of the Jesuits, was the strongest, and the onely bond, whereby Catesby afterwards kept and retained all the Traitors in that so abominable and detestable a Confederacy. For in March following, Catesby, Thomas Winter, and others, resolve upon the Powder-plot, and Fawkes, as being a man unknown, and withall a desperate person, and a Soldier, was resolved upon, as fit for the executing thereof; to which purpose he was, in April following, by Thomas Winter sought and fetched out of Flanders into England. In May, in the second year of his Majesty, Catesby, Percy, Iohn Wright, Thomas

Winter, and Fawkes meet, and having upon the holy Evangelists taken an Oath of secresie and constancy to this effect;

You shall swear by the blessed Trinity, and by the Sacrament you now purpose to receive, never to disclose, directly or indirectly, by word or circumstance, the matter that shall be proposed to you to keep secret, nor desist from the execution thereof, until the rest shall give you leave.

They all were Confessed, had Absolution, and received thereupon the Sacrament, by the hands of Gerrard the Jesuit then present.

In Iune following Catesby and Greenwel the Jesuit confer about the Powder-treason. And at Midsummer Catesby having speach with Garnet of the Powder-treason; they said that it was so secret, as that it must prevail, before it could be discovered. Then Garnet seemed to desire that the Popes consent might be obtained; But Catesby answered, that he took that as granted by the Pope in the two Buls or Briefs before; For that said he, if it were lawfull not to receive, or to repell him, as the said Buls or Briefs did import, then it is lawfull also to expell or cast him out. Upon the 7th. of Iuly 1604, was the Parliament Prorogued untill the 7th. of February; and in November following, Thomas Bates, being (as hath been declared more at large in the former Arraignment) fetched in by Catesby his master, to participate in the Powder-treason, for better assurance of his secrecy, and prosecution thereof, is by Greenwel the Jesuit confessed, encouraged and told, that being for a good cause, he might and ought not onely conceal it, as committed unto him in secret by his master, but further said, that it was no offence at all, but justifiable and good. About this time was Robert Keyes taken into the Confederacy, and by Catesby resolved of the lawfulness thereof from the Jesuits.

In the 11th. of December they entred the Mine: and in March following, which was in 1605, was Guy Fawks sent over to Sir William Stanley with letterts from Garnet, ro Baldwine the Legier Jesuit there, to take order that against the time of the Blow, the forces might be brought near to the Sea side, to the end that they might suddenly be transported into England. And there doth Fawkes by consent of the confederates, give Owen the Oath of secrecy and perseverance, and then acquaints him with the whole Treason: Who having been a most malicious and inveterate Traitor, greatly applauded it, and gave his consent and counsel for the furtherance thereof. In May 1605, fell out certain Broils in Wales by the Romish Catholiques, at what time also Rookewood was by Catesby acquainted with the Powder-treason, and resolved of the lawfulness of the fact by him as from the Jesuits. Now doth Garnet write to the Pope, that commandment might come from his Holiness, or els from Aquaviva the General of the Jesuits, for the staying of all commotions of the Catholiques here in England, intending indeed to set their whole rest of the Catholique Romish cause, upon the Powder-plot, and in the mean time to lull us asleep in security, in respect of their dissembled quitness and conformity, as also least impediment might be offered to this main

Plot by reason of any suspicion of the stirring of Papists, or of inquiry after them upon occasion of any petty commotions or broils. But when he further desired, that it might be so enjoyned upon censures, that latter request was not granted, least it might indeed be an impediment to the Powder-plot.

In Iune following doth Greenwel the Jesuit consult with Garnet his Superior, of the whole course of the Powder-treason at large. Wherein observe the politique and subtil dealing of this Garnet. First he would not (as he saith) confer of it with a lay man (other than Catesby whom he so much trusted) why so? because that might derogate from the reverence of his Place, That a Jesuit, and a Superior of them, should openly joyn with Laymen in cause of so much bloud; And therefore secondly, as he would consult of it with a Priest, and a Jesuit, one of his own order and his subject; so for his further security, he would consult thereof with Greenwel the Jesuit, as in a disguised confession. And being informed, that the discourse would be too long to repeat kneeling, he answered that he would consult with him of it in confession walking; and so accordingly in an ambulatory confession, he at large discoursed with him of the whole Plot of the Powder-treason; And that a Protector (after the Blow given) should be chosen out of such of the Nobility as should be warned and reserved.

In this Moneth likewise was there a great conference and consultation betwixt Garnet; Catesby, and Francis Tresham, concerning the strength of the Catholicks in England, to the end that Garnet might by Letters send direct Advertisement thereof to the Pope; for that his Holiness would not be brought to shew his inclination concerning any Commotion or rising of the Catholick part, until such time as he should be certainly informed that they had sufficient and able Force to prevail.

And in August following, Garnet, in a conference had about acquainting of the Pope with the Powder-treason, named and appointed Sir Edmund Baynam for to carry [...]at message to the Pope, yet not to him as Pope, but to him [...] a temporal Prince, and by him doth Garnet write Letters in that behalf; as also for staying of Commotions, under pain of Censures, well knowing that before his Letters could be answered, the House of Parliament (according to their designs) should have been blown up, and the whole State overthrown. But this trick he used like a thief, that going to steal and take Partriches with a setting dog, doth rate his dog for questing or going too near, until he have laid his net over them, for fear the game should be sprung, and the purpose defeated.

In this Moneth also doth Garnet write to Baldwine the Legier Jesuit in the Low-Countreys, in the behalf of Catesby, that Owen should move the Marquess for a Regiment of horses for him the said Catesby, not with any intent, as it was agreed, that Catesby should undertake any such charge, but that under colour of it, horses and other necessaries might be provided without suspition to furnish the Traitors.

In September following doth Parsons the Jesuit write to Garnet, to know the particulars of the Project in hand, for the journey to Saint Winifrides Well in this

Moneth. It was but a Jergon, to have better opportunity by colour thereof, to confer and retire themselves to those parts.

In October doth Garnet meet the other Traytors at Coughton in Warwickshire, which was the place of Rendevouz, whither they resorted out of all Countreys.

Upon the [...]st of November, Garnet openly prayeth for the good success of the great Action, concerning the Catholick cause in the beginning of the Parliament; and prayer is more then consent. For, Nemo orat sed qui sperat & credit. He in the prayer used two verses of a Hymn, Gentem auferte perfidam credentium de finibus, ut Christo laudes debitas persolvamus alacriter.

Now was the Letter with the Lord Mountegle, whose memory shall be blessed, on the fourth of November, by the providence of the Almighty, not many hours before the Treason should have been executed, was it fully discovered.

On the 5th of November, being the time when the Traitors expected that their devilish practise should have taken effect, they convented at Dunchurch under colour of a great hunting match, appointed by Sir Everard Digby, as being a man of quality and accompt thereabout, purposing by this means to furnish themselves with company for their intended Insurrection and Rebellion; for that men being gathered together, and a tumult suddenly raised, the Traitors thought, that every or most of them would follow the present fortune, and be easily persuaded to take part with them, and that they might easily surprise the person of the Lady Elisabeth, then being in those parts, in the Lord Harringtons house.

Upon the 6th of November, early in the Morning, Catesby and the said Confederates dispatched Thomas Bates with a Letter to Garnet the superior of the Jesuits, who was (as they well knew) then ready at Coulton near unto them, earnestly intreating his help and assistance, for the raising of Wales, and putting so many as he could into open Rebellion. At what time Garnet, and Greenwell (who then of purpose was there with Garnet,) then certainly perceiving that the Plot was indeed discovered, and knowing themselves to be the chiefest Authors thereof, prophesied the overthrow of the whole order of the Jesuits, saying that they feared that the discovery and miscarrying of this practice, would utterly undo and overthrow the whole Society of the Jesuits. But Greenwel the Jesuit being carried with a more violent and firy spirit, posteth up and down, to incite such as he could to rise up in open Rebellion. And meeting in Master Abingtons house with Hall another Jesuit, adviseth him the said Hall likewise to loose no time, but forthwith to seek to raise and stir up so many as he could. But Hall seeming to deliberate thereof, whether seeing no end of so rash an attempt, or fearing by that means to be himself apprehended, Tesmond told him that he was a Flegmatic[...] fellow, and said, A man may herein see the difference betwixt a Flegmatick man (such as he meant Hall was) and a Cholerick, as he said himself was; and further added, that he was resolved to do his best endevors for the raising of a Rebellion, under this false pretext and colour, That it was concluded that the throats of all the Catholicks in England should be cut. So persuading himself to incite them to take Arms for to stand upon their Guard and Defence; and with this device he posted away into the County of Lancaster: afterwards Hall the Jesuit, othertherwise called Oldcorn, being urged by Humphrey Littleton with the evil success of their intended Treason, that surely God was displeased and offended with such bloody and barbarous courses, in stead of an humble acknowledgment of the Justice of God, and a sense of the wickedness of the Treason, fell rather Satanically to argue for the justification of the same, and said, Ye must not judge the cause by the event: for the eleven Tribes of Israel were by God himself commanded to go and fight against Benjamin, yet were they twice overthrown. So Lewes of France fighting against the Turk, his Army was scattered, and himself died of the Plague. And lastly, the Christians defending the Rhodes, were by the Turks overcome. And these he applyed to the Powder-treason, and persuaded Littleton not to judge it ungodly or unlawful by the event.

Observe here a double consequent of this Powder-treason: 1. Open Rebellion, as hath been shewed both immediately before, and more at large in the former Arraignment: and since that blasphemy in Garnet, the Superior of the Jesuits: for he having liberty in the Tower to write, and sending a Letter (which Letter was openly shewed in the Court before him) to an acquaintance of his in the Gatehouse, there was nothing therein to be seen but ordinary matter, and for certain necessaries: but in the Margent, which he made very great and spacious, and underneath where there remained clean paper, he wrote cunningly with the Juice of an Orange, or of a Lemmon, to publish his Innocency, and concerning his usage, and there denieth those things which before he had freely and voluntarily confessed, and said, that for the Spanish Treason, he was freed by his Majesties Pardon, and as for the Powder-treason, he hoped for want of proof against him, to avoid that well enough: but concludeth blasphemously, applying the words which were spoken of our blessed Saviour, to himself in this damnable Treason, and saith, Necesse est ut unus homo moriatur pro populo, It is necessary that one man die for the people; which words Caiphas spake of Christ. Wherein note his Prevarication and Equivocation; for before the Lords Commissioners, he truly and freely confessed his Treasons, being (as himself under his own hand confessed) overwhelmed tanta nube testium, and yet ad faciendum populum, in his Letters which he wrote abroad, he cleareth himself of the Powder-Treason. And thus much concerning the two Circumstances subsequent, which were Rebellion and Blasphemy.

The Circumstances concurring, are concerning the Persons offending and offended. For the principal Person offending here at the Bar, he is, as you have heard, a man of many names, Garnet, Wallye, Darcy, Roberts, Farmer, Phillips: and surely I have not commonly known or observed a true man, that hath had so many false Appellations. He is by Countrey an Englishman, by Birth a Gentleman, by Education a Scholar, afterwards a Corrector of the Common Law Print, with Mr. Tottle the Printer, and now is to be corrected by the Law. He hath many Gifts and Endowments of Nature, by Art Learned, a good Linguist, and by

Profession a Jesuit, and a Superior, as indeed he is Superior to all his Predecessors in devillish Treason; a Doctor of Jesuits, that is, a Doctor of five Dd. as, Dissimulation, Deposing of Princes, Disposing of Kingdoms, Daunting and deterring of Subjects, and Destruction. Their Dissimulation appeareth out of their Doctrine of Equivocation. Concerning which it was thought fit to touch something of that which was more copiously delivered in the former Arraignment, in respect of the presence of Garnet there, who was the Superior of the Jesuits in England, concerning the Treatise of Equivocation, seen and allowed by Garnet, and by Blackwell the Arch Priest, wherein under the pretext of the lawfulness of a mixt proposition to express one part of a mans mind, and retain another, people are indeed taught not only simple lying, but fearful and damnable Blasphemy. And whereas the Jesuits ask why we convict and condemn them not for Heresie; it is for that they will Equivocate, and so cannot that way be tryed or judged according to their words.

Now for the antiquity of Equivocation, it is indeed very old, within little more then 300. years after Christ, used by Arrius the Heretick, who having in a general Counsel been condemned, and then by the commandment of Constantine the Emperor sent into Exile, was by the said Emperor upon instant intercession for him, and promise of his future conformity to the Nicene faith, recalled again: who returning home, & having before craftily set down in writing his Heretical belief, & put it into his bosom, when he came into the presence of the Emperor, and had the Nicene faith propounded unto him, and was thereupon asked, whether he then did indeed, and so constantly would hold that faith; he (clapping his hand upon his bosom where his paper lay) answered and vowed, that he did, and so would constantly profess and hold that Faith (laying his hand on his bosom where the paper of his Heresie lay) meaning fraudulently (by the way of Equivocation) that faith of his own, which he had written and carried in his bosom. For these Jusuits, they indeed make no vow of speaking truth, and yet even this Equivocating, and lying is a kind of unchastity, against which they vow and promise: For as it hath been said of old, Cor linguae faederat naturae sanctio, veluti in quodam certo Connubio: Ergo cum dissonent cor & loquutio, Sermo concipitur in Adulterio, that is, The law and Sanction of Nature, hath (as it were) married the heart and tongue, by joyning and knitting of them together in a certain kind of marriage; and therefore when there is discord between them two, the speech that proceeds from them, is said to be conceived in Adultery; and he that breeds such bastard children, offends against Chastity. But note the heavy and wofull fruit of this Doctrine of Equivocation. Francis Tresham being near his natural death in the Tower, had of charity his wife permitted (for his comfort) to come unto him: who understanding that her husband had before directly and truly accused Garnet of the Spanish Treason, least belike her husband should depart this life, with a conscience that he had revealed any thing concerning the Superior of the Iesuits, a very little before he died, drew him to this, that his own hand being so feeble as that he could not write himself, yet he caused his servant then attending on him, to write that which he did dictate, and therein protested upon his salvation, that he had not seen the said Garnet of 16. years before, and thereupon prayed that his former confession to the contrary might in no wise take place. And that this paper of his Retractation which he had weakly, and dyingly subscribed, might after his death be delivered to the Earl of Salisbury: Whereas Master Garnet himself hath clearly confessed the Spanish Treason, and now acknowledged the same at the Bar; and he and Mistress Vaux and others directly confess and say, that Garnet and Tresham had within two years space been very often together, and also many times before. But Qualis vita, finis ita. And Garnet himself being at the Bar afterwards, urged to say what he thought of such the departure of Francis Tresham out of this life, answered only this, I think he meant to Equivocate. Thus were they stayned with their own works, and went a whoring with their own Inventions, as it is in the Psalm. So that this is indeed Gens perfida, according to the Hymn, a perfidious people, and therefore Jurat? crede minùs, non Jurat? credere noli. Iurat, non Iurat hostis, ab hoste cave.

For their Doctrine of Deposing of Princes, Simanca and Philopater are plain (as hath in the former Arraignment been more amply declared, and was now again at large to Garnets face repeated.) If a Prince be an Heretick, then he is Excommunicated, Cursed, and Deposed, his children deprived of all their Right of Succession, himself not to be restored to his Temporal Estate upon repentance; and by an Heretick they profess that he is intended and meant, namely, whosoever doth not hold the Religion of the Church of Rome. Nay there is an easier and a more expedite way then all these to fetch off the Crown from off the head of any King Christened whatsoever, which is this, That Princeps indulgendo haereticis amittit Regnum, If any Prince shall but tolerate or favour Hereticks, he loseth his Kingdom: Nay whereas Garnet in defence of this usurped power of the high Priest of Rome, alledged, Nos Sanctorum, &c. out of the Decretals, in the very next Title before that, there is another Decree that passeth all we have recited, wherein it is shewed, that Zachary the Pope deposed Childerick of France, for nothing else there specified, Sed quia Inutilis, but onely for that he was reputed unprofitable to Govern.

Now as concerning their daunting and deterring of Subjects, which is a part of the Jesuits profession: It were good that they would know & remember, how that the most Noble & famous Kings of England, never were afraid of Popes Bulls, no not in the very midnight of Popery, as Edward the Confessor, Hen. 1. Edw. 1. Ric. 2. Hen. 5. Hen. 4. &c. And in the time of Henry the seventh, and in all their times, the Popes Legate never passed Callis, but stayed there, and came not to England, untill he had taken a solemn Oath to do nothing to the detriment of the Crown or State.

For the persons offended, they were these: First the King, of whom I have spoken often, but never enough: A King of High and most Noble ancient descent, as hath been briefly declared, and in himself full of all Imperial vertues; Religion, Justice, Clemency, Learning, Wisdom, Memory, Affability, and the rest.

Then the Queen, and she in respect of her happy fruitfulness, is a great blessing, in so much that of her in that respect, may be said that she is, Ortu magna, viro major, sed maxima Prole, Great in Birth, Greater in her Marriage, but to all posterity greatest in the blessed fruit of her Womb, as having brought forth the greatest Prince that ever England had. 3 The Noble Prince, of whom we may say with the Poet, Quae te tam laeta tulere secula? qui tanti talem genuere parentes? Never Prince, true heir Apparent to the Imperial Crown, had such a father, nor ever King had such a son. Then the whole Royal Issue, the Councel, the Nobility, the Clergy, nay our Religion it self, and specially this City of LONDON, that is famous for her Riches, more famous for her People, (having above five hundred thousand souls within her and her Liberties) most famous for her Fidelity, and more then most famous of all the Cities in the world for her true Religion and service of God. Hold up thy head (Noble City) and advance thy self, for that never was thy Brow blotted with the least taint or touch, or suspicion of Disloyalty: Thou mayest truly say with the Prophet David, I will take no wicked thing in hand, I hate the sin of unfaithfulness, there shall no such cleave unto me: Therefore for thy Fidelity thou art honoured with the Title of THE KINGS CHAMBER, as an inward place of his greatest safety: And for thy comfort and joy this day, hath BRITAINS great King honoured thee with the proceeding upon this great and Honourable Commission, after the heavy and dolefull Rumours this other day, when it was certainly known that King IAMES was in safety, well did the fidelity of this City appear, (whereof I was an eye-witness) Vna voce conclamaverunt omnes, Salva Londinum, salva Patria, salva Religio; Iacobus Rex noster salvus: Our City, our Countrey, our Religion is safe, for our King IAMES is in safety.

The observations are many, and only in a word to be touched. The first is, that in the Spanish Treason before mentioned, and this Powder-treason, there was the same order, cause, and end. The order was, first to deal by secret practise and Treason, and then by force and invasion. The cause which they pretend, was the Romish Catholick Religion. The end was the finall destruction of the Royal succession, yea even Occidere regnum, to overthrow and dissolve the whole Kingdom.

2. Note, that even the Enemy hath acknowledged that our State is so setled and established, as neither strength nor Stratagem can prevail, unless there be a party made in England.

3. We shall never have Bull more to come from Rome to England, because they shall never have a party strong enough to incounter with so many Lions.

4. All their Canons, Decrees, and new-found Doctrines tend to one of these two ends: either worldly pride, or wicked policy, for the amplitude and inlargement of the Popes authority, and for the safety of the Jesuits, Priests, &c.

5. Observe that Baynam, a Layman, and one of the Damned crue, and so naming himself, was sent to inform the Pope as a temporal Prince.

6. I conceive their fall to be near at hand, both by Divinity and by Philosophy. For the first, there are now in England about 400. Priests: so many were there in Israel in the days of Achab. Who, saith God, shall go and deceive Achab, that he may fall? a lying spirit in the mouths of his 400. Prophets undertook and effected it; their fall was near, when once a lying Spirit had possessed the Priests, according to the vision of Micheas, as now it hath possessed the Jesuits. 2. The imitation of good for the most part comes short of the pattern: but the imitation of evil ever exceeds the example. Now no imitation can exceed this fact, and therefore their time is at an end.

7. Many condemn it now, that would have commended it, if it had taken effect, for this, say they, is Enumero eorum quae non laudantur nisi peracta.

8. They and their adherents spread abroad false rumors; as that the King should have broken promise with them concerning toleration: which mixture of Gods service rather then he would suffer, he would lose Children, Crown, Life, and all. Nay, they may see there is no such hope left, for that his Majesty bringeth up his Royal Issue in the true Religion and service of the Almighty.

Lastly observe the wonderful providence of God in the admirable discovery of this Superior Jesuit to be party to this Treason, and that in two respects.

First, in respect of the means of secrecy used by him in conference only with Catesby of the Laity.

Secondly, They had a strong and a deep Oath given them both for secrecy and perseverance.

Thirdly, They hereupon received the holy Sacrament.

Fourthly, They were allowed and taught by the Jesuits, to equivocate upon Oath, salvation or otherwise, and how then should it be discovered?

Fiftly, their secret intelligence was such, as that it was unpossible by the wit of man to be found out. And therefore the second thing is, how this Treason, being long sithence plotted, the providence of God did continually from time to time divert and put off the executing thereof, by unexpected putting off the times of assembly in Parliament. For the Parliament begun the 19th of March in the first year of his Majesties Reign, and continued till the 7th of Iuly following, before which time the Conspirators could not be ready; from thence it was proroged untill the 7th of February, against which time, they could not make the Myne ready, in respect that they could not dig there, for that the Commissioners of the Union sare near the place, and the wall was thick, and therefore they could not be provided before the 7th of February; and on the 7th of February the Parliament was proroged untill the 5th of October. After this they found another Course, and altered the place from the Myne to the Cellar. O blessed Change of so wicked a work! Oh but these fatal Engineers are not yet discovered, and yet all things are prepared! Oh prorogue it once more: and accordingly God put it into his Majesties heart (having then not the least suspicion of any such matter) to prorogue the Parliament, and further to open and inlighten his understanding, out of a mystical and dark Letter, like an Angel of God to point to the Cellar, and command that to be searched, so that it was discovered thus miraculously, but even a few hours before the Design should have been executed.

The Conclusion therefore shall be this, Qui cum Iesu itis, non itis cum Iesuitis: for they courage themselves in mischief, and commune among themselves secretly, how they may lay snares, and say, that no man shall see them. But God shall suddenly shoot at them with a swift arrow, that they shall be wounded; In so much that whoso seeth it, shall say, This hath God done; for they shall perceive that it is his work.

Then were repeated the proofs for every of the particular accusations aforesaid, by the express and voluntary confessions of Garnet, and of his Complices themselves, and of two credible witnesses sworn at the Bar, and openly heard viva voce, and acknowledged by Garnet himself to be men without exception.

Then Mr. Garnet having licence of the Court to answer what he could for himself, spake, and divided all which had been objected, to his remembrance, into 4 parts, viz.

Containing matter of

1 Doctrine.

2 Recusants.

3 Iesuits in general.

4 Himself in particular.

In doctrine he remembered two points.

1. Concerning Equivocation, whereunto he answered, that their Church condemned all lying, but especially if it be in cause of Religion and faith, that being the most pernicious lye of all others, and by St. Augustine condemned in the Priscillianists: Nay, to lie in any cause is held a sin, and evil, Howsoever of 8 degrees which St. Augustine maketh, the lowest indeed is to lie for to procure the good of some without hurting of any: So then our Equivocation is not to maintain lying, but to defend the use of certain Propositions. For a man may be asked of one, who hath no Authority to interrogate, or examined concerning something which belongeth not to his cognisance who asketh, As what a man thinketh, &c. So then no man may Equivocate, when he ought to tell the truth, Otherwise he may; And so St. Augustine upon John saith, That Christ denied he knew the day of Iudgment, viz. with purpose to tell it to his Disciples; and so St. Thomas and others, who handle this matter. Chiefly under the Title of Confession. 2. For the second point, which was the Power of the Pope in deposing of Princes, his Answer was three-fold. 1. That therein he onely propounded and followed the general Doctrine of the Church. 2. That this

Doctrine of the Power of the Pope, was by all other Catholick Princes tolerated without grievance. 3. That yet for his own part, he always made a difference in the matter of Excommunicating and Deposing of Princes, betwixt the condition and state of our King, and of others, who having sometimes been Catholicks, did, or shall afterwards fall back. As for Simanca and other Writers, whatsoever they set down of the Deposing of Hereticks, it is to be understood of those Princes, who having sometimes professed the Faith of the Church of Rome, do afterwards make a defection from the same.

2. For Recusant[...], 1. I desire them not to impute any offence or crime of mine, to the prejudice of the cause of Religion. 2. Concerning their not going to Church, whereas it was urged by Mr. Attorney, that the grounds of their not going to Church, was the Excommunication and Bull of Pius Quintus, and that now they may go, for that his Majesty is not denounced Excommunicate; I answer, That it followeth not; for the Arrians and Catholicks had the same Service in their Churches, yet came they not together. And I know divers my self, who before that Bull, refused to go to Church all the time of Queen Elizabeth, though perhaps most Catholicks did indeed go to Church, before it was about the end of the Council of Trent, where this matter was discussed by twelve learned men, and concluded not lawful. And this was occasioned, for that Calvin himself held it not lawful for any Protestant to be present, not onely at our Mass, wherein perhaps they may say there is Idolatry, but not at our Even-song, being the same with theirs.

3. Concerning the Iesuits, he saith, That if any were privy to such horrible Treasons, it was impious, especially in men of their profession: But said, That he talked with some of them about it, and that they denied it.

4. Touching my self, The Negociation into Spain was indeed propounded unto me, and I was also acquainted with the Negociation for Money, but ever intending it should be bestowed for the relief of poor Catholicks: But when they were there, they moved for an Army; which when they afterwards acquainted me withall, I misliked it, and said, It would be much disliked at Rome. Onely I must needs confess, I did conceal it, after the example of Christ, who commands us, when our Brother offends, to reprove him, for if he do amend, we have gained him: Yet I must needs confess, that the Laws made against such concealing are very good and just, for it is not fit the safety of a Prince should depend upon any other mans Conscience. So that I am verily perswaded, if they yielded to me, it had been good. But what their intent and meaning was in desiring an Army, I knew not; and I was charged not to meddle therein, no not with the money which was to be sent for Pensions, though it was to maintain the Title of the King.

The Earl of Salisbury then demanded, To maintain whose Title?

Garnet answered, The Title of the King of Spain.

The Earl of Northampton asked him, Why he did not oppose himself against it, and forbid it, as he might have done? For, Qui cum possit non prohibet, jubet.

Whereupon Garnet answered, That he might not do it; and for sending of Letters, and commending some Persons thereby, he confessed he did it often, as they were commended to him, without knowing either their Purposes, or some of their Persons: for he never knew Mr. Wright for whom he writ.

The Earl of Salisbury then replied to Garnet, I must now remember you, how little any of your Answers can make for your purpose, when you would seek to colour your dealing with Baynham, by professing to write to Rome to procure a countermand of Conspiracies. And yet you know, when he took his journey towards Rome, the blow must needs have been passed before the time he could have arrived to the Popes presence, (such being your zeal and his haste for any such prevention) as it was about the 20th. of our October when he passed by Florence towards Rome.

To which Garnet made no great answer, but let it pass. And then went on with his defence of sending· Letters in commendation of many of those with which he had been formerly charged; and so confessed, that he had written in commend[...]tion of Fawkes, thinking that he went to serve as a Soldier, not knowing then of any other purpose he had in hand. And as for Sir Edmond Baynham, what he or Mr. Catesby intended, he knew not in particular; onely Mr. Catesby asked him in general the question, of the lawfulness to destroy Innocents with Nocents, as having been before objected against him; which at first, I thought, said Garnet, had been an idle question· though afterwards I did verily think, he intended something that was not good. Whereupon having shortly after this received Letters from Rome, to prohibit all Insurrections intended by Catholicks, which might perturb this State· Garnet informed Catesby thereof, and told him That if he proceeded against the Pope's will, h[...] could not prevail. But Catesby refused, an[...] said, He would not take notice of the Pope's pleasure by him. Notwithstanding he shewed to Catesby the general Letter which he had received from Rome; but said, he would infor[...] the Pope, and tell Garnet also in particular what attempt he had in hand, if he would hear it which afterwards he offered to do, but Garnet refused to hear him, and at two several times re-quested him to certifie the Pope what he intende[...] to do.

And when Sir Edmond Baynham (as [...] pretended) was to go over into Flanders for [...] Soldier, Garnet thought good to send him to th[...] Popes Nuncio, and to commend him to othe[...] friends of his, That they should send him to in[...] form the Pope of the distressed estate of the Ca[...] tholicks in England: the rather, that the Po[...] having a Lay-man there, might be acquainte[...] with all their proceedings: And that Baynha[...] might then learn of the Pope, what course [...] would advise the Catholicks in England to take for their own good; but wished Baynham in no case to use Garnet's name to the Nuncio in that behalf.

Then were the two Witnesses called for, both of them Persons of good estimation, that overheard the Interlocution betwixt Garnet and Hall the Iesuit, viz. Mr. Fauset, a man learned, and a Iustice of Peace; and Mr. Lockerson. But Mr. Fauset being not present, was sent for to appear; and in the mean time Mr. Lockerson, who being deposed before Garnet, delivered upon his Oath, that they heard Garnet say to Hall, They will charge me with my Prayer for the good success of the great Action, in the beginning of the Parliament, and with the Verses which I added in the end of my Prayer,

"Gentem auferte perfidam

"Credentium de finibus,

"Ut Christo laudes debitas.

"Persolvamus alacriter.

It is true indeed (said Garnet) that I prayed for the good success of that great Action; but I will tell them, that I meant it in respect of some sharper Laws, which I feared they would then make against Catholicks: And that Answer shall serve well enough.

Here Garnet replied, That for the two Gentlemen that heard the Interlocution, he would not charge them with Perjury, because he knew them to be honest men; yet he thought they did mistake some things, though in the substantial parts he confessed, he could not deny their relation. And for the main Plot, he confessed, that he was therewithall acquainted by Greenwell particularly, and that Greenwell came perplexed unto him to open something, which Mr. Catesby with divers others intended: To whom he said, He was contented to hear by him what it was, so[...] as he would not be a[...]known to Mr. Catesby, or to any other, that he was made privy to it. Whereupon Father Greenwell told him the whole Plot, and all the particulars thereof, with which he protested that he was very much distempered, and could never sleep quietly afterwards, but sometimes prayed to God that it should not take effect.

To that the Earl of Salisbury replied, That he should do well to speak clearly of his devotion in that point; for otherwise he must put him in remembrance, that he had confessed to the Lords, That he had offered Sacrifice to God for stay of that Plot, unless it were for the good of the Catholick Cause; and in no other fashion (said his Lordship) was this State beholding to you for your Masses and Oblations. Adding thus much further, That he wondred why he would not write to his Superiour Aquaviva, as well of this particular Powder-Treason, as to procure prohibition for other smaller matters.

Garnet faintly answered, He might not disclose it to any, because it was matter of secret Confession, and would endanger the life of divers men.

Whereunto the Earl of Northampton replied, That that matter of Confession, which before he refused to confess, because he would save lives, he confessed it now to endanger his own life; and therefore his former Answer was idle and frivolous.

Then Garnet told the Lords, That he commanded Greenwell to disswade Catesby, which he thought he did; and if Catesby had come to him upon Allhallow-day, he thought he could so far have ruled him, as he would have been perswaded to desist.

Then said the Earl of Salisbury, Why did you refuse to hear Catesby tell you all the particulars, when he would have told you, if you had been desirous to prevent it?

Garnet replied, That after Greenwell had told him what it was which Catesby intended, and that he called to mind what Catesby said to him, at his first breaking with him in general terms, his Soul was so troubled with mislike of that particular, as he was loath to hear any more of it.

Well then (said the Earl of Salisbury) you see his heart. And then turning to the Lords Commissioners, he desired leave of them, that he might use some speech concerning the proceeding of the State in this great cause, from the first beginning until that hour; and so began to this effect, That although the Evidence had been so well distributed and opened by Mr. Attorney, as he had never heard such a mass of matter better contracted, nor made more intelligible to the Jury, to whom it was not his part to speak, nor his purpose to meddle with Mr. Garnet in Divinity, or in the Doctrine of Aequivocation, in which latter he saw how he had plaid his Master-prise: yet because he had been particularly used in this service with other of the Lords Commissioners, by whom, nothing was more desired, next the glory of God, than to demonstrate to the world with that sincerity and moderation his Majesties Justice was carried in all points, he would be bold to say somewhat of the manner of this Arraignment, and of the place where it was appointed. For the first, he said, That seeing there was nothing to which this State might more attribute the infinite goodness and blessings of God, than to the protection of the true Religion, which had groaned so long under the bitter persecutions of men of his profession; he confessed, that he held himself greatly honoured to be an Assistant amongst so many great Lords, at the Seat of Justice, where Gods Cause should receive so much honour, by discrediting the person of Garnet, on whom the common Adversary had thought to confer the usurpation of such an eminent Jurisdiction: For otherwise, who did not know, that the quality of poor Henry Garnet might have undergone a more ordinary form of Trial, and happily in some other place of less note and observation? And so his Lordship took an occasion to declare, That the City of London was so dear to the King, and his Majesty so desirous to give it all honour and comfort, as when this opportunity was put into his hands, whereby there might be made so visible an Anatomy of Popish Doctrine, from whence these Treasons have their source and support, he thought he could not chuse a fitter Stage than the City of London, which was not onely rightly termed, The Chamber of his Empire, but was by his Majesty esteemed as his greatest and safest Treasury, who accounteth no Riches comparable to his Subjects Hearts; and acknowledgeth, That such a Circuit did never contain so many faithful Subjects within the Walls: a matter well appearing to his own eyes amongst others, upon the decease of the late Queen of precious memory, when he attending most of the Peers and Privy Counsellors of this Kingdom, who were accompanied with no small number of Noble and Faithful Gentlemen, had seen them all stayed from entry within the Gates of this City, until they had publickly declared with one voice, That they would live and die with the King our Sovereign Lord. To you therefore, Mr. Garnet, (said the Earl of Salisbury) must I address my self, as the man in whom it appeareth best what horrible Treasons have been covered under the Mantle of Religion, which heretofore had been Petty-Treason for a Protestant to have affirmed: such hath been the iniquity of false tongues, who have always sought to prove the Truth a liar: of which impudent calumnies the State is so tender, as you do best know (Mr. Garnet) that since your apprehension even till this day, you have been as Christianly, as courteously, and as carefully used, as ever man could be, of any quality, or any profession: Yea, it may truly be said, that you have been as well attended for health or otherwise, as a Nurse-child. Is it true or no, said the Earl?

It is most true, my Lord (said Garnet) I confess it.

Well then (said the Earl) if your strange Doctrine of Equivocation be observed, and your hardiness of heart to deny all things; let it not be forgotten, that this Interlocution of yours with Hall, over-heard by others, appears to be Digitus Dei; for thereby had the Lords some light and proof of matter against you, which must have been discovered otherwise by violence and coertion, a matter ordinary in other Kingdoms, though now forborn here; but it is better as it is for the Honour of the State, for so were your own words, that you thought it best to tell the truth at last, when you saw you were confounded Tanta nube testium. In which I protest, that I do confidently assure my self, that you would as easily have confessed your self to be Author of all the Action, as the Concealer, but that his Majesty, and my Lords, were well contented to draw all from you without Racking, or any such bitter torments. Then speaking to Garnet, he said, I pray you, Mr. Garnet, what encouraged Catesby that he might proceed, but your resolving him in the first Proposition? What warranted Fawks, but but Catesby's Explication of Garnet's Arguments? as appears infallibly by Winter's Confession, and by Fawkes, that they knew the point had been resolved to Mr. Catesby, by the best Authority.

Then Garnet answered, That Mr. Catesby was to blame to make such application.

To that the Earl replied, That he must needs be bold with him, to drive him from the trust he had, to satisfie the world by his denials, by putting him in mind, how after the Interlocution betwixt him and Hall, when he was called before all the Lords, and was asked, not what he said, but whether Hall and he had conference together, desiring him not to equivocate; how stifly he denied it upon his Soul, reiterating it with so many detestable execrations, as the Earl said, it wounded their hearts to hear him; and yet as soon as Hall had confessed it, he grew ashamed, crying the Lords mercy, and said, he had offended, if Equivocation did not help him.

To this Garnet answered, That when one is asked a question before a Magistrate, he was not bound to answer before some Witnesses he produced against him, Quia nemo tenetur prodere seipsum. Then Garnet falling into some professions of his well-wishing to his Majesty, and being put in mind of the answer he had made concerning the Excommunication of Kings, wherein he referred himself to the Canon of Nos Sanctorum, he answered, That his Majesty was not yet Excommunicated.

Then the Earl of Salisbury bad him deal plainly, for now was the time, Whether in case the Pope, per sententiam Orthodoxam, should Excommunicate the Kings Majesty of Great Britain, his Subjects were bound to continue their obedience?

To this he denied to answer, by which the hearers might see his mind.

From that matter he began to make request, that where he had confessed the receiving of two Brieves or Bulls from the Pope, in the Queens time, by which all Catholicks were forbidden to adhere to any Successor that was not obedient to the Church of Rome; his Majesty would be pleased to make a favourable interpretation, because he had shewed them to very few Catholicks in England, in the Queens time; and when he understood that the Pope had changed his mind, then he burnt the Bulls.

To that it was said, That belike the Pope changed his mind, when the King was so safely possessed of his Estate, and Garnet with his Accomplices began to feel their own impiety; and so, as Catesby said to Percy, did resolve roundly of that Treason, which would speed all at once.

Then Garnet began to use some speeches, that he was not consenting to the Powder-treason.

Whereupon the Earl of Salisbury said, Mr. Garnet, give me but one Argument that you were not consenting to it, that can hold in any indifferent mans ear or sense, besides your bare Negative. But Garnet replied not.

Then Mr. Attorney General spake in Answer of Garnet more particularly to this effect. 1. For Equivocation, it is true indeed, that they do outwardly to the world condemn lying and perjury, because the contrary were too palpable, and would make them odious to all men: But it is open and broad lying and forswearing, not secret and close lying and perjury, or swearing a falshood which is most abominable, and without defence or example. And if they allow it not generally in others, yet at least in themselves, their confederates and associates in treasonable practises, they will both warrant and defend it, especially when it may serve their turn, for such purposes and ends as they look after. 2. Concerning the usurped power of the Pope in deposing of Princes, neither is it the general Doctrine of the Church, as he falsly said, neither allowed or tolerated by all Princes, who are otherwise of their Religion, as may appear out of the French discourse written to the French King against the re-admitting of the Jesuitical Faction. And whereas he would pick a thank, in seeming to spare and exempt King Iames our Sovereign; it is not possible to avoid their distinction of being Excommunicated de jure, if not de facto; howsoever if it be true also, that the Pope doth, de facto, every year once curse all Hereticks. For Recusants not going to Church, the example of the Catholicks not joyning in service and prayer with the Arrians, who denied a main Article of the Christian Creed, doth no ways hold, neither can it agree to us, of whom no such impious blasphemy can be shewed or imagined. That Garnet said, He knew some, who, before the Bull came, went not to Church, it may be true perhaps in some one or two perverted and perverse men like himself: But whereas he produced the Council of Trent, as if there the matter had been determined, and thereupon inferreth, that after that all Romish Catholicks refused to meet with us at Church in time of prayer, it is a gross error; for the last Session of that Council was in the year of our Lord 1563, which was in the fifth year of Queen Elizabeth; whereas I shewed, and am able to justifie and prove, That their Romish English Catholicks came to our Service in our Churches until the nineteenth year of her Majesty, which was many years after that Council was ended.

Concerning Garnet himself: First, for that answer of his, that he knew of the Powder-Treason by Confession; it is true which before was spoken, that such Acts as this is, Non laudantur nisi peracta, are then onely commended when they are performed; but otherwise, first, Greenwel's was no Sacramental Confession, for that the Confitent was not Penitent: nay, himself hath clearly delivered under his hand, That the Powder-Treason was told him, not as a fault, but by way of consultation and advice. 2. It was a future thing to be done, and not already then executed. 3. Greenwel told it not of himself that he should do it, but of Fawkes, Percy, Catesby, Winter, and others; and therefore he ought to have discovered them, for that they were no Confitents. 4. He might and ought to have discovered the mischief, for preservation of the State, though he had concealed the persons. 5. Catesby told it unto him extra confessionem, out of Confession, saying, They might as w[...]ll turn him out, as have kept him out. Lastly, by the Common Law, howsoever it were (it being crimen laesae Majestatis) he ought to have disclosed it. Now for that Garnet denied, that he was a principal Author and Procurer of this Treason, but onely that he had received knowledge thereof; the contrary is clear and manifest, both out of his own Confessions, by himself acknowledged, and apparently proved, in that he resolved Catesby concerning the lawfulness and merit thereof, and that he prayed for the good success of the Powder-Treason, which is more than either consultation or consent. Besides, he must remember him of the old Versicle, Qui non prohibet quod prohibere potest, consentire videtur. Garnet might have commanded Greenwell that told him of the Powder-Treason, to have desisted, but did not: but Greenwell went still on with the Treason, and when it was disclosed, went into the Countrey to move Rebellion, which doubtless he would never have done, if Garnet had forbidden him: therefore he said, he might say with the Orator Tully, *Cui adsunt testimonia rerum, quid opus est verbis?* Moreover Mr. Attorney added, how Garnet writ first for Thomas Winter, then for Kit Wright, after that for Guy Fawkes, then for Sir Edward Bainham, and afterwards for Catesby for a Regiment of Horse; and that Garnet was for the Infanta, and by his Breeves intended to keep out the King, except he should tolerate and swear to maintain the Romish Religion. Then Mr. Attorney spake of the Interlocution betwixt Garnet and Hall, and said, That in all their speeches they never named God, nor confessed their innocency; but as soon as they spake together, Hall spake first, and then Garnet said, He suspected one, whose name, they that were set to over-hear them, could not hear, to have disclosed something against them. But it may be otherwise, for he said he was much subject to that frailty of suspicion. He said, He received a Note from Rookwood, that Greenwell was gone over-Seas; and another, that Gerard was gone to father Parsons, and that Mistress Anne was in Town (meaning Mrs. Anne Vaux) and many other things were by them uttered in that conference.

By this time came in Mr. Forset, who being deposed, affirmed likewise, that their examination, and the matter therein contained were true; saying further, that both of them took notes of that which they heard of Garnet and Hall, as near as possibly they could, and set down nothing in their examinations, but those things, wherein both their notes, and perfect memories agreed and assented, and that many things that were very material; and of great moment, were left out of their examinations, because both their notes and memories did not perfectly agree therein.

And now one of the Letters, which were written with sack, was shewed to the Court, by which appeared that Hall and Garnet had interlocution together. Mr. Atturney here inferred that the necessary end of Justice was, *vt poena ad paucos, metus ad omnes perveniat,* and urged the examination of Garnet, wherein he confessed that when Tesmond alias Greenwell, made relation to him of the great blow by the Powder-treason, who should have the protection, Greenwell said, the Lords that should be left alive should choose a Protector. And further Mr. Atturney urged the writing of another Letter written with sack to Sayer, alias Rockwood, a Priest in the Gate-house; But of this point much is formerly mentioned.

Here Mr. Attorney ending, my Lord of Northampt. spake to the Prisoner this speech following.

Though no man alive can be less apt or willing than my self, to add the least grain or scurple of improvement to the weight of any mans calamity, that groans under the heavy burthen of a distressed state, *Vel gravatis addere gravamina,* whereof I have as many witnesses as the world hath eyes: yet as the case stands now in this trial, Mr. Garnet, between my dear Soveraign, *ex cuius spiritu,* as one of Alexander said, nos omnes spiritum ducimus, and you that were so well content to let the course of conspiracy run forward to the stopping of this breath before the time, which God by nature doth prescribe between his honour, and your error, his just proceedings and your painted shews, his sincerity and your hypocricy; I could wish it possible that in a person of some other quality, you might hear the Ecchoes of your unperfect and weak answers, and thereupon judge more indifferently and evenly of the true state of your cause than you have done hitherto, being distracted with fear, or forestalled by prejudice, or, to borrow your own phrase, which is more proper to the point than any I can use, oppressed tanta nube testium, with so thick a cloud of witnesses, as concur with one voice, heart and spirit, for the conviction of your audacity.

I confess that never any man in your state gave less hold or advantage to examiners, than you have done in the whole course of proceeding, to us that were in Commission: sometime by forswearing, as upon the confession of Hall your fellow: sometime by dissembling, as about the places of your Rendezvous, which was the lapwings neast: sometimes by earnest expostulation: sometime by artificial Equivocation: sometime by Sophisticating true substances: sometime by adding false qualities: yet sat superest, as may appear, to the defeat of your inventions, and the defence of the Kings Majesty, quia magna est veritas, & praevalet.

Your parts by nature simply considered, and in another person, would rather move compassion, than exasperate humanity: for whom would not the ruine of such a person touch, as is in apparance temperate, and in understanding ripe? But our end at this time is the same with Decius in Livie, ut quem vos obrutum reliquistis, ignem &c. that we may quench that fire by prevention, which you have only raked up in ashes, ut novum daret incendium, that it might cause a new combustion so soon as it might hit upon matter that were fit and sutable. Wherefore I must rather draw your answers to the true touch for discharge of rumors, than verberare aërem, beat the air: For the substance of all your evasions and slie shifts, is as the Inn-keepers of Chalcis confessed of his dishes to his guests, admiring tantam fer[...]ulorum diversitatem, that they were only compounded of pork, howsoever your fine cookery may vary them.

The two Buls that in the late Queens time entred the land (with a purpose by their lowd lowing to call all their calves together, for the making of a strong party, at the shutting up of the evening against our dead Soveraign) were grased in your pastures, Mr. Garnet, or to speak more properly (because they durst neither endure the light, nor admit the air) they were staul-fed at your crib, as your self confess, and therefore, Serve nequam, ex ore tuo te judico. And what answer make you to this? mary that the purpose was imparted to very few: so much the worse: For out of publication grows discovery; and yet experience hath justified, that those very few were the very souls and spirits of that pack of Conspirators, and such as for want of patience and temperance to tary the time, when the game had been brought to bearing, should have played the chiefest parts in the late smoaking Tragedy. You say the Buls were after sacrificed in the fire by your self. But not before the Kings good Angel had cut their throats, and the best part of their proof were past, and your hopes dead of that good which in likelihood they should have brought with them. For to what use could these dumb beasts serve in seeking to prevent that lawful and undoubted right, which heaven had now proclaimed, and earth acknowledged? But let the proof be what it will, I look into the root. I wonder Mr. Garnet, what Apostle warrants you in undertaking wicked Plots, in hope that good may follow; neglecting what all Laws (and the Laws of England above all) what all States and Nations conclude of men, that slily practise, and combine for anticipation of the future rights of lawfull Successors.

In excuse of Letters written with your own hand by Thomas Winter to father Creswell, when he was employed about the procurement of an Army to Invade, with supplies of Treasure proportionable for the quicker execution of so desperat an Enterprise, you answer, that the Persons were commended in your Letters, not the Plot: spectatum admissi risum teneatis amici? as though the minister had any other errand or instruction, than the main Plot it self: as though you, Mr. Garnet; being then Magister in Israel, and Rector chori, could or would be ignorant of their prefixed end; as though so grave a Person as your self, were likely to set his hand to Blancks like a baby, and to leave the rest to the disposition of a man wholly transported with fiery humors: Or as though in this very point other mens confession in particular, beside your own in generality, had not left us marks and traces evident and plain enough to descry doubleness with diversity. You confess privity to a practice, but not for an Army: foreknowledge of a course for getting Treasure, but with a purpose, as you conceived, to employ it wholly for the relief of Catholicks. So as the reason of the reservedness of Catesby, Winter and the rest toward you, must be undoubtedly their suspicion of your over great affection and duty to the Queen; For otherwise it is certain they would have trusted you as well with their intention, as with their means: with their hopes, as with their instruments: especially considering how hard it was for them to compass their own vast desires, without help both of your credit, and of your industry.

Wright was in like manner, and with like expedition commended by you afterward for the quickening of Winters project, if any life were in it, upon the slacking of the passions of Spain, with the propositions of peace, that no time might be lost, no stone left unremoved, that might give a knock to the peace of our policy: your head wrought upon all offers, your hand walked in all Regions, your spirit steered all attempts and undertakings: and yet if protestations, qualified and protected by Equivocations, may cary weight; all this while your mind was, as good pastors to be, patient, your thoughts were obedient, and your counsels innocent. But now to search your cunning somewhat nearer to the quick, we must observe, that when your hopes of Invasion began to cool by likelyhood of peace, your desires of supplies by the cold answers that came from Spain, your expectation of new mischief to be wrought at home without

Complots abroad: when malice it self was cast into so desperate a swoun, as neither Rosa solis when Spain relented, nor Iscobah when Tyrone submitted, nor dissention within the Kingdom when discontentments ended, could put it by any fresh adventure into life, when you for your own part, Mr. Garnet, having bin once washed and regenerated in the fountain of the Kings free Pardon, from the leprous spots of former Treasons, were determined to begin upon another stock, and return as a dog to the vomit (though washing can avail no man (as the Preacher warns) that iterum tangit mortuum, toucheth the dead the second or third time after he hath been made clean:) for secretly Catesby resorts to you, as Mahomet might to Sergius, (for now I speak according to the matter, and not the men) to enquire whether it were lawful, considering the necessiity of the time, to undertake an enterprise, for the advancement of the Catholick Religion, though it were likely that among many that were nocent, some should perish that were innocent. A man that is Religious in any kind, or but morally honest in his own kind, would expect that a Priest, a Iesuit, (which title doth imply salvation, and not destruction, nay, the Superior of English Iesuits) upon this rash demand, should have resorted for a safe resolution to Gods own Book, where he should have found, that God was pleased to withdraw his wrathful hand from Sodom, so as there had been only decem justi, ten justmen within that Town, and for their sakes; that the wise housholder in St. Matthew, marking how hard it would be, when the corn was ripe, to make separation, gave order to his servants to abstain from plucking up the tares, ne simul eradicarent triticum, least withall they plucked up the wheat by the Roots. Ye should have found in the stories of the Church, that the godly Bishops in the first spring of Religion, suspended process against the Priscillian Hereticks, ne Catholici cum illis perirent, least the Catholicks might also perish with them. And the Church of Millain taxed Theodosius the Emperor, quod insontes unâ cum sontibus trucidâsset, that he had proceeded both against the guilty, and the guiltless with one stroke, and with one measure of severity. But far beside the Holy writ, or holy presedents, your answer, Mr. Garnet, was such, as I both abhor to think, and quake to utter, that if any great advantage were to grow to the Church this way, they might destroy them all.

Tantae ne animis coelestibus irae? O Mr. Garnet, be not offended though I ask of you, as a worthy Emperor did once of a Traitor, in a case by many degrees inferior to this, Quid facit in pectore humano lupi feritas, canis rabies, serpentis venenum? But that which ought most to torture and afflict the spirit (if you be the child of him, whose Name and Badge you bear) is, that your Doctrine was confidently delivered, and so speedily digested, and converted to nutriment from such a mouth as yours, considering that (according to the Prophet) knowledge should depend upon the lips of the Priest, as Rookwood, Bates and others, that did shrink at the horror of the Project when it was first laid down, received satisfaction upon the very sound of your assent, though masked with the title of a man as grave and learned, as any in the land. And Catesby doubting of the fickleness of mens affections, in cases that concern the soul, used your admittance as a charm or spell, to keep quick spirits within the circle of combined faith, which otherwise perhaps when Hell brake loose, would have sought liberty. Your Charter only (whereupon I beseech you for your own souls health, to meditate for the time you tarry in this world) was the Base whereon some grounded their bad conscience in proceeding with this Plot, not only to the destruction of their bodies, but to the perill of their souls, without sound and true repentance, which by the merit of Christs passion, will serve in quacunque hora peccator ingemuerit. For though Christ were joyfull that he had not lost one of those whom his father gave him in charge, and came to save, and not to destroy; yet your advise was to destroy them all: Such was your burning charity.

Some man surprised with a question upon the sudden, might answer sharply and shrewdly at some time, I confess, without thinking or intending ill: But this man, Mr. Garnet, cannot be you, that having confessed clearly under your own h[...] [...] suspicion and fear of some [...]sch[...] [...] [...]nd intended in their hearts, by t[...] [...] of Nocents and Innoce[...]ts and [...] [...]uod dubitas ne feceris. It seems the heart of Catesby was a fertile soil for sprowting of stinking weeds hastily, into which the seed of your securing confidence was cast. For the Powder-plot which in Ianuary was barly embryo, became formatus foetus in the March next following, it quickened the next December, when the Pioneers began to dig in the thick wall: Catesby not long after imparted his conceipt secretly to you, of the great likelihood he foresaw of a lucky time of birth, and thereupon was Guy Fawks sent over by your knowledge and encouragement, to deal with Sir William Stanley, about the drawing down of Forces somewhat nearer to the Sea side for speedy transport, which if need were, might carry torches at the solemnity. But what is your answer to this employment of Guy Fawks? Forsooth that your purpsoe was only, to commend him as a Souldier, but not as a Conspirator. O unlucky Treason, that comes to be excused by so poor an Advocate! when Fawks himself meant nothing else than to be a Souldier, having so strange a part to play soon after in the Powder-train, but used this retreat as a colour to disguise the secret purpose that did onely tarry time, and to eschew those watchful eyes, that nearer hand would have observed both his inlets and his outlets in that place more narrowly. The point is clear, the confessions are direct, the purpose is palpable. All the lines of your level are drawn to the centre of the Powder-mine. All Letters are either drawn or enterlined manu Scorpionis, to use the word of Hierome; and yet under pain of censure we must believe, that all this while you were in charity, because all this while (which it grieves me to remember) you were not afraid to communicate.

But now to weigh your Answers that concern the Powder-plot it self, which is paramount in respect of the Longitude and Latitude to all that have been, or shall ever be: Your self cannot deny, Mr. Garnet, that Green-wel's overture, as you say in Confession, coming after the notice which you took of Catesbies question about Innocents, was but a fruit of your own Doctrine, an effect of your own instruction, and a conclusion drawn wholly out of your own propositions and principles. Now when we press to know what reason drew you to the concealment of a Project so pernicious both to Prince and State, without revealing it either to the King himself, tanquam praecellenti, to use St. Peter's term, or to his Ministers subordinate; you start to the shift of Confession for a formal help, which comes too short in respect of Catesby's first discovery, which your own words aver plainly to have wrought with you. I will not argue in this place what course a Confessor should take, or how far he ought to strain for the securing of a Princes life, that otherwise is sure to perish by the rage and ignorance invincible of a base Villain, (whose life answers not in value the least hair of a Princes head) because time suffers not: But I am sure, that for a matter of less weight than this, and a crime of less importance than the life both of Prince and State, Confession received a deep wound for a long time, more than a thousand years past, in the Church of Constantinople. For God forbid that matters of such weight should hang by such feeble threeds. But to this excuse of tenderness in the point of Confession, I would answer by making a great doubt, Whether this course of conference were a Confession or not: for against your bare words, which Equivocation supports, I object some likelihood, That since you kneeled sometimes, and sometimes walked up and down; since matter of conspiracy were interlaced with matter of Confession, not for ease of conscience, as should appear, but for advice in execution; since Greenwel was absolved instantly, which excludes the shift of reference; and Greenwel should be found to lie to the holy Ghost, in case this were a true Confession, in promising (Mr. Garnet) as you say, to disswade the project, which he prosecuted even to the last point, as is evident: and after the Powder Camp brake up, I conclude, that though this discovery were by confession, yet it was no Supersedeas to your former knowledge from Catesby, your trusty friend: and if it were none, then it can be no protection for faith putrified. What need we seek light through cobweb-lawns, when the drift of your whole device in seeking to conclude from one what you learned of another, and from all what you affected and abetted in your heart, doth evidently prove your counsels to have been carried along with such a temper of reservedness, as whensoever mischief should be brought to light, the world might rather wonder at your caution, than commend your fidelity.

By shaping such weak answers to demonstrations so manifest, you must either work by the Ring of Giges, in making your audacity and presumption invisible; or hold a very weak conceit of our capacities, in supposing that they can be either dazled or deluded by such poor Sophistry. For though you pretend to have received a deep wound in Conscience at the first revealing of the plot, to have lost your sleep with vexation of spirit, to have offered and prayed to God for his preventing grace, to have required Greenwel's help and furtherance in crossing and diverting the design; yet all this while you suffered the project to proceed, you helped and assisted their endeavours that were labourers, you wrote earnestly Letters both to Baldwin and to Creswel for their furtherance of ordinary means, you gave order for a prayer to be said by Catholicks for their prosperous success, you kept measure with the two first dimensions of Frier Bacon's Brasen Head, Time is, Time was, till (thanks be to God) the third time was past; you had ever an ear open to listen for the crack, and were in the same agony for the Powder-plot, that Charles the Fifth was for the Popes duress, giving order in all his Dominions, that Prayers should be made for his release, when in the mean time he kept and held him in his own hand prisoner: the least word of your mouth, or labour of your pen, might have secured both Prince and State; while you pretend to have broken both your sleeps and your brains, and that with a greater advantage to the cause which you would advance, than can ever grow by combustion and conspiracy. But your tenderness herein was suitable with another dutiful desire of yours to disswade Catesby from the Plot, at his coming into Warwickshire, who never meant to come thither, but as to the Rendezvous when the Parliament had been blown up, and the storm had been blown over. It may be that your mind was perplexed and disquieted upon the meditation of strange events, for so was the mind of Cain, Achitophel, and Iudas that betray'd his Master: the reason is very pregnant in the Word of God it self, that cum sit timidia nequitia, dat testimonium condemnationis, since wickedness is cowardly and timorous, it gives evidence of condemnation against it self: Et semper praesumit saeva perturbata conscientia; but Sathan prevailing, his Angels execute.

I will now conclude this address to you, Mr. Garnet, by observing some special points, how strangely and preposterously the Devil, in this last project of Powder, hath altered his old properties. For the curse that God laid upon the Serpent, after the first transgression, was, Ut gradiretur super pectus suum, to creep upon his breast; but now we find him mounted upon the wings of an Espray, to the highest Region of the Air, and among the Fire-works. The other part of his curse was, that he should eat Pulverem, that is, dust or powder: But now since Sodom was destroyed by Sulphure, and the Wife of Lot transmuted into Salt, the proper materials of that mean by which Satan wrought in this hot fire, it appears that the Serpent from eating powder (which was a plain devise) fell, for a worse purpose, to snuff Gun-powder. Then the Serpent did insidiari calcaneo, now capiti, from which the body draweth both sense sense and influence. Then he began to Eve with a modest question, Cur praecepit Deus, Why hath God commanded? now with a resolution, Praecepit Deus, God hath commanded. His words in those carried a flourish of great comfort, Nequaquam moriemini; but now terror, Moriemini, for a great advantage destroy them all. The Devil at that time did onely nibble about the Text of holy Writ, tanquam mus ponticus, as Tertullian terms Martian; but now he draws the grounds of Equivocation concerning Princes lives: Out of the very Scripture, and by Scholastical Authority, Sathan tempted Christ with a fair offer, Dandi omnia, of giving all upon the top of the Pinacle: But now he sets upon the great Lieutenant of Gods Authority and Dignity, with an auferam tibi omnia, both Life and Crown, ex penetralibus ubi Christus non est, as we are taught by his Evangelist. The Dragons ambition extended no further, than the sweeping away with his tail of the third part of the Stars in the Firmament: But now the plot of him and his Disciples was, to sweep away the Sun, the Moon, and the Stars, both out of Star-

Chamber and Parliament, that no light be given in this Kingdom to the best Labourers. In the time of Saul, the Devil was so modest as to suspend his Illusions and Oracles, till the Visions of the Prophets began to cease: But now though we have both Moses and the Prophets, & firmiorem sermonem propheticum, yet he ruffles among the robes, & inaudita fundit oracula. In the beginning of the Christian Church, the very name of Christ was sufficient to make Sathan pack, and to quit the possession of tormented men; but he hath learned a more cunning trick of late, under the banner of Christ, to fight against the Lieutenants of his Imperial Majesty. In one point I find no change, that is, in labouring and working by all means, to draw men from their trust in Gods direction, to a tickle kind of confidence in themselves, and their own weak knowledge of good and ill. And as that error was the cause of Adams exile from Paradise, which was hortus conclusus; so had such another almost divided us and our heirs both from our lives and Estates, Et penitus toto divisos orbe Britannos.

I have stood the longer on this point, to let you know how idlely, and yet how wilfully you strive against both the Providence of God, and the Justice of the Land; Quae tuo te jugulavit gladio. The more you labour to get out of the Wood, having once lost the right way, the further you creep in. For the wisdom of the world is folly before God; and unpossible it is, that those counsels or proceedings should either have good proof in this world, or reward in the next, that are embrued with blood, and pursued with tyranny. If then there be no other way to Heaven than by the destruction of Gods Annointed and their Heirs, I will conclude with you, Mr. Garnet, as Constantius did with Ascesius, Erigito tibi scalam, & in coelum solus ascendito; set up a Ladder for your self, and climb up to Heaven alone, for Loyal minds will not sute themselves with such bad company. The worst I wish to your person standing now to be convicted at the Bar, is remorse and repentance, for the safeguard of your Soul; and for the rest, Fiat justitia, currat lex, & vincat Veritas.

Hereunto Garnet said, That he had done more than he could excuse, and he had dealt plainly with them; but he was bound to keep the secrets of Confessions, and to disclose nothing that he heard in Sacramental Confession.

Whereupon the Earl of Nottingham asked him, if one confessed this day to him, that to morrow morning he meant to kill the King with a dagger, if he must conceal it?

Whereunto Garnet answered, That he must conceal it.

Then the Earl of Salisbury desired liberty of him to ask him some questions of the nature of Confessions.

Garnet said, His Lordship might, and he would answer him as well as he could.

Why then (said he) must there not be Confession and Contrition before Absolution?

Yes, (said Garnet.)

Then he demanded, Whether Greenwel were absolved by him or no?

Garnet said, He was.

The Earl then asked him, What Greenwel had done, to shew that he was sorry for it, and whether he did promise to desist?

Garnet answered, that Greenwel said, He would do his best.

To that the Earl replied, That it could not be so; for as soon as Catesby and Percy were in Arms, Greenwel came to them from Garnet, and so went from them to Hall at Mr. Abington's house, inviting them most earnestly to come and assist those Gentlemen in that action. Hereby (saith he) it appears, that either Greenwel told you out of Confession, and then there needs no secrecie; or if it were in Confession, he professed no penitency, and therefore you could not absolve him. To which the Earl added, That this one circumstance must still be remembred, and cannot be cleared, That when Greenwel told you what Catesby meant in particular, and you then called to mind also what Catesby had spoken to you in the general before, if you had not been so desirous to have the Plot take effect, you might have disclosed it out of your general knowledge from Catesby: but when Catesby offered to deliver you the particulars himself, as he had done to Greenwel, you refused to hear him, lest your tongue should have betrayed your heart.

To this Garnet weakly replied, That he did what he could to disswade it, and went into Warwickshire with a purpose to disswade Mr. Catesby, when he should have come down. And for Mr. Greenwel's going to Father Hall, to perswade him to joyn, Garnet said, he did very ill in so doing.

To that the Earl of Salisbury replied, That his first answer was most absurd, seeing he knew Catesby would not come down till the 6th. of November, which was the day after the blow should have been given; and Garnet went into the Countrey ten days before. And for the second, he said, That he was onely glad, that the world might now see, that Jesuits were condemned by Jesuits; and Treason and Traitors laid naked by the Traitors themselves; yea, Jesuits by that Jesuit, that governs all Jesuits here, and without whom, no Jesuit in England can do any thing.

Garnet (as it should seem) being here mightily touched with remorse of his offence, prayed God and the King, that other Catholicks might not fare the worse for his sake.

Then the Earl of Salisbury said, Mr. Garnet, is it not a lamentable thing, that if the Pope, or Claudius Aquaviva, or your self, command poor Catholicks any thing, that they must obey you, though it be to endanger both body and soul? And if you maintain such Doctrine amongst you, how can the King be safe? Is it not time therefore the King and the State should look to you, that spend your time thus in his Kingdom?

Garnet said very passionately, My Lord, I would to God I had never known of the Powder-Treason.

Hereupon the Lord Chief Justice of England said, Garnet, you are Superior of the Jesuits;

and if you forbid, must not the rest obey? Was not Greenwel with you half an hour at Sir Everard Digby's house, when you heard of the discovery of your Treason? and did you not there confer and debate the matter together? Did you not send him to Hall, to Mr. Abington's house, to stir him up to go to the Rebels, and encourage them? Yet you seek to colour all this, but that's but a meer shift in you; and notwithstanding all this you said, No man living but one did know that you were privy to it; then belike some that are dead did know it. Catesby was never from you, (as the Gentlewoman that kept your house with you confessed) and by many apparent proofs, and evident presumptions, you were in every particular of this action, and directed and commanded the Actors; nay, I think verily, you were the chief that moved it.

Garnet said, No, my Lord, I did not.

Then it was exceedingly well urged by my Lord Chief Justice, how he writ his Letters for Winter, Wright, Fawkes, Baynham, and Catesby, principal Actors in this matchless Treason. Besides, his Lordship told him of his keeping the two Bulls to prejudice the King, and to do other mischief in the Realm; which, when he saw the King peaceably to come in, then being out of hope to do any good, he burnt them.

Here Mr. Attorney caused to be read the Confession of Hall, alias Oldcorn the Jesuit, under his own hand, (which, he said, was Omni exceptione majus) against him, wherein he confessed, That Humfrey Littleton told him, That Catesby and others were sore hurt with Powder, and said that he was exceeding sory that things took no better effect; whereat Hall wished him not to be discouraged, nor to measure the cause by the event: For though the xi. Tribes of Israel went twice by the special commandment of God against the Tribe of Benjamin, yet they both times received the overthrow. So Lewis the French king in his voyage into the Holy-land against the Infidels, was overthrown, and his whole Army discomfitted, though his cause were good. And so likewise the Christians when they defended Rhodes against the Turks, lost the City, and the Turks had the upper hand. And this he confessed, and applied to the fact of Catesby and others for the Powder-treason, and said, It would have been commendable when it had been done, though not before.

After this Mr. Attorney opened, how Francis Tresham, a dilinquent Romanist, even in articulo mortis (a fearful thing) took it upon his salvation, That he had not seen Garnet in sixteen years before, when Garnet himself had confessed he had seen him often within that time: and likewise, that Garnet knew not of the

Spanish Invasion, which Garnet himself confessed also, and which two things Tresham himself had formerly confessed to the Lords; yet for a recantation of these two things upon his death bed, he commanded Vavasor his man, (whom I think (said Mr. Attorney) deeply guilty in this Treason) to write a Letter to the Earl of Salisbury: And to shew this his desperate recantation, Mr. Treshams Letter was offered to be read.

But before the reading thereof, my Lord of Salisbury said, Because there was matter incident to him, and to that which should be read, he thought fit to say something. To which purpose he said his desire was, truly to lay open what cause there was for any faith to be given to these mens protestations, when they, to colour their own impieties, and to slander the Kings Justice, would go about to excuse all Jesuits, how foul soever, out of an opinion that it is meritorious so to do, at such time as they had no hope of themselves. Such is it to be doubted that Sir Everard Digbies protestations might be at the Bar, who sought to clear all Jesuits of those practices, which they themselves have now confessed ex ore proprio. That such was also Treshams labour, who being visited with sickness, and his wife in charity suffered to come to him, this Letter was hatched by them, and signed by himself some few hours before his death, wherein he taketh that upon his salvation, which shall now by Garnet be disproved.

Then the Letter was read, being to this effect, That whereas since the Kings time he had had his pardon, and that to satisfie the Lords who heretofore examined him, he had accused Garnet; that now, he being weak, desired that his former examinations might be called in, because they were not true: and set down upon his salvation, that he had not seen Garnet in sixteen years before.

Then my Lord of Salisbury shewed and said, It was a lamentable thing: for within three hours after he had done this, he died; and asked Garnet what interpretation he made of this testamental protestation?

Garnet answered, It may be, my Lord, he meant to Equivocate. Here was the examination and confession of Mrs. Anne Vaux offered to be read also, to confirm Treshams perjury, who confessed that she had seen Mr. Tresham with Garnet at her house, three or four times since the Kings coming in, and divers times before; and that he had dined with him, and that Garnet always gave him good counsel, and would say sometimes to him, and others, Good Gentlemen, be quiet: for we must obtain that which you desire by prayer. She confessed also, that they were at Erith together the last Sommer.

After all this, Garnet being demanded, if these examinations were true, he affirmed they were. And then were his own examinations likewise read to the same effect, wherein he both confessed the seeing of Mr. Tresham, and his sending into Spain about an Invasion.

Here my Lord of Salisbury concluded, That that which was said of Mr. Tresham, and others, was not done against charity to the dead, but upon inevitable necessity, to avoid all their slanderous reports and practises: for he said, That even now there was currant throughout the Town, a report of a Retractation under Bates his hand, of his accusation of Greenwel; which are strange and grievous practises to think upon. But this day shall witness to the world, that all is false, and your self condemned not by any but by your self, your own confessions and actions. Alass, Mr. Garnet, why should we be troubled all this day with you, poor man, were it not to make the cause appear as it deserveth? wherein, God send you may be such an example, as you may be the last Actor in this kind.

Hereupon my Lord Admiral said to Garnet, that he had done more good this day in that Pulpit which he stood in (for it was made like unto a Pulpit wherein he stood) than he had done all the days of his life time in any other Pulpit.

Then was another examination of Mrs. Anne Vaux read, wherein she confessed that Mr. Garnet and she were not long since with Mr. Tresham, at his house in Northamptonshire, and stayed there.

After this, my Lord of Salisbury said, Mr. Garnet, if you have not yet done, I would have you to understand that the King hath commanded, that whatsoever made for you, or against you, all should be read, and so it is, and we take of you what you will. This Gentlewoman that seems to speak for you in her confessions, I think would sacrifice her self for you to do you good, and you likewise for her: Therefore, good Mr. Garnet, whatsoever you have to say, say on a Gods name, and you shall be heard.

Then Garnet desired the Iury, that they would allow of, and believe those things he had denied, and affirmed, and not to give credit unto those things, whereof there was no direct proof against him, not to condemn him by circumstances or presumptions.

The Earl of Salisbury demanded of him, saying, Mr. Garnet, is this all you have to say?

if it be not, take your time, no man shall interrupt you.

To whom Garnet answered, Yea, my Lord.

Mr. Attorney humbly desired all the Lords Commissioners, that if he had forgotten to speak of any thing material, that their Lordships would be pleased to put him in mind of it: Who was assured by my Lord of Salisbury, that he had done very well, painfully, and learnedly.

Then Mr. Attorney desired the Jury might go together, who upon his motion going together forth of the Court, within less than a quarter of an hour returned, and found Henry Garnet guilty.

Whereupon Mr. Sergeant Crook prayed judgment.

Then Mr. Waterhouse the Clerk of the Crown demanding what he could say for himself, why judgment should not be given against him?

Garnet made answer, that he could say nothing, but referred himself to the mercy of the King, and God Almighty.

After this, the Earl of Northampton made a Learned Speech, which in it self was very copious; and the intention being to contract this Volume as much as might be, and to keep onely to matter of Fact, it was thought convenient to omit the same.

Then the Lord Chief Justice making a pithy preamble of all the apparent proofs and presumptions of his guiltiness, gave Judgment, that he should be drawn, hanged, and quartered.

And my Lord of Salisbury demanded, if Garnet would say any thing else?

Garnet answered, No, my Lord. But I humbly desire your Lordships all, to commend my life to the Kings Majesty, saying, That at his pleasure he was ready either to die or live, and do him service.

And so the Court arose.

A true Relation of all such things as passed at the Execution of Mr. Garnet, the Third of May, Anno 1606.

On the Third of May, Garnet, according to his Judgment, was executed upon a Scaffold, set up for that purpose, at the West end of St. Paul's Church. At his arise up the Scaffold, he stood much amazed, (fear and guiltiness appearing in his face.) The Deans of Pauls and Winchester being present, very gravely and Christianly exhorted him to a true and lively faith to Godward, a free and plain acknowledgment to the World of his offence; and if any further Treason lay in his knowledge, to unburthen his Conscience, and shew a sorrow and detestation of it. But Garnet impatient of perswasions, and ill pleased to be exhorted by them, desired them not to trouble him; he came prepared, and was resolved. Then the Recorder of London (who was by his Majesty appointed to be there) asked Garnet if he had any thing to say unto the people before he died; it was no time to dissemble, and now his Treasons were too manifest to be dissembled: therefore if he would, the world should witness, what at last he censured of himself, and of his fact; it should be free to him to speak what he listed. But Garnet unwilling to take the offer, said, His voice was low, his strength gone, the people could not hear him, though he spake to them; but to those about him on the Scaffold, he said, The intention was wicked, and the fact would have been cruel, and from his Soul he should have abhorred it, had it effected. But he said, He onely had a general knowledge of it by Mr. Catesby, which in that he disclosed not, nor used means to prevent it, herein he had offended; what he knew in particulars was in Confession, as he said. But the Recorder wished him to be remembered, That the Kings Majesty had under his hand-writing these four points amongst others:

1. That Greenway told him of this, not as a fault, but as a thing which he had intelligence of, and told it him by way of consultation.

2. That Catesby and Greenway came together to him to be resolved.

3. That Mr. Tesmond and he had conference of the particulars of the Powder-Treason in Essex long after.

4. Greenway had asked him, who should be the Protector? But Garnet said, That was to be referred till the blow was past.

These prove your privity besides Confession, and these are extant under your hand. Garnet answered, Whatsoever was under his hand was true. And for that he disclosed not to his Majesty the things he knew, he confessed himself justly condemned, and for this did ask forgivness of his Majesty. Hereupon the Recorder led him to the Scaffold to make his Confession publick.

Then Garnet said, Good Countrey-men, I am come hither this blessed day of The Invention of the holy Cross, to end all my crosses in this life: The cause of my suffering is not unknown to you; I confess I have offended the King, and am sorry for it, so far as I was guilty, which was in concealing it, and for that I ask pardon of his Majesty. The Treason intended against the King and State was bloody, my self should have detested it had it taken effect; and I am heartily sorry, that any Catholicks ever had so cruel a design. Then turning himself from the people to them about him, he made an Apology for Mrs. Ann Vaux, saying, There is such an honourable Gentlewoman, who hath been much wronged in report; for it is suspected and said, that I should be married to her, or worse; but I protest the contrary, she is a vertuous Gentlewoman, and for me a perfect pure Virgin. For the Popes Breeves, Sir Edmond Baynams going over Seas, and the matter of the Powdertreason, he referred himself to his Arraignment, and his Confessions; for whatsoever is under my hand in any of my Confessions, said he, is true.

Then addressing himself to Execution, he kneeled at the Ladder foot, and asked if he might have time to pray, and how long? It was answered, he should limit himself, none should interrupt him. It appeared, he could not constantly or devoutly pray, fear of death, or hope of pardon, even then so distracted him; for oft in those Prayers he would break off, turn and look about him, and answer to what he over-heard, while he seemed to be praying. When he stood up, the Recorder finding in his behaviour as it were an expectation of a Pardon, wished him not to deceive himself, nor beguile his own Soul; he was come to die, and must die; requiring him not to equivocate with his last breath, if he knew any thing that might be danger to the King or State, he should now utter it. Garnet said, It is now no time to equivocate; how it was lawful, and when, he had shewed his mind else-where. But, saith he, I do not now equivocate, and more than I have confessed, I do not know. At his ascending up the Ladder, he desired to have warning before he was turned off. But it was told him, He must look for no other turn but death. Being upon the Gibbet, he used these words, I commend me to all good Catholicks, and I pray God preserve his Majesty, the Queen, and all their Posterity, and my Lords of the Privy Council, to whom I remember my humble duty, and I am sorry that I did dissemble with them; but I did not think they had had such proof against me, till it was shewed me: but when that was proved, I held it more honour for me at that time to confess, than before to have accused. And for my Brother Greenway, I would the truth were known; for the false reports that are, make him more faulty than he is. I should not have charged him, but that I thought he had been safe. I pray God the Catholicks may not fare the worse for my sake; and I exhort them all to take heed they enter not into any Treasons, Rebellions, or Insurrections against the King. And with this, ended speaking, and fell to praying: and crossing himself, said, In nomine Patris, & Filii, & Spiritus sancti; and prayed, Maria mater Gratiae, Maria mater misericordiae, T[...] me à malo protege, & hora mortis suscipe. Then, In manus tuas, Domine, commendo spiritum meum. Then, Per crucis hoc signum, (crossing himself) fugiat procul omne malignum. Infige crucem tuam in corde meo Domine. Let me always remember the Cross. And so returned again to Maria mater Gratiae, and then was turned off, and hung till he was dead.

A complex story! It does not matter if the story is old or accurate, so much as its influence on history. We are not concerned with authorship, only that it exists in the "theatre". How does such a story work on the mind, the soul, the life? How do we celebrate the Great Deliverance so that it will persist efficiently in centuries to come?

Matthaus Merian, Chronicle, 1660